The Hudson River Valley Reader

The Hudson River Valley Reader

Edited by *Edward C. Goodman*

CIDER MILL PRESS

BOOK PUBLISHERS

Kennebunkport, Maine

13-Digit ISBN: 978-1-60433-037-3
10-Digit ISBN: 1-60433-037-6

Library of Congress Control Number: 2008934070

This book may be ordered by mail from the publisher. Please include $2.75 for postage and handling.

Please support your local bookseller first!

Books published by Cider Mill Press Book Publishers are available at special discounts for bulk pur-chases in the United States by corporations, institutions, and other organizations. For more informa-tion, please contact the publisher.

Cider Mill Press Book Publishers
"Where good books are ready for press"
12 Port Farm Road
Kennebunkport, Maine 04046

Visit us on the web!
www.cidermillpress.com

Designed by PonderosaPineDesign.com, Vicky Vaughn Shea

Typography: Adobe Garamond Pro, Aquiline, Avenir, Linotype Decorations, Olduvai

Photography and illustration credits: cover see page 6; page 8–9 Library of Congress (dig-pga0344); pages 12–13 Library of Congress (ppmsca17157); page 14 Library of Congress (Kaaterskill Falls, by Thomas Cole, 1826); pages 24, 30, 121, 128, 145, 172, 190, 196, 269, 401 *The Hudson, From the Wilderness to the Sea*, published originally in 1866 by H.B. Nims & Co., Troy, New York; page 32 Library of Congress (3a31182u); page 34 Library of Congress (6a11243u); page 36 Library of Congress (cph3a43382); page 41 Library of Congress (cph3b19440); page 49 Library of Congress (det4a16097); page 67 Library of Congress (cph3a07364); page 68 Library of Congress (cph3b42490); page 79 Library of Congress (cph3a45461); page 90 Library of Congress (3b42490u); page 95 Library of Congress (3b01948u); page 98 Library of Congress (cph3b44356); page 100 Library of Congress (chp3a22185); page 106 Library of Congress (det4a16094); page 114 Library of Congress (pga00210); page 123 Library of Congress (02693u); pages 126–127 Library of Congress (cph3c13127); page 152 Library of Congress (cai2a12440); page 156 Library of Congress (det4a09636); page 170 Library of Congress (cph3c07822); page 176 Library of Congress (3b50896u); page 179 Library of Congress (3g06074u); page 186 Library of Congress (pga02705); page 204 Library of Congress (cph3a06608); pages 220–221 Library of Congress (cph3a43789); page 222 Library of Congress (ppmsca17489u); page 258 Library of Congress (cph3a07639); page 263 Library of Congress (cph3a43889); page 310 Library of Congress (cph3a44799); page 322 Library of Congress (cph3a46996); page 339 Library of Congress (cph3c12464); page 360 Library of Congress (det4a24572); page 369 Library of Congress (cph3g08981u); page 372 Library of Congress (det4a25913); page 402 Library of Congress (03449u); pages 404–405 Library of Congress (cph3c12790); end sheets Library of Congress (3b49764u & LC-USZ62-43545)

Printed in China

1 2 3 4 5 6 7 8 9 0

First Edition

Acknowledgments

I would like to thank my publisher John F. Whalen and Carlo De Vito for their valuable suggestions and support. Additionally, thanks to Vicky Vaughn Shea of Ponderosa Pine Design for her terrific design in a challenging timeframe.

My thanks to my parents Harry and Shirley Goodman for their continued support, my sister Helen, and my friends Daniel Starr and Gary Miller who have a home in the Hudson Valley which I frequently visit.

COVER IMAGE: John Bunyan Bristol (1826–1909),
Hudson River Scene (not dated). Oil on canvas, 14 x 22 in.
Collection of the Hudson River Museum, gift of Mr. and
Mrs. Richard Manney. 69.23.1

Table of Contents

Foreword

The Hudson River Valley encompasses the canyon of the Hudson River and its adjacent communities in New York and New Jersey, generally from northern Westchester County northward to Albany. Originally populated by the Mahican Native American tribe, the Hudson River was explored by Henry Hudson in 1609. The Dutch settled the region, establishing New Amsterdam as a port in 1625.

In 1664, the territory came under the rule of Great Britain and was named New York. During the French and Indian War in the 1750s and early 1760s, the northern end of the valley became the bulwark of the British defense against French invasion from Canada.

The Hudson River Valley was a strategic battleground during the Revolutionary War, involving famous leaders and figures such as George Washington and the treacherous Benedict Arnold.

Through the stories of Washington Irving, James Fenimore Cooper, and John Burroughs, as well as the poems of William Cullen Bryant, Joseph Rodman Drake, George P. Morris, and

Thomas Cole, the Hudson Valley grew quite popular. In the 1830s–70s, the area was an inspiration to the painters of the Hudson River School, such as Frederic E. Church, who built his residence at Olana overlooking the river with views of the Catskill Mountains.

It also was the location of the estates of many wealthy New Yorkers, including John D. Rockefeller, Frederick William Vanderbilt, and President Franklin D. Roosevelt.

The beauty of the Hudson Valley earned a portion of it in New York's Dutchess and Columbia counties the designation National Historic Landmark.

The essays in this work were compiled from various original texts published from the 1800s to the 1920s. We have not brought the texts into conformity with contemporary spelling and usage, preferring instead to let the authors speak in their unique and eloquent voices.

—Edward C. Goodman

PART I

History

The Highlands from Newburgh and Butler
Hill with the Hudson River. Watercolor over
graphite underdrawing, July 24, 1846.

There is no spot in all the world where poetry and romance are so closely blended with the heroic in history as along the banks of our Hudson.

—Wallace Bruce

Kaaterskill Falls, by Thomas Cole, 1826, oil on canvas. Collection of the Wadsworth Atheneum.

Amid thy forest solitudes one climbs
O'er crags, that proudly tower above the deep,
Along the verge of the cliff, and he can hear
The low dash of the wave with startled ear.

—Fitz-Greene Halleck

The Hudson has often been styled "The Rhine of America." There is, however, little of similarity and much of contrast. The Rhine from Dusseldorf to Manheim is only twelve hundred to fifteen hundred feet in breadth. The Hudson from New York to Albany averages more than five thousand feet from bank to bank. At Tappan Zee the Hudson is ten times as wide as the Rhine at any point above Cologne. At Bonn the Rhine is barely one-third of a mile, whereas the Hudson at Haverstraw Bay is over four miles in width. The average breadth of the Hudson from New York to Poughkeepsie is almost eight thousand feet.

The mountains of the Rhine also lack the imposing character of the Highlands. The far-famed Drachenfels, the Landskron, and the Stenzleburg are only seven hundred and fifty feet above the river; the Alteberg eight hundred, the Rosenau nine hundred, and the great Oelberg thirteen hundred and sixty-two. According to the latest United States Geological Survey the entire group of mountains at the northern gate of the Highlands is from fourteen hundred to sixteen hundred and twenty-five feet in height, not to speak of the Catskills from three thousand to almost four thousand feet in altitude.

The Hudson is in fact a vast estuary of the sea; the tide rises two feet at Albany and six inches at Troy.

The State of New York is to the geologist what the Holy Land is to the Christian, and the works of her Palaeontologist are the Old Testament Scriptures of the science. It is a Laurentian, Cambrian, Silurian and Devonian State, containing all the groups and all the formations of these long ages, beautifully developed in belts running nearly across the state in an east and west direction, lying undisturbed, as originally laid down.

A series of great dislocations with upthrows on the east side traverse eastern North America from Canada to Alabama. One of these great faults has been traced from near the mouth of the St. Lawrence River, keeping mostly under the water up to Quebec just north of the fortress, thence by a gently curving line to Lake Champlain or through western Vermont across Washington County, New York, to near Albany. It crosses the river near Rhinebeck 15 miles north of Poughkeepsie and continues on southward into New Jersey and runs into another series of faults probably of a later date, which extends as far as Alabama. It brings up the rocks of the so called Quebec group on the east side of the fracture to the level of the Hudson River and Trenton.

The rock of New York Island is gneiss, except a portion of the north end, which is limestone. The south portion is covered with deep alluvial deposits, which in some places are more than 100 feet in depth. The natural outcroppings of the gneiss appeared on the surface about 16th Street, on the east side of the city, and run diagonally across to 31st Street on 10th Avenue. North of this, much of the surface was naked rock. It contains a large proportion of mica, a small proportion of quartz and still less feldspar, but generally an abundance of iron pyrites in very minute crystals, which, on exposure, are decomposed. In consequence of these ingredients it soon disintegrates on exposure, rendering it unfit for the purposes of building. The erection of a great city, for which this island furnishes a noble site, has very greatly changed its natural condition. The geological age of the New York gneiss is undoubtedly very old, not the Laurentian or oldest, nor the Huronian, but it belongs to the third or White Mountain series, named by Dr. Hunt the Montalban. It is the same range which is the basis rock of nearly all the great cities of the Atlantic coast. It crosses New Jersey where it is turned to clay, until it appears under

Trenton, and it extends to Philadelphia, Baltimore, Washington and Richmond, Va., and probably Boston, Massachusetts, is founded on this same formation.

Names of the Hudson—The Iroquois called the river the "Cohatatea." The Mahicans and Lenapes the "Mahicanituk," or "the ever-flowing waters." Verrazano in 1524 styled it Rio de Montaigne. Gomez in 1525 Rio San Antonio. Hudson styled it the "Manhattes" from the tribe at its mouth. The Dutch named it the "Mauritius," in 1611, in honor of Prince Maurice of Nassau, and afterwards "the Great River." It has also been referred to as the "Shatemuck" in verse. It was called "Hudson's River" not by the Dutch, as generally stated, but by the English, as Hudson was an Englishman, although he sailed from a Dutch port, with a Dutch crew, and a Dutch vessel. It was also called the "North River," to distinguish it from the Delaware, the South River. It is still frequently so styled, and the East River almost "boxes the compass" as applied to Long Island Sound.

Height of Hills and Mountains—It is interesting to hear the opinions of different people journeying up and down the Hudson as to the height of mountains along the river. The Palisades are almost always under-estimated, probably on account of their distance from the steamer. It is only when we consider the size of a house at their base, or the mast of a sloop anchored near the shore, that we can fairly judge of their magnitude. Various guides, put together in a day or a month, by writers who have made a single journey, or by persons who have never consulted an authority, have gone on multiplying blunder upon blunder, but the United States Geological Survey furnishes reliable information. According to their maps the Palisades are from 300 to 500 feet in height, the Highlands from 785 to 1625, and the Catskills from 3000 to 3885 feet.

The Palisades

At Fort Lee	300 feet
Opposite Mt. St. Vincent	400 "
Opposite Hastings	500 "

The Highlands

Sugar Loaf	785 feet
Dunderberg	865 "
Anthony's Nose	900 "
Storm King	1368 "
Old Cro' Nest	1405 "
Bull Hill	1425 "
South Beacon	1625 "

The Catskills

North Mountain	3000 feet
Plaaterkill	3135 "
Outlook	3150 "
Stoppel Point	3426 "
Round Top	3470 "
High Peak	3660 "
Sugar Loaf	3782 "
Plateau	3855 "

Sources of the Hudson—The Hudson rises in the Adirondacks, and is formed by two short branches. The northern branch (17 miles in length), has its source in Indian Pass, at the base of Mount McIntyre; the eastern branch, in a little lake poetically called the "Tear of the Clouds," 4,321 feet above the sea under the summit of Tahawus, the noblest mountain of the Adirondacks, 5,344 feet in height. About thirty miles below the junction it takes the waters of Boreas River, and in the southern part of Warren County, nine miles east of Lake George, the tribute of the Schroon. About fifteen miles north of Saratoga it receives the waters of the Sacandaga, then the streams of the Battenkill and the Walloomsac; and a short distance above Troy its largest tributary, the Mohawk. The tide rises six inches at Troy and two feet at Albany, and from Troy to New York, a distance of one hundred and fifty miles, the river is navigable by large steamboats.

Principal streams—The principal streams which flow into the Hudson between Albany and New York are the Norman's Kill, on west bank, two miles south of Albany; the Mourdener's Kill, at Castleton, eight miles below Albany, on the east bank; Coxsackie Creek, on west bank, seventeen miles below Albany; Kinderhook Creek, six miles north of Hudson; Catskill Creek, six miles south of Hudson; Roeliffe Jansen's Creek, on east bank, seven miles south of Hudson; the Esopus Creek, which empties at Saugerties; the Rondout Creek, at Rondout; the Wappingers, at New Hamburgh; the Fishkill, at Matteawan, opposite Newburgh; the Peekskill Creek, and Croton River. The course of the river is nearly north and south, and drains a comparatively narrow valley.

Spuyten Duyvil Creek—Above Washington Heights, on the east bank, the Spuyten Duyvil meets the Hudson. This stream is the northern boundary of New York Island, and a short distance east of the Hudson bears the name of Harlem River. Its course is southeast and joins the East River at Randall's Island, just above Hell Gate. It is a curious fact that this modest stream should be bounded by such suggestive appellations as Hell Gate and Spuyten Duyvil. This is the first point of special legendary interest to one journeying up the Hudson and it takes its name according to the veracious Knickerbocker, from the following incident: It seems that the famous Antony Van Corlear was despatched one evening with an important message up the Hudson. When he arrived at this creek, the wind was high, the elements were in an uproar, and no boatman at hand. "For a short time," it is said, "he vapored like an impatient ghost upon the brink, and then, bethinking himself of the urgency of his errand, took a hearty embrace of his stone bottle, swore most valorously that he would swim across 'en spijt en Duyvil' (in spite of the Devil), and daringly plunged into the stream. Scarce had he buffeted half way over when he was observed to struggle violently, as if battling with the spirit of the waters. Instinctively he put his trumpet to his mouth, and giving a vehement blast—sank forever to the bottom."

It is emphatically the "River of the Mountains," as it rises in the Adirondacks, flows seaward east of the Helderbergs, the Catskills, the Shawangunks, through twenty miles of the Highlands and along the base of the Palisades.

The Five Divisions of the Hudson—which possess interest for all, as they present an analysis easy to be remembered—divisions marked by something more substantial than sentiment or fancy, expressing five distinct characteristics:

1. THE PALISADES, an unbroken wall of rock for fifteen miles—GRANDEUR.
2. THE TAPPAN ZEE, surrounded by the sloping hills of Nyack, Tarrytown, and Sleepy Hollow—REPOSE.
3. THE HIGHLANDS, where the Hudson for twenty miles

plays "hide and seek" with "hills rock-ribbed and ancient as the sun"—SUBLIMITY.

4. THE HILLSIDES for miles above and below Poughkeepsie— THE PICTURESQUE.

5. THE CATSKILLS, on the west, throned in queenly dignity—BEAUTY.

The Palisades, or Great Chip Rock—as they were known by the old Dutch settlers, present the same bold front to the river that the Giant's Causeway does to the ocean. Their height at Fort Lee, where the bold cliffs first assert themselves, is three hundred feet, and they extend about seventeen or eighteen miles to the hills of Rockland County. A stroll along the summit reveals the fact that they are almost as broken and fantastic in form as the great rocks along the Elbe in Saxon-Switzerland.

As the basaltic trap-rock is one of the oldest geological formations, we might still appropriately style the Palisades "a chip off the old block." They separate the valley of the Hudson from the valley of the Hackensack. The Hackensack rises in Rockland Lake opposite Sing Sing, within two or three hundred yards of the Hudson, and the rivers flow thirty miles side by side. Some geologists think that originally they were one river, but they are now separated from each other by a wall more substantial than even the 2,000 mile structure of the "Heathen Chinee."

It might also be interesting to note Prof. Newberry's idea

The Palisades

that in pre-glacial times this part of the continent was several hundred feet higher than at present, and that the Hudson was a very rapid stream and much larger than now, draining as it did the Great Lakes: that the St. Lawrence found its way through the Hudson Channel following pretty nearly the line of the present Mohawk, and the great river emptied into the Atlantic some 80 miles south of Staten Island. This idea is confirmed by the soundings of the coast survey which discover the ancient page of the Hudson as here indicated on the floor of the sea far out where the ocean is 500 feet in depth. A speculation of what a voyager a few million years ago would have then seen might, however, as Hamlet observes, be "to consider somewhat too curiously" for ordinary up-to-date tourists. But even, granting all this to be true, the Palisades were already old, thrown up long ages before, between a rift in the earth's surface, where it cooled in columnar form. The rocky mould which held it, being of softer material, finally disintegrated and crumbled away, leaving the cliff with its peculiar perpendicular formation.

A recent writer has said: "The Palisades are among the wonders of the world. Only three other places equal them in importance, but each of the four is different from the others, and the Palisades are unique. The Giant's Causeway on the north coast of Ireland, and the cliffs at Kawaddy in India, are thought by many to have been the result of the same upheaval of nature as the Palisades; but the Hudson rocks seem to have preserved their entirety—to have come up in a body, as it were—while the Giant's Causeway owes its celebrity to the ruined state in which the Titanic forces of nature have left it. The third wonder is at Staffa, in Scotland, where the rocks have been thrown into such a position as to justify the name of Fingal's Cave, which they bear, and which was bestowed on them in the olden times before Scottish history began to be written. It is singular how many of the names which dignify, or designate, favorite spots of the Giant's Causeway have been duplicated in the Palisades.

Among the Hudson rocks are several 'Lady's Chairs,' 'Lover's Leaps,' 'Devil's Toothpicks,' 'Devil's Pulpits,' and, in many spots on the water's edge, especially those most openly exposed to the weather, we see exactly the same conformations which excite admiration and wonder in the Irish rocks."

Croton River—known by the Indians as Kitchawonk, joins the Hudson in a bay crossed by the New York Central Railroad Croton draw-bridge. East of this point is a water shed having an area of 350 square miles, which supplies New York with water. The Croton Reservoir is easily reached by a pleasant carriage drive from Sing Sing, and it is a singular fact that the pitcher and ice-cooler of New York, or in other words, Croton Dam and Rockland Lake, should be almost opposite.

About fifty years ago the Croton first made its appearance in New York, brought in by an aqueduct of solid masonry which follows the course of the Hudson near the Old Post Road, or at an average distance of about a mile from the east bank. Here and there its course can be traced by "white stone ventilating towers" from Sing Sing to High Bridge, which conveys the aqueduct across the Harlem River. Its capacity is 100,000,000 gallons per day, which however began to be inadequate for the city and a new aqueduct was therefore begun in 1884 and completed in 1890, capable of carrying three times that amount, at a cost of $25,000,000. The water-shed is well supplied with streams and lakes. Lake Mahopac, one of its fountains, is one of the most beautiful sheets of water near the metropolis, and easily accessible by a pleasant drive from Peekskill, or by the Harlem Railroad from New York. The old Indian name was Ma-cook-pake, signifying a large inland lake, or perhaps an island near the shore. The same derivation is also seen in Copake Lake, Columbia County. On an island of Mahopac the last great "convention" of the southern tribes of the Hudson was held. The lake is about 800 feet above tide, and it is pleasant to know that the bright waters of Mahopac and the clear streams of Putnam and Westchester are conveyed to New York even as the poetic waters of Loch Katrine to the city of Glasgow. The Catskill water supply, the ground of which was broken in 1907, is referred to in our description of Cold Spring and the Catskills.

❦

The Dunderberg—the dread of the Dutch mariners. This hill, according to Irving, was peopled with a multitude of imps, too great for man to number, who wore sugar-loaf hats and short doublets, and had a picturesque way of "tumbling head over heels in the rack and mist." They were especially malignant toward all captains who failed to do them reverence, and brought down frightful squalls on such craft as failed to drop the peaks of their mainsails to the goblin who presided over this shadowy republic. It was the dread of the early navigators—in fact, the Olympus of Dutch mythology. Verditege Hook, the Dunderberg, and the Overslaugh, were names of terror to even the bravest skipper. The old burghers of New York never thought of making their week's voyage to Albany without arranging their wills, and it created as much commotion in New Amsterdam as a modern expedition to the north pole. Dunderberg, in most of the Hudson Guides and Maps, is put down as 1,098 feet, but its actual altitude by the latest United States Geological Survey is 865 feet.

Anthony's Nose—Strangely enough, the altitude of the mountains at the southern portal of the Highlands has been greatly overrated. The formerly accepted height of Anthony's Nose has been reduced by the Geological Survey from 1,228 feet to 900. It has, however, an illustrious christening, and according to various historians several godfathers. One says it was named after St. Anthony the Great, the first institutor of monastic life, born A. D. 251, at Coma, in Heraclea, a town in Upper Egypt. Irving's humorous account is, however, quite as probable that it was derived from the nose of Antony Van Corlear, the illustrious trumpeter of Peter Stuyvesant. "Now thus it happened that bright and early in the morning the good Antony, having washed his burly visage, was leaning over the quarter-railing of the galley, contemplating it in the glassy waves below. Just at this moment the illustrious sun, breaking in all his splendor from behind a high bluff of the Highlands, did dart one of his most potent beams full upon the refulgent nose of the sounder of brass, the reflection of which shot straightway down hissing hot into the water, and killed a mighty sturgeon that was sporting beside the vessel. When this astonishing miracle was made known to the Governor, and he tasted of the unknown fish, he marveled exceedingly; and, as a monument thereof, he gave the name of Anthony's Nose to a stout promontory in the neighborhood, and it has continued to be called Anthony's Nose ever since." It was called by the Indians "Kittatenny," a Delaware term, signifying "endless hills." The stream flowing into the river south of Anthony's Nose is known as the Brocken Kill, broken into beautiful cascades from mountain source to mouth.

Storm King—The first European name given to Storm King was Klinkersberg (so called by Hendrick Hudson, from its glistening and broken rock). It was styled by the Dutch "Butter Hill," from its shape, and, with Sugar Loaf on the eastern side below the point, helped to set out the tea-table for the Dunderberg goblins. It was christened by Willis, "Storm King," and may well be regarded the El Capitan of the Highlands. Breakneck is opposite, on the east side, where St. Anthony's Face was blasted away.

This section was known by the Indians as "Wequehache," or, "the Hill Country," and the entire range was called by the Indians "the endless hills," a name not inappropriate to this mountain bulwark reaching from New England to the Carolinas.

The Catskills—were called by the Indians *On-ti-o-ras*, or mountains of the sky, as they sometimes seem like clouds along the horizon. This range of mountains, 3,800 feet high, was supposed by the Indians to have been originally a monster who devoured all the children of the red men, until the great spirit touched him when he was going down to the salt lake to bathe, and here he remains. "Two little lakes upon the summit were regarded the eyes of the monster, and these are open all the summer; but

At the Foot of the Storm King

in the winter they are covered with a thick crust or heavy film; but whether sleeping or waking tears always trickle down his cheeks. In these mountains, according to Indian belief, was kept the great treasury of storm and sunshine, presided over by an old squaw spirit who dwelt on the highest peak of the mountains. She kept day and night shut up in her wigwam, letting out only one at a time. She manufactured new moons every month, cutting up the old ones into stars," and, like the old Aeolus of mythology, shut the winds up in the caverns of the hills.

᠗

Kaaterskill Falls—The upper fall 175 feet, lower fall 85 feet. The amphitheatre behind the cascade is the scene of one of Bryant's finest poems:

"From greens and shades where the Kaaterskill leaps From cliffs
where the wood flowers cling;"

and we recall the lines which express so beautifully the well-nigh fatal dream

"Of that dreaming one
By the base of that icy steep,
When over his stiffening limbs begun
The deadly slumber of frost to creep."

About half-way up the old mountain carriage road, is the place said to be the dreamland of Rip Van Winkle—the greatest character of American mythology, more real than the heroes of Homer or the massive gods of Olympus.

Lake George—called by the French "Lac St. Sacrament," was discovered by Father Jacques, who passed through it in 1646, on his way to the Iroquois, by whom he was afterward tortured and burned. It is 36 miles long by three miles broad. Its elevation is 243 feet above the sea. The waters are of remarkable transparency; romantic islands dot its surface, and elegant villas line its shores. Fort William Henry and Ticonderoga, situated at either end of the lake, were the salients respectively of the two most powerful nations upon the globe. France and England sent great armies, which crossed each other's track upon the ocean, the one entering the St. Lawrence, the other the harbor of New York.

The dramatic natural beauty of Lake George

Their respective colonies sent their thousands to swell the number of trained troops, while tribes of red men from the south and the north were marshalled by civilized genius to meet in hostile array upon these waters, around the walls of the forts, and at the base of the hills. In 1755, General Johnston reached Lake St. Sacrament, to which he gave the name of Lake George, "not only in honor of his Majesty, but to assert his undoubted dominion here."

At its widest point, Lake George measures about four miles, but at other places it is less than one mile in width. It is dotted with islands; how many we do not know exactly—nobody does; but tradition, which passes among the people of the district for history and truth, says there is exactly one island for every day in the year, or 365 in all. Whatever their real number they all are beautiful, although some of them are barely large enough to support a flagstaff, and they all seem to fit into the scene so thoroughly that each one seems necessary to complete the charm. On either side are high hills, in some places rising gently from the shores, and in others beetling up from the surface of the water with a rugged cliff, or time-worn mass of rocks, which reminds one of the wild bits of rocky scenery that make up the savage beauty of the Isle of Skye.

Lake Champlain—The western shore of Lake Champlain forms the margin of the most varied and altogether delightful wilderness to be found anywhere upon this continent east of the Rocky Mountains. The serried peaks to the westward are in plain view from its shores, their foot-hills ending in lofty and often abrupt ridges where they meet the lake. Three impetuous rivers, the Saranac, the Salmon and the Ausable, flow down from the cool, clear lakes, hidden away in the wildwood, and, breaking through this barrier at and in the vicinity of Plattsburgh, contribute not only to the lucid waters of Lake Champlain but to the picturesque variety of the region.

୧୦

Albany—The clay beds at Albany are more than 100 feet thick, and between that city and Schenectady they are underlaid by a bed of sand that is in some places more than 50 feet thick. There is an old glacial clay and boulder drift below the gravel at Albany, but Professor Hall says it is not the estuary stratified clay.

The steamship "Hendrick Hudson" traveling downriver, circa 1909

The Hudson Tide—The Hudson River is the continuation of the tide-wave, which comes up from the ocean through New York Bay, and is carried by its own momentum 160 miles, growing, of course, constantly smaller, until it is finally stopped by the dam at Troy. The crest of this wave, or top high water, is ten hours going from New York to Troy. The average rise and fall of the tides in New York is five and one-half feet, and in Troy, about two feet.

Flood tide may carry salt water, under the most favorable circumstances, so that it can be detected at Poughkeepsie; ordinarily the water is fresh at Newburgh.

Discovery of the Hudson. Henry Hudson's ship the "Half Moon," dropping anchor in the Hudson River, greeted by Indians in canoes. Photogravure of painting by Warren Sheppard, c. 1895.

The prow of the "Half-Moon" has left a broadening wake whose ripples have written an indelible history, not only along the Hudson's shores, but have left their imprint on kingdoms over the sea.

—William Wait

CHAPTER 2

Discovery/ Dutch Period

Henry Hudson—If ever a compelling Fate set its grip upon a man and drove him to an accomplishment beside his purpose and outside his thought, it was when Henry Hudson—having headed his ship upon an ordered course northeastward—directly traversed his orders by fetching that compass to the southwestward which ended by bringing him into what now is Hudson's River, and which led on quickly to the founding of what now is New York.

Hudson sought, as from the time of Columbus other navigators had sought, a short cut to the Indies; but his search was made, because of what those others had accomplished, within narrowed lines. In the century and more that had passed between the great Admiral's death and the beginning of Hudson's explorations, one important geographical fact had been established: that there was no water-way across America between, roughly, the latitudes of 40 deg. South and 40 deg. North. Of necessity, therefore—since to round America south of 40 deg. South would make a longer voyage than by the known route around the Cape of Good Hope—exploration that might produce practical results had to be made north of 40 deg. North, either westward from the Atlantic or eastward from the North Sea.

Even within those lessened limits much had been determined before Hudson's time. To the eastward, both Dutch and English searchers had gone far along the coast of Russia; passing between that coast and Nova Zembla and entering the Kara Sea. To the westward, in the year 1524, Verazzano had sailed along the American coast from 34 deg. to 50 deg. North; and in the course of that voyage had entered what now is New York Bay. In the year 1598, Sebastian Cabot had coasted America from 38 deg. North to the mouth of what now is Hudson's Strait. Frobisher had entered that Strait in the year 1577; Weymouth had sailed into it nearly one hundred leagues in the year 1602; and Portuguese navigators, in the years 1558 and 1569, probably had passed through it and had entered what now is Hudson's Bay.

As the result of all this exploration, Hudson had at his command a mass of information—positive as well as negative—that at once narrowed his search and directed it; and there is very good reason for believing that he actually carried with him charts of a crude sort on which, more or less clearly, were indicated the Strait and the Bay and the River which are regarded as his discovery, and which bear his name.

It is Hudson's third voyage—the one that brought him into our own river, and that led on directly to the founding of our own city—that has the deepest interest to us of New York. He made it in the service of the Dutch East India Company: but how he came to enter that service is one of the unresolved problems of his career.

In itself, there was nothing out of the common in those days in an English shipmaster going captain in a Dutch vessel. But Hudson—by General Read's showing—was so strongly backed by family influence in the Muscovy Company that it is not easy to understand why he took service with a corporation that in a way was the Muscovy Company's trade rival. Lacking any explanation, I am inclined to link it with the action of the English Government—when he returned from his voyage and made harbor at Dartmouth—in detaining him in England and in ordering him to serve only under the English flag; and to infer that his going to Holland was the result of a falling out with the directors of the Muscovy Company; and that at their request, when the chances of the sea brought him within English jurisdiction, he was detained in his own country—and so was put in the way to take up with the adventure that led him straight onward to his death. In all of which may be seen the working-out of that fatalism which to my mind is so apparent in Hudson's doings, and which is most apparent in his third voyage: that evidently had its origin in a series of curious mischances, and that ended in his doing precisely what those who sent him on it were resolved that he should not do.

Mr. Henry C. Murphy—to whose searchings in the archives of Holland we owe so much—found at The Hague a manuscript history of the East India Company, written by P. van Dam in the seventeenth century, in which a copy of Hudson's contract with the Company is preserved. The contract reads as follows:

> *"On this eighth of January, in the year of our Lord one thousand six hundred and nine, the Directors of the East India Company of the Chamber of Amsterdam of the ten years reckoning of the one part, and Master Henry Hudson, Englishman, assisted by Jodocus Hondius[1], of the other part, have agreed in manner following, to wit: That the said Directors shall in the first place equip a small vessel or yacht of about thirty lasts [60 tons] burden, well provided with men, provisions and other necessaries, with which the above named Hudson shall, about the first of April, sail in order to search for a passage by the north, around the north side of Nova Zembla, and shall con-*

Replica of the "Half Moon" in New York Harbor during the 300-year anniversary celebrations of the discovery of the Hudson. Stereograph, c. 1909.

tinue thus along that parallel until he shall be able to sail southward to the latitude of sixty degrees. He shall obtain as much knowledge of the lands as can be done without any considerable loss of time, and if it is possible return immediately in order to make a faithful report and relation of his voyage to the Directors, and to deliver over his journals, log-books, and charts, together with an account of everything whatsoever which shall happen to him during the voyage without keeping anything back.

"For which said voyage the Directors shall pay the said Hudson, as well for his outfit for the said voyage as for the support of his wife and children, the sum of eight hundred guilders [say $336]. And in case (which God prevent) he does not come back or arrive hereabouts within a year, the Directors shall farther pay to his wife two hundred guilders in cash; and thereupon they shall not be farther liable to him or his heirs, unless he shall either afterward or within the year arrive and have found the passage good and suitable for the Company to use; in which case the Directors will reward the before named Hudson for his dangers, trouble, and knowledge, in their discretion.

"And in case the Directors think proper to prosecute and continue the same voyage, it is stipulated and agreed with the before named Hudson that he shall make his residence in this country with his wife and children, and shall enter into the employment of no other than the Company, and this at the discretion of the Directors, who also promise to make him satisfied and content for such farther service in all justice and equity. All without fraud or evil intent. In witness of the truth, two contracts are made hereof ... and are subscribed by both parties and also by Jodocus Hondius as interpreter and witness."

Hudson sailed from the Texel in the "Half Moon" (possibly accompanied by a small vessel, the "Good Hope," that did not pursue the voyage) on March 27–April 6, 1609; and for more than a month—until he had doubled the North Cape and was well on toward Nova Zembla—went duly on his way. Then came the mutiny that made him change, or that gave him an excuse for changing, his ordered course.

The log that has been preserved of this voyage was kept by Robert Juet; who was Hudson's mate on his second voyage, and who was mate again on Hudson's fourth voyage—until his mutinous conduct caused him to be deposed. What rating he had on board the "Half Moon" is not known; nor do we know whether he had, or had not, a share in the mutiny that changed the ship's course from east to west. With a suspicious frankness, he wrote in his log:

> "Because it is a journey usually knowne I omit to put downe what passed till we came to the height of the North Cape of Finmarke, which we did performe by the fift of May (stilo novo), being Tuesday." To this he adds the observed position on May 5th, 71 deg. 46' North, and the course, "east, and by south and east," and continues: "After much trouble, with fogges sometimes, and more dangerous ice. The nineteenth, being Tuesday, was close stormie weather, with much wind and snow, and very cold. The wind variable between the north north-west and north-east. We made our way west and by north till noone."

> "The first of September, faire weather, the wind variable betweene east and sooth; we steered away north north west. At noone we found our height [a little north of Cape May] to bee 39 degrees 3 minutes.... The second, in the morning close weather, the winde at south in the

morning. From twelve untill two of the clocke we steered north north west, and had sounding one and twentie fathoms; and in running one glasse we had but sixteene fathoms, then seventeene, and so shoalder and shoalder untill it came to twelve fathoms. We saw a great fire but could not see the land. Then we came to ten fathoms, whereupon we brought our tacks aboord, and stood to the eastward east south east, foure glasses. Then the sunne arose, and we steered away north againe, and saw the land [the low region about Sandy Hook] from the west by north to the north west by north, all like broken islands, and our soundings were eleven and ten fathoms. Then we looft in for the shoare, and faire by the shoare we had seven fathoms. The course along the land we found to be north east by north. From the land which we had first sight of, untill we came to a great lake of water [the Lower Bay] as we could judge it to be, being drowned land, which made it to rise like islands, which was in length ten leagues. The mouth of that land hath many shoalds, and the sea breaketh on them as it is cast out of the mouth of it. And from that lake or bay the land lyeth north by east, and we had a great streame out of the bay; and from thence our sounding was ten fathoms two leagues from the land. At five of the clocke we anchored, being little winde, and rode in eight fathoms water.... This night I found the land to hall the compasse 8 degrees. For to the northward off us we saw high hils [Staten Island and the Highlands]. For the day

before we found not above two degrees of variation. This is a very good land to fall with, and a pleasant land to see."

"The third, the morning mystie, untill ten of the clocke. Then it cleered, and the wind came to the south south east, so wee weighed and stood to the northward. The land is very pleasant and high, and bold to fall withal. At three of the clocke in the after noone, we came to three great rivers [the Raritan, the Arthur Kill and the Narrows]. So we stood along to the northermost [the Narrows], thinking to have gone into it, but we found it to have a very shoald barre before it, for we had but ten foot water. Then we cast about to the southward, and found two fathoms, three fathoms, and three and a quarter, till we came to the souther side of them; then we had five and sixe fathoms, and anchored. So wee sent in our boate to sound, and they found no lesse water than foure, five, sixe, and seven fathoms, and returned in an houre and a halfe. So we weighed and went in, and rode in five fathoms, oze ground, and saw many salmons, and mullets, and rayes, very great. The height is 40 degrees 30 minutes."

That is the authoritative account of Hudson's great finding. It has been quoted in full partly because of the thrilling interest that it has for us, but more to show that the record of his explorations—the "Half Moon's" log being written throughout with the same definiteness and accuracy—gave what neither Gomez nor Verrazano gave: clear directions for finding with certainty the haven that he, and those earlier navigators, had found by chance.

On that fact, and on the other fact that his directions promptly were utilized, rests his claim to be the practical discoverer of the harbor of New York.

For more than a week the "Half Moon" lay in the Lower Bay and in the Narrows. Then, on the eleventh of September, she passed fairly beyond Staten Island and came out into the Upper Bay: and Hudson saw the great river—which on that day became his river—stretching broadly to the north. I can imagine that when he found that wide waterway, leading from the ocean into the heart of the continent—and found it precisely where his friend Captain John Smith had told him he would find it, "under 40 degrees"—his hopes were very high. The first part of the story being confirmed, it was a fair inference that the second part would be confirmed; that presently, sailing through the "strait" that he had entered, he would come out, as Magellan had come out from the other strait, upon the Pacific—with clear water before him to the coasts of Cathay.

That glad hope must have filled his heart during the ensuing fortnight; and even then it must have died out slowly through another week—while the "Half Moon" worked her way northward as far as where Albany now stands. Twice in the course of his voyage inland—on September 14th, when his run was from Yonkers to Peekskill—he reasonably may have believed that he was on the very edge of his great discovery. As the river widened hugely into the Tappan Sea, and again widened hugely into Haverstraw Bay, it well may have seemed to him that he was come to the ocean out-

let—and that in a few hours more he would have the waters of the Pacific beneath his keel. Then, as he passed through the Southern Gate of the Highlands, and thence onward, his hope must have waned—until on September 22d it vanished utterly away. Under that date Juet wrote in his log: "This night, at ten of the clocke, our boat returned in a showre of raine from sounding the river; and found it to bee at an end for shipping to goe in."

That was the end of the adventure inland. Juet wrote on the 23d:

"At twelve of the clocke we weighed, and went downe two leagues"; and thereafter his log records their movements and their doings—sometimes meeting with "loving people" with whom they had friendly dealings; sometimes meeting and having fights with people who were anything but loving—as the "Half Moon" dawdled slowly down the stream. By the 2d of October they were come abreast of about where Fort Lee now stands. There they had their last brush with the savages, killing ten or twelve of them without loss on their own side.

After telling about the fight, Juet adds:

"Within a while after wee got downe two leagues beyond that place and anchored in a bay [north of Hoboken], cleere from all danger of them on the other side of the river, where we saw a very good piece of ground [for anchorage]. And hard by it there was a cliffe [Wiehawken] that looked of the colour of a white greene, as though it were either copper or silver myne. And I thinke it to be

one of them, by the trees that grow upon it. For they be all burned, and the other places are greene as grasse. It is on that side of the river that is called Manna-hata. There we saw no people to trouble us, and rode quietly all night, but had much wind and raine."

In that entry the name Manna-hata was written for the first time, and was applied, not to our island but to the opposite Jersey shore. The explanation of Juet's record seems to be that the Indians known as the Mannahattes dwelt— or that Juet thought that they dwelt—on both sides of the river. That they did dwell on, and that they did give their name to, our island of Manhattan are facts absolutely established by the records of the ensuing three or four years.

During October 3d the "Half Moon" was storm-bound. On the 4th, Juet records "Faire weather, and the wind at north north west, wee weighed and came out of the river into which we had runne so farre." Thence, through the Upper Bay and the Narrows, and across the Lower Bay—with a boat out ahead to sound—they went onward into the Sandy Hook channel.

"And by twelve of the clocke we were cleere of all the inlet. Then we took in our boat, and set our mayne sayle and sprit sayle and our top sayles, and steered away east south east, and south east by east, off into the mayne sea."

Juet's log continues and concludes—passing over unmentioned the mutiny that occurred before the ship's course definitely was set eastward—in these words:

"We continued our course toward England, without seeing any land by the way, all the rest of this moneth of October. And on the seventh day of November (stilo novo), being Saturday, by the grace of God we safely arrived in the range of Dartmouth, in Devonshire, in the yeere 1609."

New Amsterdam—The delectable accounts given by the great Hudson and Master Juet of the country they had discovered excited not a little talk and speculation among the good people of Holland. Letters patent were granted by Government to an association of merchants, called the West India Company, for the exclu-

Replica of the "Half Moon" entering New York Harbor, c. 1909.

sive trade on Hudson River, on which they erected a trading-house called Fort Aurania, or Orange, from whence did spring the great city of Albany. But I forbear to dwell on the various commercial and colonizing enterprises which took place; among which was that of Mynheer Adrian Block, who discovered and gave a name to Block Island, since famous for its cheese—and shall barely confine myself to that which gave birth to this renowned city.

It was some three or four years after the return of the immortal Hendrick that a crew of honest Low Dutch colonists set sail from the city of Amsterdam for the shores of America. It is an irreparable loss to history, and a great proof of the darkness of the age and the lamentable neglect of the noble art of book-making, since so industriously cultivated by knowing sea-captains and learned supercargoes, that an expedition so interesting and important in its results should be passed over in utter silence.

The ship in which these illustrious adventurers set sail was called the Goede Vrouw, or good woman, in compliment to the wife of the president of the West India Company, who was allowed by everybody, except her husband, to be a sweet-tempered lady—when not in liquor. It was in truth a most gallant vessel, of the most approved Dutch construction, and made by the ablest ship-carpenters of Amsterdam, who, it is well known, always model their ships after the fair forms of their country-women. Accordingly, it had one hundred feet in the beam, one hundred feet in the keel, and one hundred feet from the bottom of the stern-post to the taffrail. Like the beauteous model, who was declared to be the greatest belle in Amsterdam, it was full in the bows, with a pair of enormous catheads, a copper bottom, and withal a most prodigious poop.

The architect, who was somewhat of a religious man, far from decorating the ship with pagan idols, such as Jupiter, Neptune or Hercules, which heathenish abominations, I have no doubt, occasion the misfortunes and shipwreck of many a noble vessel, he I say, on the contrary, did laudably erect for a head, a goodly image of St. Nicholas, equipped with a low, broad-brimmed hat, a huge pair of Flemish trunk hose, and a pipe that reached to the end of the bow-sprit. Thus gallantly furnished, the staunch ship floated sideways, like a majestic goose, out of the harbor of the great city of Amsterdam, and all the bells that were not otherwise engaged, rung a triple bobmajor on the joyful occasion.

The voyage was uncommonly prosperous, for, being under the especial care of the ever-revered St. Nicholas, the Goede Vrouw seemed to be endowed with qualities unknown to common vessels. Thus she made as much leeway as headway, could get along very nearly as fast with the wind a head as when it was a-poop, and was particularly great in a calm; in consequence of which singular advantage she made out to accomplish her voyage in a very few months, and came to anchor at the mouth of the Hudson, a little to the east of Gibbet Island.

Here lifting up their eyes they beheld, on what is at present called the Jersey shore, a small Indian village, pleasantly embowered in a grove of spreading elms, and the natives all collected on the beach, gazing in stupid admiration at the Goede Vrouw. A boat was immediately dispatched to enter into a treaty with them, and, approaching the shore, hailed them through a trumpet in the most friendly terms; but so horribly confounded were these poor savages at the tremendous and uncouth sound of the Low Dutch language that they one and all took to their heels, and scampered over the Bergen Hills: nor did they stop until they had buried themselves, head and ears, in the marshes on the other side, where they all miserably perished to a man; and their bones being collected and decently covered by the Tammany Society of that day, formed that singular mound called Rattlesnake Hill, which rises out of the center of the salt marshes a little to the east of the Newark Causeway.

Animated by this unlooked-for victory, our valiant heroes sprang ashore in triumph, took possession of the soil as conquerors, in the name of their High Mightinesses the Lords States General; and marching fearlessly forward, carried the village of Communipaw by storm, not withstanding that it was vigorously defended by some half a score of old squaws and pappooses. On looking about them they were so transported with the excellences of the place that they had very little doubt the blessed St. Nicholas had guided them thither as the very spot whereon to settle their colony. The softness of the soil was wonderfully adapted to the driving of piles; the swamps and marshes around them afforded ample opportunities for the constructing of dykes and dams; the shallowness of the shore was peculiarly favorable to the building of docks; in a word, this spot abounded with all the requisites for the foundation of a great Dutch City.

On making a faithful report, therefore, to the crew of the Goede Vrouw, they one and all determined that this was the destined end of their voyage. Accordingly, they descended from the Goede Vrouw, men, women and children, in goodly groups, as did the animals of yore from the ark, and formed themselves into a thriving settlement, which they called by the Indian name Communipaw.

Communipaw is at present but a small village, pleasantly situated among rural scenery, on that beauteous part of the Jersey shore which was known in ancient legends by the name of Pavonia, and commands a grand prospect of the superb bay of New York. It is within but half an hour's sail of the latter place, provided you have a fair wind, and may be distinctly seen from the city.

Communipaw, in short, is one of the numerous little villages in the vicinity of this most beautiful of cities, which are so many strongholds and fastnesses whither the primitive manners of our Dutch forefathers have retreated, and where they are cherished with devout and scrupulous strictness. The dress of the original settlers is handed down inviolate from father to son—the identical broad-brimmed hat, broad-skirted coat, and broad-bottomed breeches continue from generation to generation; and several gigantic knee-buckles of massy silver are still in wear that made gallant display in the days of the patriarchs of Communipaw. The language likewise continues unadulterated by barbarous innovations; and so critically correct is the village schoolmaster in his dialect that his reading of a Low Dutch psalm has much the same effect on the nerves as the filing of a hand-saw.

The original name of the island whereon the squadron of Communipaw was thus propitiously thrown is a matter of some dispute, and has already undergone considerable vitiation—a melancholy proof of the instability of all sublunary things, and the vanity of all our hopes of lasting fame; for who can expect his name will live to posterity, when even the names of mighty islands are thus soon lost in contradiction and uncertainty!

The name most current at the present day, and which is likewise countenanced by the great historian Vander Donck, is Manhattan, which is said to have originated in a custom among the squaws, in the early settlement, of wearing men's hats, as is still done among many tribes. "Hence," as we are told by an old governor, who was somewhat of a wag, and flourished almost a century since, and had paid a visit to the wits of Philadelphia, "hence arose the appellation of *man-hat-on*, first given to the Indians, and afterwards to the island"—a stupid joke!—but well enough for a governor.

Among the more venerable sources of information on this subject is that valuable history of the American possessions, written by Master Richard Blome, in 1687, wherein it is called the Manhadaes and Manahanent; nor must I forget the excellent little book, full of precious matter, of that authentic historian, John Josselyn, gent., who expressly calls it Manadaes.

Another etymology still more ancient, and sanctioned by the countenance of our ever to be lamented Dutch ancestors, is that found in certain letters, still extant, which passed between the early governors and their neighboring powers, wherein it is called indifferently Monhattoes, Munhatos, and Manhattoes, which are evidently unimportant variations of the same name; for our wise forefathers set little store by those niceties, either in orthography or orthoepy, which form the sole study and ambition of many learned men and women of this hypercritical age. This last name is said to be derived from the great Indian spirit Manetho, who was supposed to make this island his favorite abode, on account of its uncommon delights. For the Indian traditions affirm that the bay was once a translucid lake, filled with silver and golden fish, in the midst of which lay this beautiful island, covered with every variety of fruits and flowers, but that the sudden irruption of the Hudson laid waste these blissful scenes, and Manetho took his flight beyond the great waters of Ontario.

The land being thus fairly purchased of the Indians, a circumstance very unusual in the history of colonization, and strongly illustrative of the honesty of our Dutch progenitors, a stockade fort and trading house were forthwith erected on an eminence in front of the place where the good St. Nicholas had appeared in a vision to Oloffe the Dreamer; and which, as has already been observed, was the identical place at present known as the Bowling Green.

Around this fort a progeny of little Dutch-built houses, with tiled roofs and weathercocks, soon sprang up, nestling themselves under its walls for protection, as a brood of half-fledged chickens nestle under the wings of the mother hen. The whole was surrounded by an enclosure of strong palisadoes, to guard against any sudden irruption of the savages. Outside of these extended the corn-fields and cabbage-gardens of the community, with here and there an attempt at a tobacco plantation; all covering those tracts of country at present called Broadway, Wall Street, William Street, and Pearl Street.

And now the infant settlement having advanced in age and stature, it was thought high time it should receive an honest Christian name. Hitherto it had gone by the original Indian name of Manna-hata, or, as some will have it, "The Manhattoes;" but this was now decried as savage and heathenish, and as tending to keep up the memory of the pagan brood that originally possessed it. Many were the consultations held upon the subject without coming to a conclusion, for though everybody condemned the old name, nobody could invent a new one. At length, when the council was almost in despair, a burgher, remarkable for the size and squareness of his head, proposed that they should call it New Amsterdam. The proposition took everybody by surprise; it was so striking, so apposite, so ingenious. The name was adopted by acclamation, and New Amsterdam the metropolis was thenceforth called. Still, however, the early authors of the province continued to call it by the general appelation of "The Manhattoes," and the poets fondly clung to the euphonious name of Manna-hata; but those are a kind of folk whose tastes and notions should go for nothing in matters of this kind.

Having thus provided the embryo city with a name, the next was to give it an armorial bearing or device, as some cities have a rampant lion, others a soaring eagle; emblematical, no doubt, of the valiant and high-flying qualities of the inhabitants: so after mature deliberation a sleek beaver was emblazoned on the city standard as indicative of the amphibious origin and patient persevering habits of the New Amsterdamers.

The houses of the higher class were generally constructed of wood, excepting the gable end, which was of small black and yellow Dutch bricks, and always faced on the street, as our ancestors, like their descendants, were very much given to outward show, and were noted for putting the best leg foremost. The house was always furnished with abundance of large doors and small windows on every floor, the date of its erection was curiously designated by iron figures on the front, and on the top of the roof was perched a fierce little weathercock, to let the family into the important secret which way the wind blew. These, like the weathercocks on the tops of our steeples, pointed so many different ways, that every man could have a wind to his mind;—the most staunch and loyal citizens, however, always went according to the weathercock on the top of the governor's house, which was certainly the most correct, as he had a trusty servant employed every morning to climb up and set it to the right quarter.

In those good days of simplicity and sunshine, a passion for cleanliness was the leading principle in domestic economy, and the universal test of an able housewife—a character which formed the utmost ambition of our unenlightened grandmothers. The front door was never opened except on marriages, funerals, new year's days, the festival of St. Nicholas, or some such great occasion. It was ornamented with a gorgeous brass knocker, curiously wrought, sometimes in the device of a dog, and sometimes of a lion's head, and was daily burnished with such religious zeal, that it was oft-times worn out by the very precautions taken for its preservation. The whole house was constantly in a state of inundation, under the discipline of mops and brooms and scrubbing brushes; and the good housewives of those days were a kind of amphibious animal, delighting exceedingly to be dabbling in water—insomuch that an historian of the day gravely tells us, that many of his townswomen grew to have webbed fingers like unto a duck; and some of them, he had little doubt, could the matter be examined into, would be found to have the tails of mermaids; but this I look upon to be a mere sport of fancy, or, what is worse, a wilful misrepresentation.

The grand parlor was the "sanctum sanctorum," where the passion for cleaning was indulged without control. In this sacred apartment no one was permitted to enter excepting the mistress and her confidential maid, who visited it once a week, for the purpose of giving it a thorough cleaning, and putting things to rights; always taking the precaution of leaving their shoes at the door, and entering devoutly on their stocking feet.

After scrubbing the floor, sprinkling it with fine white sand, which was curiously stroked into angles, and curves, and rhomboids with a broom; after washing the windows, rubbing and polishing the furniture, and putting a bunch of evergreens in the fireplace—the window shutters were again closed to keep out the flies, and the room carefully locked up until the revolution of time brought round the weekly cleaning day.

As to the family, they always entered in at the gate, and most generally lived in the kitchen. To have seen a numerous household assembled round the fire, one would have imagined that he was transported back to those happy days of primeval simplicity, which float before our imaginations like golden visions. The fireplaces were of a truly patriarchal magnitude, where the whole family, old and young, master and servant, black and white, nay, even the very cat and dog, enjoyed a community of privilege, and had each a right to a corner. Here the old burgher would sit in perfect silence, puffing his pipe, looking into the fire with half-shut eyes, and thinking of nothing for hours together; the goede vrouw, on the opposite side, would employ herself diligently in spinning yarn or knitting stockings. The young folks would crowd around the hearth, listening with breathless attention to some old crone of a negro, who was the oracle of the family, and who, perched like a raven in the corner of a chimney, would croak forth for a long winter afternoon a string of incredible stories about New England witches, grisly ghosts, horses without heads, and hair-breadth escapes and bloody encounters among the Indians.

In those happy days a well-regulated family always rose with the dawn, dined at eleven, and went to bed at sunset. Dinner was invariably a private meal, and the fat old burghers showed incontestable signs of disapprobation and uneasiness at being surprised by a visit from a neighbor on such occasions. But though our worthy ancestors were thus singularly averse to giving dinners, yet they kept up the social bands of intimacy by occasional banquettings, called tea-parties.

These fashionable parties were generally confined to the

higher classes, or noblesse: that is to say, such as kept their own cows and drove their own waggons. The company commonly assembled at three o'clock, and went away about six, unless it was in winter time, when the fashionable hours were a little earlier, that the ladies might get home before dark. The tea-table was crowned with a huge earthen dish, well stored with slices of fat pork, fried brown, cut up into morsels, and swimming in gravy. The company being seated round the genial board, and each furnished with a fork, evinced their dexterity in launching at the fattest pieces in this mighty dish—in much the same manner as sailors harpoon porpoises at sea, or our Indians spear salmon in the lakes. Sometimes the table was graced with immense apple-pies, or saucers full of preserved peaches and pears; but it was always sure to boast an enormous dish of balls of sweetened dough, fried in hog's fat, and called doughnuts, or olykoeks— a delicious kind of cake, at present scarce known in this city, except in genuine Dutch families.

The tea was served out of a majestic delf teapot, ornamented with paintings of fat little Dutch shepherds and shepherdesses, tending pigs, with boats sailing in the air, and houses built in the clouds, and sundry other ingenious Dutch fantasies. The beaux distinguished themselves by their adroitness in replenishing this pot from a huge copper tea-kettle, which would have made the pigmy macaronies of these degenerate days sweat merely to look at it. To sweeten the beverage, a lump of sugar was laid beside each cup, and the company alternately nibbled and sipped with great decorum; until an improvement was introduced by a shrewd and economic old lady, which was to suspend a large lump directly over the tea-table by a string from the ceiling, so that it could be swung from mouth to mouth—an ingenious expedient, which is still kept up by some families in Albany, but which prevails without exception in Communipaw, Bergen Flatbush, and all our uncontaminated Dutch villages.

At these primitive tea parties the utmost propriety and dignity of deportment prevailed. No flirting nor coquetting—no gambling of old ladies, nor hoyden chattering and romping of young ones—no self-satisfied struttings of wealthy gentlemen with their brains in their pockets—nor amusing conceits and monkey divertissements of smart young gentlemen with no brains at all. On the contrary, the young ladies seated themselves demurely in their rush-bottomed chairs, and knit their own woollen stockings; nor ever opened their lips excepting to say "yah Mynheer," or "yah ya Vrouw," to any question that was asked them; behaving, in all things, like decent, well-educated damsels. As to the gentlemen, each of them tranquilly smoked his pipe, and seemed lost in contemplation of the blue and white tiles with which the fireplaces were decorated; wherein sundry passages of Scripture were piously portrayed—Tobit and his dog figured to great advantage, Haman swung conspicuously on his gibbet, and Jonah appeared most manfully bouncing out of the whale like Harlequin through a barrel of fire.

The parties broke up without noise and without confusion. They were carried home by their own carriages, that is to say, by the vehicles nature had provided them, excepting such of the wealthy as could afford to keep a wagon. The gentlemen gallantly attended their fair ones to their respective abodes, and took leave of them with a hearty smack at the door; which, as it was an established piece of etiquette, done in perfect simplicity and honesty of heart, occasioned no scandal at that time, nor should it at the present. If our great-grandfathers approved of the custom, it would argue a great want of reverence in their descendants to say a word against it.

Peter Stuyvesant—was the last, and, like the renowned Wouter Van Twiller, the best of our ancient Dutch governors; Wouter having surpassed all who preceded him, and Pieter, or Piet, as he was sociably called by the old Dutch burghers, who were ever prone to familiarize names, having never been equalled by any successor. He was, in fact, the very man fitted by Nature to retrieve the desperate fortunes of her beloved province, had not the Fates, those most potent and unrelenting of all ancient spinsters, destined them to inextricable confusion.

His wooden leg, was the only prize he had gained in bravely fighting the battles of his country, but of which he was so proud, that he was often heard to declare he valued it more than all his other limbs put together; indeed, so highly did he esteem it, that he had it gallantly enchased and relieved with silver devices, which caused it to be related in divers histories and legends that he wore a silver leg.

He was, in fact, the very reverse of his predecessors, being neither tranquil and inert, like Walter the Doubter, nor restless and fidgeting, like William the Testy; but a man, or rather a governor, of such uncommon activity and decision of mind, that he never sought nor accepted the advice of others, depending bravely upon his single head, as would a hero of yore upon his single arm, to carry him through all difficulties and dangers. To tell the simple truth, he wanted nothing more to complete him as a statesman than to think always right, for no one can say but that he always acted as he thought. He was never a man to flinch when he found himself in a scrape, but to dash forward through thick and thin, trusting, by hook or by crook, to make all things straight in the end. In a word, he possessed in an eminent degree that great quality in a statesman, called perseverance by the polite, but nicknamed obstinacy by the vulgar. A wonderful salve for official blunders; since he who perseveres in error without flinching gets the credit of boldness and consistency, while he who wavers, in seeking to do what is right, gets stigmatised as a trimmer. This much is certain, and it is a maxim well worthy the attention of all legislators great and small, who stand shaking in the wind, irresolute which way to steer, that a ruler who follows his own will pleases himself, while he who seeks to satisfy the wishes and whims of others runs great risk of pleasing nobody. There is nothing, too, like putting down one's foot resolutely when in doubt, and letting things take their course. The clock that stands still points right twice in the four-and-twenty hours, while others may keep going continually, and be continually going wrong.

Nor did this magnanimous quality escape the discernment

of the good people of Nieuw Nederlandts; on the contrary, so much were they struck with the independent will and vigorous resolution displayed on all occasions by their new governor, that they universally called him Hard Koppig Piet, or Peter the Headstrong, a great compliment to the strength of his understanding.

This most excellent governor commenced his administration on the 29th of May, 1647; a remarkably stormy day, distinguished in all the almanacks of the time which have come down to us by the name of "Windy Friday." As he was very jealous of his personal and official dignity, he was inaugurated into office with great ceremony, the goodly oaken chair of the renowned Wouter Van Twiller being carefully preserved for such occasions, in like manner as the chair and stone were reverentially preserved at Scone, in Scotland, for the coronation of the Caledonian monarchs.

The very first movements of the great Peter, on taking the reins of government, displayed his magnanimity, though they occasioned not a little marvel and uneasiness among the people of the Manhattoes. Finding himself constantly interrupted by the opposition, and annoyed by the advice of his privy council, the members of which had acquired the unreasonable habit of thinking and speaking to themselves during the preceding reign, he determined at once to put a stop to such grievous abominations. Scarcely, therefore, had he entered upon his authority, than he turned out of office all the meddlesome spirits of the factious cabinet of William the Testy; in place of whom he chose unto himself councillors from those fat, somniferous, respectable burghers who had flourished and slumbered under the easy reign of Walter the Doubter. All these he caused to be furnished with abundance of fair long pipes, and to be regaled with frequent corporation dinners, admonishing them to smoke, and eat, and sleep for the good of the nation, while he took the burden of government upon his own shoulders—an arrangement to which they all gave hearty acquiescence.

But the measure of the valiant Peter which produced the greatest agitation in the community was his laying his hand upon the currency. He had old-fashioned notions in favor of gold and silver, which he considered the true standards of wealth and mediums of commerce, and one of his first edicts was that all duties to government should be paid in those precious metals, and that seawant, or wampum, should no longer be a legal tender.

Here was a blow at public prosperity! All those who speculated on the rise and fall of this fluctuating currency found their calling at an end; those, too, who had hoarded Indian money by barrels full, found their capital shrunk in amount; but, above all, the Yankee traders, who were accustomed to flood the market with newly-coined oyster-shells, and to abstract Dutch merchandise in exchange, were loud-mouthed in decrying this "tampering with the currency." It was clipping the wings of commerce; it was checking the development of public prosperity; trade would be at an end; goods would moulder on the shelves; grain would rot in the granaries; grass would grow in the marketplace. In a word, no one who has not heard the outcries and howlings of a modern Tarshish, at any check upon "paper money," can have any idea of the clamor against Peter the Headstrong for checking the circulation of oyster-shells.

In fact, trade did shrink into narrower channels; but then the stream was deep as it was broad. The honest Dutchman sold less goods; but then they got the worth of them, either in silver and gold, or in codfish, tinware, apple-brandy, Weathersfield onions, wooden bowls, and other articles of Yankee barter. The ingenious people of the east, however, indemnified themselves in another way for having to abandon the coinage of oyster-shells, for about this time we are told that wooden nutmegs made their first appearance in New Amsterdam, to the great annoyance of the Dutch housewives.

The Original Manors and Patents—According to a map of the Province of New York, published in 1779, the Phillipsburg Patent embraced a large part of Westchester County. North of this was the Manor of Cortland, reaching from Tarrytown to Anthony's Nose. Above this was the Phillipse Patent, reaching to the mouth of Fishkill Creek, embracing Putnam County. Between Fishkill Creek and the Wappingers Creek was the Rombout Patent. The Schuyler Patent embraced a few square miles in the vicinity of Poughkeepsie. Above this was the purchase of Falconer & Company, and east of this tract what was known as the Great Nine Partners. Above the Falconer Purchase was the

Henry Beekman Patent, reaching to Esopus Island, and east of this the Little Nine Partners. Above the Beekman Patent was the Schuyler Patent. Then the Manor of Livingston, reaching from Rhinebeck to Catskill Station, opposite Catskill. Above this Rensselaerwick, reaching north to a point opposite Coeymans. The Manor of Rensselaer extended on both sides of the river to a line running nearly east and west, just above Troy. North and west of this Manor was the County of Albany, since divided into Rensselaer, Saratoga, Washington, Schoharie, Greene and Albany. The Rensselaer Manor was the only one that reached across the river. The west bank of the Hudson, below the Rensselaer Manor, is simply indicated on this map of 1779 as Ulster and Orange Counties.

Henry Hudson with his son and eight crew members set adrift to die after a mutiny in Hudson Bay, Canada, June, 1611.

Washington's headquarters near Newburgh, with Hudson River and mountains. Engraving by Virtue, Emmins & Co., c. 1857.

What sights and sounds at which the world has wondered
Within these wild ravines have had their birth!
Young Freedom's cannon from these glens have thundered
And sent their startling echoes o'er the earth.

—Charles Fenno Hoffman

ew York—The *Encyclopaedia Britannica* thus briefly puts the history of those far-off days when New York was a town of about 1500 inhabitants: "The English Government was hostile to any other occupation of the New World than its own. In 1621 James I. claimed sovereignty over New Netherland by right of 'occupancy.' In 1632 Charles I. reasserted the English title of 'first discovery, occupation and possession.' In 1654 Cromwell ordered an expedition for its conquest and the New England Colonies had engaged their support. The treaty with Holland arrested their operations and recognized the title of the Dutch. In 1664 Charles the Second resolved upon a conquest of New Netherland. The immediate excuse was the loss to the revenue of the English Colonies by the smuggling practices of their Dutch neighbors. A patent was granted to the Duke of York giving to him all the lands and rivers from the west side of the Connecticut River to the east side of Delaware Bay."

"On the 29th of August an English Squadron under the direction of Col. Richard Nicolls, the Duke's Deputy Governor, appeared off the Narrows, and on Sept. 8th New Amsterdam, defenseless against the force, was formally surrendered by Stuyvesant. In 1673 (August 7th) war being declared between England and Holland a Dutch squadron surprised New York, captured the City and restored the Dutch authority, and the names of New Netherland and New Amsterdam. But in July, 1674, a treaty of peace restored New York to English rule. A new patent was issued to the Duke of York, and Major Edmund Andros was appointed Governor."

On the 10th of November, 1674, the Province of New Netherland was surrendered to Governor Major Edmund Andros on behalf of his Britannic Majesty. The letter sent by Governor Andros to the Dutch Governor is interesting in this connection: "Being arrived to this place with orders to receive from you in the behalf of his Majesty of Great Britain, pursuant to the late articles of peace with the States Generals of the United Netherlands, the New Netherlands and Dependencies, now under your command, I have herewith, by Capt. Philip

Carterett and Ens. Caesar Knafton, sent you the respective orders from the said States General, the States of Zealand and Admirality of Amsterdam to that effect, and desire you'll please to appoint some short time for it. Our soldiers having been long aboard, I pray you answer by these gentlemen, and I shall be ready to serve you in what may lay in my power. Being from aboard his Majesty's ship, 'The Diamond,' at anchor near. Your very humble servant. Staten Island this 22d Oct., 1674." After nineteen days' deliberation, which greatly annoyed Governor Andros, New Amsterdam was transferred from Dutch to English authority.

෨෮

"In 1683 Thomas Dongan succeeded Andros. A general Assembly, the first under the English rule, met in October, 1683, and adopted a Charter of Liberties, which was confirmed by the Duke. In August, 1684, a new covenant was made with the Iroquois, who formally acknowledged the jurisdiction of Great Britain, but not subjection. By the accession of the Duke of York to the English throne the Duchy of New York became a royal province. The Charters of the New England Colonies were revoked, and together with New York and New Jersey they were consolidated into the dominion of New England. Dongan was recalled and Sir Edmund Andros was commissioned Governor General. He assumed his vice regal authority August 11, 1688. The Assembly which James had abolished in 1686 was reestablished, and in May declared the rights and privileges of the people, reaffirming the principles of the repealed Charter of Liberties of October 30, 1683."

◎

Captain Kidd—"My name was Captain Kidd as I sailed," are famous lines of an old ballad which was once familiar to our grandfathers. The hapless hero of the same was born about the middle of the seventeenth century, and it is thought, near Greenock, Scotland. He resided at one time in New York, near the corner of William and Cedar Streets, and was there married. In April, 1696, he sailed from England in command of the "Adventure Galley," with full armament and eighty men. He captured a French ship, and, on arrival at New York, put up articles for volunteers; remained in New York three or four months, increasing his crew to one hundred and fifty-five men, and sailed thence to Madras, thence to Bonavista and St. Jago, Madagascar, then to Calicut, then to Madagascar again, then sailed and took the "Quedah Merchant." Kidd kept forty shares of the spoils, and divided the rest with his crew. He then burned the "Adventure Galley," went on board the "Quedah Merchant," and steered for the West Indies. Here he left the "Merchant," with part of his crew, under one Bolton, as commander. Then manned a sloop, and taking part of his spoils, went to Boston via Long Island Sound, and is said to have set goods on shore at different places. In the meantime, in August, 1698, the East Indian

Company informed the Lords Justice that Kidd had committed several acts of piracy, particularly in seizing a Moor's ship called the "Quedah Merchant." When Kidd landed at Boston he was therefore arrested by the Earl of Bellamont, and sent to England for trial, 1699, where he was found guilty and executed. Now it is supposed that the crew of the "Quedah Merchant," which Kidd left at Hispaniola, sailed for their homes, as the crew was mostly gathered from the Highlands and above. It is said that they passed New York in the night, en route to the manor of Livingston; but encountering a gale in the Highlands, and thinking they were pursued, ran her near the shore, now known as Kidd's Point, and here scuttled her, the crew fleeing to the woods with such treasure as they could carry. Whether this circumstance was true or not, it was at least a current story in the neighborhood, and an enterprising individual, about fifty years ago, caused an old cannon to be "discovered" in the river, and perpetrated the first "Cardiff Giant Hoax." A New York Stock Company was organized to prosecute the work. It was said that the ship could be seen in clear days, with her masts still standing, many fathoms below the surface. One thing is certain—the company did not see it or the treasurer either, in whose hands were deposited about $30,000.

From this time on to the Revolution of 1776 there is one continual struggle between the Royal Governors and the General Assembly. The Governor General had the power of dissolving the Assembly, but the Assembly had the power of granting money. British troops were quartered in New York which increased the irritation. The conquest of Canada left a heavy burden upon Great Britain, a part of which their Parliament attempted to shift to the shoulders of the Colonies.

A general Congress of the Colonies, held in New York in 1765, protested against the Stamp Act and other oppressive ordinances and they were in part repealed.

A Page of Patriotism—During the long political agitation New York, the most English of the Colonies in her manners and feelings, was in close harmony with the Whig leaders of England. She firmly adhered to the principle of the sovereignty of the people which she had inscribed on her ancient "Charter of Liberties." Although largely dependent upon commerce she was the first to recommend a non-importation of English merchandise as a measure of retaliation against Britain, and she was the first also to invite a general congress of all the Colonies. On the breaking out of hostilities New York immediately joined the patriot cause. The English authority was overthrown and the government passed to a provincial congress.

New York Sons of Liberty—In 1767, in the eighth year of the reign of George III. there was issued a document in straight-forward Saxon, and Sir Henry Moore, Governor-in-Chief over the Province of New York, offered fifty pounds to discover the author or authors. The paper read as follows: "Whereas, a glorious stand for Liberty did appear in the Resentment shown to a Set of Miscreants under the Name of Stamp Masters, in the year 1765, and it is now feared that a set of Gentry called Commissioners (I do not mean those lately arrived at Boston), whose odious Business is of a similar nature, may soon make their appearance amongst us in order to execute their detestable office. It is therefore hoped that every votary of that celestial Goddess Liberty, will hold themselves in readiness to give them a proper welcome. Rouse, my Countrymen, Rouse! (Signed) Pro Patria."

In December, 1769, a stirring address "To the Betrayed Inhabitants of the City and County of New York," signed by a Son of Liberty, was also published, asking the people to do their duty in matters pending between them and Britain. "Imitate," the writer said, "the noble examples of the friends of Liberty in England; who, rather than be enslaved, contend for their rights with king, lords and commons; and will you suffer your liberties to be torn from you by your Representatives? tell it not in Boston; publish it not in the streets of Charles-town. You have means yet left to preserve a unanimity with the brave Bostonians and Carolinians; and to prevent the accomplishment of the designs of tyrants."

Another proclamation, offering a reward of fifty pounds, was published by the "Honorable Cadwalader Colden, Esquire, His Majesty's Lieutenant-Governor and Commander-in-Chief of the Province of New York and the territories depending thereon in America," with another "God Save the King" at the end of it. But the people who commenced to write Liberty with a capital letter and the word "king" in lower case type were not daunted. Captain Alexander McDougal was arrested as the supposed author. He was imprisoned eighty-one days. He was subsequently a member of the Provincial Convention, in 1775 was appointed Colonel of the first New York Regiment, and in 1777 rose to the rank of Major-General in the U.S. Army. New York City could well afford a monument to the Sons of Liberty. She has a right to emphasize this period of her history, for her citizens passed the first resolution to import nothing from the mother country, burned ten boxes of stamps sent from England before any other colony or city had made even a show of resistance, and when the Declaration was read, pulled down the leaden statue of George III from its pedestal in Bowling Green, and moulded it into Republican bullets.

In 1699 the population of New York was about 6,000. In 1800, it reached 60,000; and the growth since that date is almost incredible. It is amusing to hear elderly people speak of the "outskirts of the city" lying close to the City Hall, and of the drives in the country above Canal Street. In the *Documentary History of New York*, a map of a section of New York appears as it was in 1793, when the Gail, Work House, and Bridewell occupied the site of the City Hall, with two ponds to the north—East Collect Pond and Little Collect Pond,—sixty feet deep and about a quarter of a mile in diameter, the outlet of which crossed Broadway at Canal Street and found its way to the Hudson.

☙

George Washington—After the withdrawl of the American army from Long Island, it became apparent to General Washington and Hamilton that New York would have to be abandoned. General Greene and Congress believed in maintaining the fort, but future developments showed that Washington was right. The American troops, so far as clothing or equipment was concerned, were in a pitiable condition, and the result of the struggle makes one of the darkest pages of the war. On the 12th of November Washington started from Stony Point for Fort Lee and arrived the 13th, finding to his disappointment that General Greene, instead of having made arrangements for evacuating, was, on the contrary, reinforcing Fort Washington. The entire defense numbered only about 2000 men, mostly militia, with hardly a coat, to quote an English writer, "that was not out at the elbows." "On the night of the 14th thirty flat-bottomed boats stole quietly up the Hudson, passed the American forts undiscovered, and made their way through Spuyten Duyvil Creek into Harlem River. The means were thus provided for crossing that river, and landing before unprotected parts of the American works."

According to Irving, "On the 15th General Howe sent a summons to surrender, with a threat of extremities should he have to carry the place by assault." Magaw, in his reply, intimated a doubt that General Howe would execute a threat "so unworthy of himself and the British nation; but give me leave," added he, "to assure his Excellency, that, actuated by the most glorious cause that mankind ever fought in, I am determined to defend this post to the very last extremity."

"Apprised by the colonel of his peril, General Greene sent over reinforcements, with an exhortation to him to persist in his defense; and dispatched an express to General Washington, who was at Hackensack, where the troops from Peekskill were encamped. It was nightfall when Washington arrived at Fort Lee. Greene and Putnam were over at the besieged fortress. He threw himself into a boat, and had partly crossed the river, when he met those Generals returning. They informed him of the garrison having been reinforced, and assured him that it was in high spirits, and capable of making a good defense. It was with difficulty, however, they could prevail on him to return with them to the Jersey shore, for he was excessively excited."

"Early the next morning, Magaw made his dispositions for the expected attack. His forces, with the recent addition, amounted to nearly three thousand men. As the fort could not contain above a third of its defenders, most of them were stationed about the outworks."

About noon, a heavy cannonade thundered along the rocky hills, and sharp volleys of musketry, proclaimed that the action was commenced.

"Washington, surrounded by several of his officers, had been an anxious spectator of the battle from the opposite side of the Hudson. Much of it was hidden from him by intervening hills and forest; but the roar of cannonry from the valley of the Harlem River, the sharp and incessant reports of rifles, and the smoke rising above the tree-tops, told him of the spirit with which the assault was received at various points, and gave him for a time hope that the defense might be successful. The action about the lines to the south lay open to him, and could be distinctly seen through a telescope; and nothing encouraged him more than the gallant style in which Cadwalader with inferior force maintained his position. When he saw him however, assailed in flank, the line broken, and his troops, overpowered by

General Horatio Gates, Major General of the American forces in the Revolutionary War. From "An Impartial history of the war in America," 1780.

numbers, retreating to the fort, he gave up the game as lost. The worst sight of all, was to behold his men cut down and bayoneted by the Hessians while begging quarter. It is said so completely to have overcome him, that he wept with the tenderness of a child."

"Seeing the flag go into the fort from Knyphausen's division, and surmising it to be a summons to surrender, he wrote a note to Magaw, telling him if he could hold out until evening and the place could not be maintained, he would endeavor to bring off the garrison in the night. Capt. Gooch, of Boston, a brave and daring man, offered to be the bearer of the note. He ran down to the river, jumped into a small boat, pushed over the river, landed under the bank, ran up to the fort and delivered the message, came out, ran and jumped over the broken ground, dodging the Hessians, some of whom struck at him with their pieces and others attempted to thrust him with their bayonets; escaping through them, he got to his boat and returned to Fort Lee."

Washington's message arrived too late. "The fort was so crowded by the garrison and the troops which had retreated into it, that it was difficult to move about. The enemy, too, were in possession of the little redoubts around, and could have poured in showers of shells and ricochet balls that would have made dreadful slaughter." It was no longer possible for Magaw to get his troops to man the lines; he was compelled, therefore, to yield himself and his garrison prisoners of war.

The only terms granted them were, that the men should retain their baggage and the officers their swords.

The capture of Fort Clinton and Fort Montgomery was two years before Mad Anthony's successful assault on Stony Point. Early in the history of the Revolution, the British Government thought that it would be possible to cut off the eastern from the middle and southern Colonies by capturing and garrisoning commanding points along the Hudson and Lake Champlain. It was therefore decided in London, in the spring of 1777, to have Sir Henry Clinton approach from the south and Burgoyne from the north. Reinforcements, however, arrived late from England and it was September before Clinton transported his troops, about 4,000 in number, in warships and flat-boats up the river. Governor George Clinton was in charge of Fort Montgomery, and his brother James of Fort Clinton, while General Putnam, with about 2,000 men, had his headquarters at Peekskill. In addition to these forts, a chain was stretched across the Hudson from Anthony's Nose to a point near the present railroad bridge, to obstruct the British fleet. General Putnam, however, became convinced that Sir Henry Clinton proposed to attack Fort Independence. Most of the troops were accordingly withdrawn from Forts Montgomery and Clinton, when Sir Henry Clinton, taking advantage of a morning fog, crossed with 2,000 men.

"Mad" Anthony Wayne—the crossing known as King's Ferry, at and before the days of '76, was quite an avenue of travel between the Southern, Middle and Eastern States. The fort crowning a commanding headland, was captured by the British, June 1, 1779, but it was surprised and recaptured by Anthony Wayne, July 15 of the same year. A centennial was observed at the place July 15, 1879, when the battle was "refought" and the West Point Cadets showed how they would have done it if they had been on hand a century ago. Thackeray, in his "Virginians," gives perhaps the most graphic account of this midnight battle. The present light-house occupies the site of the old fort, and was built in part of stone taken from its walls. Upon its capture by the British, Washington, whose headquarters were at New Windsor, meditated a bold stroke and summoned Anthony Wayne, more generally known as "Mad Anthony," from his reckless daring, to undertake its recapture with a force of one thousand picked men. The lines were formed in two columns about 8 p.m. at "Springsteel's farm." Each soldier and officer put a piece of white paper in his hat to distinguish him from the foe. No guns were to be loaded under penalty of death.

General Wayne, at the head of the column, forded the marsh covered at the time with two feet of water. The other column led by Butler and Murfree crossed an apology for a bridge. During the advance both columns were discovered by the British sentinels and the rocky defense literally blazed with musketry. In stern silence, however, without faltering, the American columns moved forward, entered the abatis, until the advance guard under Anthony

Wayne was within the enemy's works. A bullet at this moment struck Wayne in the forehead grazing his skull. Quickly recovering from the shock, he rose to his knees, shouted: "Forward, my brave fellows"; then turning to two of his followers, he asked them to help him into the fort that he might die, if it were to be so, "in possession of the spot." Both columns were now at hand and inspired by the brave general, came pouring in, crying "The fort's our own." The British troops completely overwhelmed, were fain to surrender and called for mercy. Wayne's characteristic message to Washington antedates modern telegraphic brevity:— "Stony Point, 2 o'clock a.m. The American flag waves here.—Mad Anthony." There were twenty killed and sixty wounded on each side. Some five hundred of the enemy were captured and about sixty escaped. "Money rewards and medals were given to Wayne and the leaders in the assault. The ordinance and stores captured were appraised at over $180,000 and there was universal rejoicing" throughout the land. "Stony Point State Park" was dedicated by appropriate ceremony July 16, 1902. At the close of Governor Odell's address the flag was raised by William Wayne, a lineal descendant of the hero, and the cruiser "Olympia" of Manila fame boomed forth her tribute. Verplank's Point, on the east bank (now full of brick-making establishments), was the site of Fort Lafayette. It was here that Baron Steuben drilled the soldiers of the American army. Back from Green Cove above Verplanck's Point is "Knickerbocker Lake."

Benedict Arnold—At Tarrytown, 26 miles from New York on the Old Post Road, now called Broadway, a little north of the village, Major Andre was captured and Arnold's treachery exposed. A monument erected on the spot by the people of Westchester County, October 7, 1853, bears the inscription:

> *ON THIS SPOT, THE 23D DAY OF SEPTEMBER,*
> *1780, THE SPY,*
> *MAJOR JOHN ANDRE,*
> *Adjutant-General of the British Army, was captured by*
> *JOHN PAULDING, DAVID WILLIAMS, AND*
> *ISAAC VAN WART.*
> *ALL NATIVES OF THIS COUNTY.*

The following quaint ballad-verses on the young hero give a realistic touch to one of the most providential occurrences in our history:

> *He with a scouting party*
> *Went down to Tarrytown,*
> *Where he met a British officer,*
> *A man of high renown,*
> *Who says unto these gentlemen,*
> *"You're of the British cheer,*
> *I trust that you can tell me*
> *If there's any danger near?"*

Then up stept this young hero,
John Paulding was his name,
"Sir, tell us where you're going
And also whence you came?"
"I bear the British flag, sir;
I've a pass to go this way,
I'm on an expedition,
And have no time to stay."

Young Paulding, however, thought that he had plenty of time to linger until he examined his boots, wherein he found the papers, and, when offered ten guineas by Andre, if he would allow him to pursue his journey, replied: "If it were ten thousand guineas you could not stir one step."

The centennial anniversary of the event was commemorated in 1880 by placing, through the generosity of John Anderson, on the original obelisk of 1853, a large statue representing John Paulding as a minute man.

Almost opposite Irvington about two miles southwest of Piermont, is old Tappantown, where Major Andre was executed October 2, 1780. The removal of his body from Tappan to Westminster was by a special British ship, and a singular incident was connected with it. The roots of a cypress tree were found entwined about his skull and a scion from the tree was carried to England and planted in the garden adjoining Windsor Palace. It is a still more curious fact that the tree beneath which Andre was captured was struck by lightning on the day of Benedict Arnold's death in London.

That overruling Providence which has so often and so remarkably interposed in our favor, never manifested itself more conspicuously than in the timely discovery of Arnold's treachery.

—George Washington

Beverley House—at Cohn's Hook, pronounced Connosook, is where Benedict Arnold had his headquarters when in command of West Point. The old house, a good specimen of colonial times, was unfortunately burned in 1892, and with it went the most picturesque landmark of the most dramatic incident of the Revolution.

It will be remembered that Arnold returned to the Beverley House after his midnight interview with Andre at Haverstraw, and immediately upon the capture of Andre the following day, that Colonel Jamison sent a letter to Arnold, advising him of the fact. It was the morning of September 4th. General Washington was on his way to West Point, coming across the country from Connecticut. On arriving, however, at the river, just above the present station of Garrison, he became interested in examining some defenses, and sent Alexander Hamilton forward to the Beverley House, saying that he would come later, requesting the family to proceed with their breakfast and not to await his arrival.

Alexander Hamilton and General Lafayette sat gayly chatting with Mrs Arnold and her husband when the letter from Jamison was received. Arnold glanced at the contents, rose and excused himself from the table, beckoning to his wife to follow him, bade her good-bye, told her he was a ruined man and a traitor, kissed his little boy in the cradle, rode to Beverley Dock, and ordered his men to pull off and go down the river. The "Vulture," an English man-of-war, was near Teller's Point, and received a traitor, whose miserable treachery branded him with eternal infamy on both continents.

It is said that he lived long enough to be hissed in the House of Commons, as he once took his seat in the gallery, and he died friendless and despised. It is also said, when Talleyrand arrived in Havre on foot from Paris, in the darkest hour of the French Revolution, pursued by the bloodhounds of the reign of terror, and was about to secure a passage to the United States, he asked the landlord of the hotel whether any Americans were staying at his house, as he was going across the water, and would like a letter to a person of influence in the New World. "There is a gentleman up-stairs from Britain or America," was the response. He pointed the way, and Talleyrand ascended the stairs. In a dimly lighted room sat a man of whom the great minister of France was to ask a favor. He advanced, and poured forth in elegant French and broken English, "I am a wanderer, and an exile. I am forced to fly to the New World without a friend or home. You are an American. Give me, then, I beseech you, a letter of yours, so that I may be able to earn my bread." The strange gentleman rose. With a look that Talleyrand never forgot, he retreated toward the door of the next chamber. He spoke as he retreated, and his voice was full of suffering: "I am the only man of the New World who can raise his hand to God and say, 'I have not a friend, not one, in America!'" "Who are you?" he cried—"your name?" "My name is Benedict Arnold!"

○○

Alexander Hamilton—The duel between Hamilton and Burr occurred near Weehauken. A monument once marked the spot, erected by the St. Andrews Society of New York City on the ledge of rock where Hamilton fell early in the morning of the eleventh of July, 1804. The quarrel between this great statesman and his malignant rival was, perhaps, more personal than political. It is said that Hamilton, in accordance with the old-time code of honor, accepted the challenge, but fired into the air, while Burr with fiendish cruelty took deliberate revenge. Burr was never forgiven by the citizens of New York and from that hour walked its streets shunned and despised. Among the many poetic tributes penned at the time to the memory of Hamilton, perhaps the best was by a poet whose name is now scarcely remembered, Mr. Robert C. Sands. A fine picture of Hamilton will be found in the New York Chamber of Commerce where the writer was recently shown the following concise paragraph from Talleyrand: "The three greatest men of my time, in my opinion, were Napoleon Bonaparte, Charles James Fox and Alexander Hamilton and the greatest of the three was Hamilton."

○○

End of Revolutionary War—In the spring of 1782 Washington made his headquarters at Newbergh and remained here until August 18, 1783, on the morning of which day he took his departure. At this place he passed through the most trying period of the Revolution: the year of inactivity on the part of Congress, of distress throughout the country, and of complaint and discontent in the army, the latter at one time bordering on revolt among the officers and soldiers.

It was at this place, on the 22d day of May, 1782, that Colonel Nicola, on behalf of himself and others, proposed that Washington should become king, for the "national advantage," a proposal that was received by Washington with "surprise and astonishment," "viewed with abhorrence," and "reprehended with severity." The temptation which was thus repelled by Washington, had its origin with that portion of the officers of the army, who while giving their aid heartily to secure an independent government, nevertheless believed that that government should be a monarchy. The rejection of the proposition by Washington was not the only significant result. The rank and file of the army rose up against it, and around their camp-fires chanted their purpose in Billings' song, "No King but God!" From that hour a republic became the only possible form of government for the enfranchised Colonies.

With silvered locks and eyes grown dim,

As victory's sun proclaimed the morn,

He pushed aside the diadem

With stern rebuke and patriot scorn.

—*Wallace Bruce*

୬୦

The inattention of Congress to the payment of the army, during the succeeding winter, gave rise to an equally important episode in the history of the war. On the 10th of March, 1783, the first of the famous "Newburgh Letters" was issued, in which, by implication at least, the army was advised to revolt. The letter

Washington's headquarters near Newburgh

was followed by an anonymous manuscript notice for a public meeting of officers on the succeeding Tuesday. Washington was equal to the emergency. He expressed his disapprobation of the whole proceeding, and with great wisdom, requested the field officers, with one commissioned officer from each company, to meet on the Saturday preceding the time appointed by the anonymous notice. He attended this meeting and delivered before it one of the most touching and effective addresses on record. When he closed his remarks, the officers unanimously resolved "to reject with disdain" the infamous proposition contained in the anonymous address.

The meeting of officers referred to was held at the New Building or "Temple" as it was called, in New Windsor, but Washington's address was written at his headquarters. The "Newburgh Letters," to which it was a reply, were written by Major John Armstrong, aid-de-camp to General Gates. The anonymously called meeting was not held. The motives of its projectors we will not discuss; but its probable effect, had it been successful, must be considered in connection with Washington's encomium of the result of the meeting which he had addressed: "Had this day been wanting, the world had never known the height to which human greatness is capable of attaining.'

Notice of the cessation of hostilities was proclaimed to the army April 19, 1783. It was received with great rejoicings by the troops at Newburgh, and under Washington's order, was the occasion of an appropriate celebration. In the evening, signal beacon lights proclaimed the joyous news to the surrounding country. Thirteen cannon came pealing up from Fort Putnam, which were followed by a "feu-de-joie" rolling along the lines. The mountain sides resounded and echoed like tremendous peals of thunder, and the flashing from thousands of fire-arms, in the darkness of the evening, was like unto vivid flashes of lightning from the clouds. From this time furloughs were freely granted to soldiers who wished to return to their homes, and when the army was finally disbanded those absent were discharged from service without being required to return. That portion of the army, which remained at Newburgh on guard duty, after the removal of the main body to West Point in June, were participants here in the closing scenes of the disbandment, when, on the morning of November 3, 1783, "the proclamation of Congress and the farewell orders of Washington were read, and the last word of command given."

From Monell's "Handbook of Washington's Headquarters" we also quote a general description of the house and its appearance when occupied by the commander-in-chief. "Washington's family consisted of himself, his wife, and his aid-de-camp, Major Tench Tilghman. The large room, which is entered from the piazza on the east, known as 'the room with seven doors and one window,' was used as the dining and sitting-room.

The northeast room was Washington's bedroom and the one adjoining it on the left was occupied by him as a private office. The family room was that in the southeast; the kitchen was the southwest room; the parlor the northwest room. Between the latter and the former was the hall and staircase and the store-room, so called for having been used by Colonel Hasbrouck and subsequently by his widow as a store. The parlor was mainly reserved for Mrs. Washington and her guests. A Mrs. Hamilton, whose name frequently appears in Washington's account book, was his housekeeper, and in the early part of the war made a reputation for her zeal in his service, which Thacher makes note of and Washington acknowledges in his reference to an exchange of salt. There was little room for the accommodation of guests, but it is presumed that the chambers were reserved for that purpose. Washington's guests, however, were mainly connected with the army and had quarters else-where. Even Lafayette had rooms at DeGrove's Hotel when a visitor at headquarters.

"The building is now substantially in the condition it was during Washington's occupation of it. The same massive timbers span the ceiling; the old fire-place with its wide-open chimney is ready for the huge back-logs of yore; the seven doors are in their places; the rays of the morning sun still stream through the one window; no alteration in form has been made in the old piazza—the adornments on the walls, if such the ancient host-ess had, have alone been changed for souvenirs of the heroes of the nation's independence. In presence of these surroundings, it requires but little effort of the imagination to restore the departed guests. Forgetting not that this was Washington's private residence, rather than a place for the transaction of public business, we may, in the old sitting-room respread the long oaken table, listen to the blessing invoked on the morning meal, hear the cracking of joints, and the mingled hum of conversation. The meal dispensed, Mrs. Washington retires to appear at her flower beds or in her parlor to receive her morning calls. Colfax, the captain of the life-guard, enters to receive the orders of the day— perhaps a horse and guard for Washington to visit New Windsor, or a barge for Fishkill or West Point, is required; or it may be Washington remains at home and at his writing desk conducts his correspondence, or dictates orders for army movements. The old arm-chair, sitting in the corner yonder, is still ready for its former occupant.

"The dinner hour of five o'clock approaches; the guests of the day have already arrived. Steuben, the iron drill-master and German soldier of fortune, converses with Mrs. Washington. He had reduced the simple marksmen of Bunker Hill to the discipline of the armies of Europe and tested their efficiency in the din of battle. He has leisure now, and scarcely knows how to find employment for his active mind. He is telling his hostess, in broken German-English, of the whale (it proved to be an eel) he had caught in the river. Hear his hostess laugh! And that is the voice of Lafayette, relating perhaps his adventures in escaping from France, or his mishap in attempting to attend Mrs. Knox's last party. Wayne, of Stony Point; Gates, of Saratoga; Clinton, the

Washington and Steuben, on horseback, greet Lafayette during the winter at Valley Forge, circa 1895.

Irish-blooded Governor of New York, and their compatriots—we may place them all at times beside our "Pater Patriae" in this old room, and hear amid the mingled hum his voice declare: 'Happy, thrice happy, shall they be pronounced hereafter, who have contributed anything, who have performed the meanest office in erecting this stupendous fabric of Freedom and Empire on the broad basis of independency; who have assisted in protecting the rights of human nature, and in establishing an asylum for the poor and oppressed of all nations and religions.'

"In France, some fifty years after the Revolution, Marbois reproduced, as an entertainment for Lafayette, then an old man, this old sitting-room and its table scene. From his elegant saloon he conducted his guests, among whom were several Americans, to the room which he had prepared. There was a large open fire-place, and plain oaken floors; the ceiling was supported with large beams and whitewashed; there were the seven small-sized doors and one window with heavy sash and small panes of glass. The furniture was plain and unlike any then in use. Down the center of the room was an oaken table covered with dishes of meat and vegetables, decanters and bottles of wine, and silver mugs and small wine glasses. The whole had something the appearance of a Dutch kitchen. While the guests were looking around in surprise at this strange procedure, the host, addressing himself to them said, 'Do you know where we now are?' Lafayette looked around, and, as if awakening from a dream, he exclaimed, 'Ah! the seven doors and one window, and the silver camp goblets such as the Marshals of France used in my youth. We are at Washington's Headquarters on the Hudson fifty years ago.' "

☙

Montgomery Place—formerly occupied by Mrs. Montgomery, wife of General Montgomery and sister of Chancellor Livingston. The following dramatic incident connected with Montgomery Place is recorded in Stone's "History of New York City": "In 1818 the legislature of New York—DeWitt Clinton, Governor—

ordered the remains of General Montgomery to be removed from Canada to New York. This was in accordance with the wishes of the Continental Congress, which, in 1776, had voted the beautiful cenotaph to his memory that now stands in the wall of St. Paul's Church, fronting Broadway. When the funeral cortege reached Whitehall, N. Y., the fleet stationed there received them with appropriate honors; and on the 4th of July they arrived in Albany. After lying in state in that city over Sunday, the remains were taken to New York, and on Wednesday deposited, with military honors, in their final resting place, at St. Paul's. Governor Clinton had informed Mrs. Montgomery of the hour when the steamer 'Richmond,' conveying the body, would pass her home. At her own request, she stood alone on the portico. It was forty years since she had parted from her husband, to whom she had been wedded but two years when he fell on the heights of Quebec; yet she had remained faithful to the memory of her 'soldier,' as she always called him. The steamboat halted before the mansion; the band played the 'Dead March,' and a salute was fired; and the ashes of the venerated hero, and the departed husband, passed on.

"The attendants of the Spartan widow now appeared, but, overcome by the tender emotions of the moment, she had swooned and fallen to the floor."

Hudson and Palisades from Riverside Drive. Stereograph, c. 1909.

How grateful is the sudden change
From arid pavements to the grass,
From narrow streets that thousands range
To meadows where June zephyrs pass.

—Henry T. Tuckerman

CHAPTER 4

19th Century

Greater New York—In 1830, the population of Manhattan was 202,000; in 1850, 515,000; in 1860, 805,000; in 1870, 942,000; in 1880, 1,250,000; in 1892, 1,801,739; and is now rapidly approaching three million. Brooklyn, which in 1800 had a population of only 2,000, now contributes, as the "Borough of Brooklyn," almost two million. So that Greater New York is the center of about six million of people within a radius of fifteen miles including her New Jersey suburbs with almost five millions under one municipality.

Robert Fulton—was born in 1765, and at the time of Symington's experiment in Scotland, was twenty-three years of age. He was then an artist student of Benjamin West, in London, but, after several years of study, felt that he was better adapted for engineering, and soon thereafter wrote a work on canal navigation. In 1797 he went to Paris. He resided there seven years and built a small steamboat on the Seine, which worked well, but made very slow progress.

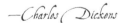

Robert Fulton, from an original painting by Chappel. Engraving by Johnson, Wilson & Co., 1874.

It is remarkable that the two most practical achievements of our century have been consummated by artists,—the telegraph by Morse after a score of "invented" failures, and the successful application of steam to navigation by Fulton.

☙❧

I was glad to think that among the last memorable beauties which have glided past us were pictures traced by no common hand, not easily to grow old or fade beneath the dust of time—the Kaatskill Mountains, Sleepy Hollow and the Tappan Zee.

—*Charles Dickens*

☙❧

Soon after his return to New York he brought his idea to successful completion. His reputation was now assured, and his invention of "torpedoes" gave him additional fame. Congress not only purchased these instruments of warfare, but also set apart $320,000 for a steam frigate to be constructed under his supervision.

Through Livingston's influence the legislature passed an act granting to Fulton the exclusive privilege of navigating the waters of the State by means of steam power. The only conditions imposed were that he should, within a year, construct a boat of not less than "twenty tons burthen," which should navigate the Hudson at a speed not less than four miles an hour, and that one such boat should not fail of running regularly between New York and Albany for the space of one year.

"The Clermont"—Named after the ancestral home of the Livingstons, the Clermont was built for "Livingston and Fulton," by Charles Brownne in New York. The machinery came from the works of Watt and Bolton, England. She left the wharf of Corlear's Hook and the newspapers published with pride that she made in speed from four to five miles an hour. She was 100 feet in length and boasted of "three elegant cabins, one for the ladies and two for the gentlemen, with kitchen, library, and every convenience." She averaged 100 passengers up or down the river. Every passenger paid $7, for which he had dinner, tea and bed, breakfast and dinner, with the liberty to carry 200 pounds of baggage.

The stars are on the running stream,
And fling, as its ripples gently flow,
A burnished length of wavy-beam
In an eel-like, spiral line below.

—*Joseph Rodman Drake*

An original letter from Robert Fulton to the minister of Bavaria at the court of France, written in 1809, upon the question of putting steamboats on the Danube, is of interest at the present day: "The distance from New York to Albany is 160 miles; the tide rises as far as Albany; its velocity is on an average 1½ miles an hour.

"We thus have the tide half the time in favor of the boat and half the time against her. The boat is 100 feet long, 16 feet wide and 7 feet deep; the steam engine is of the power of 20 horses; she runs 4½ miles an hour in still water. Consequently when the tide is 1½ miles an hour in her favor she runs 5¾ miles an hour. When the tide is against her she runs 2¾ miles an hour. Thus in theory her average velocity is 4¼ miles an hour, but in practice we take advantage of the currents. When they are against us we keep near shore in the eddies, where the current is weak or the eddy in our favor; when the tide is in our favor we take the center of the stream and draw every advantage from it. In this way our average speed is 5 miles an hour, and we run to Albany, 160 miles, in about 32 hours." Previous to the invention of the steamboat there were two modes of conveyance. One was by the common sloops; they charged 42 francs, and were on the average four days in making the passage—they have sometimes been as long as eight days. The dread of such tedious voyages prevented great numbers of persons from going in sloops. The second mode of conveyance was the mail, or stage. They charged $8, or 44 francs, and the expenses on the road were about $5, or 30 francs, so that expenses amounted to $13. The time required was 48 hours. The steamboat has rendered the communication between New York and Albany so cheap and certain that the number of passengers are rapidly increasing. Persons who live 150 miles beyond Albany know the hour she will leave that city, and making their calculations to arrive at York, stay two days to transact business, return with the boat, and are with their families in one week. The facility has rendered the boat a great favorite with the public.

∽

Hudson River Steamboats—An accurate history of the growth and development of steam navigation on the Hudson, from the building of the "Clermont" by Robert Fulton to the building of the superb steamers of the Hudson River Day Line would form a very interesting book. The first six years produced six steamers:

Clermont, built in 1807	160 tons
Car of Neptune, built in 1809	295 tons
Hope, built in 1811	280 tons
Perseverance, built in 1811	280 tons
Paragon, built in 1811	331 tons
Richmond, built in 1813	370 tons

It makes one smile to read the newspaper notices of those days. The time was rather long, and the fare rather high—thirty-six hours to Albany, fare seven dollars.

From the *Albany Gazette*, September, 1807:

"The North River Steamboat will leave Paulus Hook Ferry on Friday the 4th of September, at 9 in the morning, and arrive at Albany at 9 in the afternoon on Saturday. Provisions, good berths, and accommodation are provided. For places apply to Wm. Vandervoort, No. 48 Courtland street, on the corner of Greenwich Street, September 2d, 1807." The charge to each passenger is as follows:

To Newburg Dols. $3, time 14 hours
Poughkeepsie Dols. $4, time 17 hours
Esopus Dols. $5, time 20 hours
Hudson Dols. $5½, time 30 hours
Albany Dols. $7, time 36 hours

From the *New York Evening Post*, October 2, 1807:

"Mr. Fulton's new-invented steamboat, which is fitted up in a neat style for passengers, and is intended to run from New York to Albany as a packet, left here this morning with ninety passengers, against a strong head wind. Notwithstanding which, it is judged that she moved through the waters at the rate of six miles an hour."

∾

From the *Albany Gazette*, October 5th, 1807:

"Friday, October 2d, 1807, the steamboat (Clermont) left New York at ten o'clock a.m., against a stormy tide, very rough water, and a violent gale from the north. She made a headway beyond the most sanguine expectations, and without being rocked by the waves.

"Arrived at Albany, October 4th, at 10 o'clock p.m., being detained by being obliged to come to anchor, owing to a gale and having one of her paddle wheels torn away by running foul of a sloop."

∾

From the *Poughkeepsie Eagle*:

"To Poughkeepsie from New York in Seventeen Hours. The first steamboat on the Hudson River passed Poughkeepsie August 17th, 1807, and in June, 1808, the owners of the boat caused the following advertisement to be published in prominent papers along the river:

Robert Fulton's steamship "Clermont," c. 1909.

"Steamboat—For the information of the public. The Steamboat will leave New York for Albany every Saturday afternoon exactly at 6 o'clock, and will pass:

West Point, about 4 o'clock Sunday morning.

Newburgh, 7 o'clock Sunday morning.

Poughkeepsie, 11 o'clock Sunday morning.

Esopus, 2 o'clock in the afternoon.

Red Hook, 4 o'clock in the afternoon.

Catskill, 7 o'clock in the afternoon.

Hudson, 8 o'clock in the evening.

"She will leave Albany for New York every Wednesday morning exactly at 8 o'clock, and pass:

Hudson, about 3 in the afternoon.

Esopus, 8 in the evening.

Poughkeepsie, 12 at night.

Newburgh, 4 Thursday morning.

West Point, 7 Thursday morning.

"As the time at which the boat may arrive at the different places above mentioned may vary an hour, more or less, according to the advantage or disadvantage of wind and tide, those who wish to come on board will see the necessity of being on the spot an hour before the time. Persons wishing to come on board from any other landing than these here specified can calculate the time the boat will pass and be ready on her arrival. Innkeepers or boatmen who bring passengers on board or take them ashore from any part of the river will be allowed one shilling for each person.

Prices of Passage—from New York.

To West Point	$2.30
To Newburgh	3.00
To Poughkeepsie	3.50
To Esopus	4.00
To Red Hook	4.50
To Hudson	5.00
To Albany	7.00

From Albany.

To Hudson	$2.00
To Red Hook	3.00
To Esopus	3.50
To Poughkeepsie	4.00
To Newburgh and West Point	4.50
To New York	7.00

"All other passengers are to pay at the rate of one dollar for every twenty miles, and a half dollar for every meal they may eat.

"Children from 1 to 5 years of age to pay one-third price and to sleep with persons under whose care they are.

"Young persons from 5 to 15 years of age to pay half price, provided they sleep two in a berth, and the whole price for each one who requests to occupy a whole berth.

"Servants who pay two-thirds price are entitled to a berth; they pay half price if they do not have a berth.

"Every person paying full price is allowed sixty pounds of baggage; if less than full price forty pounds. They are to pay at the rate of three cents per pound for surplus baggage. Storekeepers who wish to carry light and valuable merchandise can be accommodated on paying three cents a pound."

Day Line Steamers—As the cradle of successful steam navigation was rocked on the Hudson, it is fitting that the Day Line

Steamers should excel all others in beauty, grace and speed. There is no comparison between these river palaces and the steamboats on the Rhine or any river in Europe, as to equipment, comfort and rapidity. To make another reference to the great tourist route of Europe, the distance from Cologne to Coblenz is 60 miles, the same as from New York to Newburgh. It takes the Rhine steamers from seven to eight hours (as will be seen in Baedeker's Guide to that river) going up the stream, and from four and a half to five hours returning with the current. The Hudson by Daylight steamers en route to Albany make the run from New York to Newburgh in three hours; to Poughkeepsie in four hours, making stops at Yonkers, West Point and Newburgh. Probably no train on the best equipped railroad in our country reaches its stations with greater regularity than these steamers make their various landing. It astonishes a Mississippi or Missouri traveler to see the captain standing like a train-conductor, with watch in hand, to let off the gang-plank and pull the bell, at the very moment of the advertised schedule.

☙❧

The "Hendrick Hudson"—The "Hendrick Hudson" steamship was built at Newburgh by the Marvel Company, under contract with the W. & A. Fletcher Company of New York, who built her engines, and under designs from Frank E. Kirby. Her principal dimensions are: length, 400 feet; breadth over all, 82 feet; depth of hold, 14 feet 5 inches, and a draft of 7 feet 6 inches.

Her propelling machinery is what is known as the 3-cylinder compound direct acting engine, and her power (6,500-horse) is applied through side wheels with feathering buckets, and steam is supplied from eight boilers.

Steel has been used in her construction to such an extent that her hull, her bulk-heads (7 in all), her engine and boiler enclosures, her kitchen and ventilators, her stanchions, girders, and deck beams, and in fact the whole essential frame work of the boat is like a great steel building. Where wood is used it is hard wood, and in finish probably has no equal in marine work.

Her scheme of decoration, ventilation and sanitation is as artistic and scientific as modern methods can produce, and at the same time her general lay out for practical and comfortable operation is the evolution of the long number of years in which the Day Line has been conducting the passenger business.

A detailed account of this steamer would be a long story, but some of the salient features are as follows: She carries the largest passenger license ever issued, namely: for 5,000 people; on her trial trip she made the fastest record through the water of any inland passenger ship in this country, namely: 23.1 miles per hour. Her shafts are under the main deck. Her mural paintings represent prominent features of the Hudson, which may not be well seen from the steamer. Her equipment far exceeds the requirements of the Government Inspection Laws.

Ice Industry—which reaches from below Staatsburgh to Castleton and Albany, well described by John Burroughs in his article on the Hudson: "No man sows, yet many men reap a harvest from the Hudson. Not the least important is the ice harvest, which is eagerly looked for, and counted upon by hundreds, yes, thousands of laboring men along its course. Ice or no ice sometimes means bread or no bread to scores of families, and it means added or diminished comforts to many more. It is a crop that takes two or three weeks of rugged winter weather to grow, and, if the water is very roily or brackish, even longer. It is seldom worked till it presents seven or eight inches of clear water ice. Men go out from time to time and examine it, as the farmer goes out and examines his grain or grass, to see when it will do to cut. If there comes a deep fall of snow the ice is 'pricked' so as to let the water up through and form snow ice. A band of fifteen or twenty men, about a yard apart, each armed with a chisel-bar, and marching in line, puncture the ice at each step, with a single sharp thrust. To and fro they go, leaving a belt behind them that presently becomes saturated with water. But ice, to be of first quality, must grow from beneath, not from above. It is a crop quite as uncertain as any other. A good yield every two or three years, as they say of wheat out west, is about all that can be counted upon. When there is an abundant harvest, after the ice houses are filled, they stack great quantities of it, as the farmer stacks his surplus hay. Such a fruitful winter was that of '74–5, when the ice formed twenty inches thick. The stacks are given only a temporary covering of boards, and are the first ice removed in the season. The cutting and gathering of the ice enlivens these broad, white, desolate fields amazingly. My house happens to stand where I look down upon the busy scene, as from a hill-top upon a river meadow in haying time, only here figures stand out much more sharply than they do from a summer meadow. There is the broad, straight, blue-black canal emerging into view, and running nearly across the river; this is the highway that lays open the farm. On either side lie the fields, or ice meadows, each marked out by cedar or hemlock boughs. The farther one is cut first, and when cleared, shows a large, long, black parallelogram in the midst of the plain of snow. Then the next one is cut, leaving a strip or tongue of ice between the two for the horses to move and turn upon. Sometimes nearly two hundred men and boys, with numerous horses, are at work at once, marking, plowing, planing, scraping, sawing, hauling, chiseling; some floating down the pond on great square islands towed by a horse, or their fellow workmen; others distributed along the canal, bending to their ice-hooks; others upon the bridges separating the blocks with their chisel bars; others feeding the elevators; while knots and straggling lines of idlers here and there look on in cold discontent, unable to get a job. The best crop of ice is an early crop. Late in the season or after January, the ice is apt to get 'sun-struck,' when it becomes 'shaky,' like a piece of poor timber. The sun, when he sets about destroying the ice, does not simply melt it from the surface—that were a slow process; but he sends his shafts into it and separates it into spikes and needles—in short, makes kindling-wood of it, so as to consume it the quicker. One of the prettiest sights about the ice harvesting is the elevator in operation. When all works well, there is an unbroken procession of the great crystal blocks slowly ascending this incline. They go up in couples, arm in arm, as it were, like friends up a stairway, glowing and changing in the sun, and recalling the precious stones that adorned the walls of the celestial city. When they reach the platform where they leave the elevator, they seem to step off like things of life and volition; they are still in pairs and separate only as they enter upon the 'runs.' But here they have an ordeal to pass through, for they are subjected to a rapid inspection and the black sheep are separated from the flock; every square with a trace of sediment or earth-stain in it, whose texture is not perfect and unclouded crystal, is rejected and sent hurling down into the abyss; a man with a sharp eye in his head and a sharp ice-hook in his hand picks out the impure and fragmentary ones as they come along and sends them quickly overboard. Those that pass the examination glide into the building along the gentle incline, and are switched off here and there upon branch runs, and distributed to all parts of the immense interior."

West Point, from above Washington Valley, looking down the river.
Painted by George Cooke, engraved by W.J. Bennett; aquatint, c. 1834.

I love thy tempests when the broad-winged blast
Rouses thy billows with his battle call,
When gathering clouds, in phalanx black and vast
Like armed shadows gird thy rocky wall.
                                        —*Knickerbocker Magazine*

CHAPTER 5

West Point—taken all in all, is the most beautiful tourist spot on the Hudson. Excursionists by the Day Boats from New York, returning by afternoon steamer, have three hours to visit the various places of history and beauty. To make an easy mathematical formula or picturesque "rule of three" statement, what Quebec is to the St. Lawrence, West Point is to the Hudson. If the citadel of Quebec is more imposing, the view of the Hudson at this place is grander than that of the St. Lawrence, and the ruins of Fort Putnam are almost as venerable as the Heights of Abraham. The sensation of the visitor is, moreover, somewhat the same in both places as to the environment of law and authority. To get the daily character and quality of West Point one should spend at least twenty-four hours within its borders, and a good hotel, the only one on the Government grounds, will be found central and convenient to everything of interest. The parade and drills at sunset hour can best be seen in this way.

The United States Military Academy—Soon after the close of the War of the Revolution, Washington suggested West Point as the site of a military academy, and, in 1793, in his annual message, recommended it to Congress, which in 1794 organized a corps of artillerists to be here stationed with thirty-two cadets, enlarging the number in 1798 to fifty-six. In 1808 it was increased to one hundred and fifty-six, and in 1812 to two hundred and sixty.

Up to 1812 only 71 cadets had been graduated. The roll of graduates now numbers about 5,000.

Each Congressman has the appointment of one cadet, supplemented by ten appointed by the President of the United States. These cadets are members of the regular army, subject to its regulations for eight years, viz: during four years of study and four years after graduating. The candidates are examined in June, each year, and must be physically sound as well as mentally qualified. The course is very thorough, especially in higher mathematics. The cadets go into camp in July and August, and this is the pleasantest time to visit the point.

‿‿

Enchanted place, hemmed in by mountain walls,

By bristling guns and Hudson's restful shore.

—*Kenneth Bruce*

The plans furnished by the architects of the new building will entirely change the appearance of the river front. The proposed massive structure crowning the cliff will "out-castle" the most massive fortifications of the walled cities of Europe. $7,500,000 has been appropriated to the work by Congress and the next generation will behold a new West Point.

In the rebuilding of the Post the Cadet Chapel, the Riding Hall, the Administration Building and some of the Officers' Quarters will be removed. Most of the old important buildings, however, will not be disturbed, and the Chapel will be placed as it were "intact" on another site. The plan leaves untouched the Cadet Barracks, the Cadet Mess, the Memorial Hall, the Library and the Officers' Mess. The tower of the new Post Headquarters will rise high and massive several stories above the other structures and present in enduring symbol the republic standing four square and firm throughout the ages.

In the "West Point Souvenir," prepared by W. H. Tripp, which every visitor will prize, are many suggestions and descriptions of value. From many visits and many sources we condense the following brevities:

The Cadet Barracks—was built in 1845–51 of native granite. In 1882 the western wing was extended adding two divisions.

The Academy Building—is immediately opposite the Head-quarters, of Massachusetts granite, erected in 1891–95, and cost about $500,000. It contains recitation and lecture rooms of all departments of instruction.

The Ordnance Museum—contains an interesting and extensive exhibit of ancient and modern firearms, also many valuable trophies from the Revolutionary, Mexican, Civil and Spanish wars.

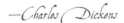

Among the fair and lovely Highlands of the Hudson, shut in by deep green heights and ruined forts, hemmed in all round with memories of Washington, there could be no more appropriate ground for the military school of America.

—Charles Dickens

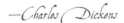

The Cadet Chapel—immediately north of the Administration Building, was erected in 1834. The chapel contains many valuable trophies of the Revolutionary and Mexican wars, including three Hessian and two British flags that were once the property of Washington. The walls have many memorial tablets and a famous "blank" of Arnold. Here also are several cannon surrendered at Saratoga, October 17, 1777.

The Administration Building—was completed in 1871.

The Library—adjoins the Cadet Chapel on the east, built of native granite in 1841, costing about $15,000. In 1900 the building was entirely reconstructed of fire-proof material by appropriation of $80,000. The exterior walls of the original building entered into the remodeled structure. The Library, founded in 1812, has about 50,000 volumes.

The Gymnasium—adjoins the Barracks on the west, erected of native granite, costing $90,000.

Memorial Hall—plainly seen from the Hudson, completed in 1899, is of Ionic architecture. The building cost $268,000, a legacy bequeathed by Gen. George W. Cullum, built of Milford granite for army trophies of busts, paintings and memorials. The bronze statute of Gen. John Sedgwick in the northwest angle of the plain was dedicated in 1868. The fine cenotaph of Italian marble was erected in 1885. It stands immediately in front of Memorial Hall.

Kosciusko's Monument—was erected in 1828. It stands in the northeast angle of Fort Clinton.

The Chain-Battery—walk runs from Kosciusko's Garden northward to Light House Point, near which was the battery that defended the chain across the river in the Revolution. The scene is of great beauty and has been known for many years by the name of "Flirtation Walk."

∽

Where Kosciusko dreamed and proud scenes bring
To mind the stormy days when Liberty
Was cradled at West Point—the Highlands' key.

—Kenneth Bruce

∽

The Battle Monument—on Trophy Point, is the most beautiful on the reservation—a column of victory in memory of 2,230 officers and soldiers of the regular army of the United States who were killed or died of wounds received in the war of the Rebellion. It is a monolith of polished granite surmounted by a figure of Fame. The shaft is 46 feet in length, 5 feet in diameter, and said to be the largest piece of polished stone in the world. The cost of the work was $66,000. The site was dedicated June 15, 1864. The monument was dedicated in 1897. The address was by Justice Brewer.

Scene of Burgoyne's Surrender

Trophy Point—on the north side of the plain, overlooking the river and commanding a majestic view of the Hudson and the city of Newburgh, has been likened by European travelers to a view on Lake Geneva. Here are the "swivel clevies" and 16 links of the old chain that was stretched across the river at this point. The whole chain, 1,700 feet long, weighing 186 tons, was forged at the Sterling Iron Works, transported to New Windsor and there attached to log booms and floated down the river to this point.

Old Fort Putnam—was erected in 1778 by the 5th Massachusetts Regiment under the direction of Col. Rufus Putnam. It was originally constructed of logs and trees with stone walls on two sides to defend Fort Clinton on the plain below. It was garrisoned by 450 men, and had 14 guns mounted. In 1787 it was dismantled, and the guns sold as old iron. Its brick arch casements overgrown with moss, vines, and shrubbery are crumbling away, but are well worth a visit. It is 495 feet above the Hudson. A winding picturesque carriage road leads up from the plain, and the pedestrian can reach the summit in 20 minutes. On clear days the Catskill Mountains are visible.

Fort Clinton—in the northeast angle of the plain, was built in 1778 under the direction of the Polish soldier, Kosciusko. Sea Coast Battery is located on the north waterfront, Siege Battery on the slope of the hill below the Battle Monument. Targets for the guns on both batteries are on the hillside about a mile distant. Battery Knox, which overlooks the river, was rebuilt in 1874 on the site of an old revolutionary redoubt.

Bright are the moments link'd with thee,

Boast of a glory-hallowed land!

Hope of the valiant and the free,

Home of our youthful soldier band!

—Anonymous

West Point seen from across the Hudson, circa 1874

While Fort Putnam was being built Washington was advised that Dubois's regiment was unfit to be ordered on duty, there being "not one blanket in the regiment. Very few have either a shoe or a shirt, and most of them have neither stockings, breeches, or overalls. Several companies of inlisted artificers are in the same situation, and unable to work in the field."

What privations were here endured to establish our priceless liberty! It makes better Americans of us all to turn and re-turn the pages of the real Hudson, the most picturesque volume of the world's history.

West Point during the Revolution was the Gibraltar of the Hudson and her forts were regarded as almost impregnable. Fort Putnam will be rebuilt as an enduring monument to the bravery of American soldiers.

The best way to study West Point, however, is not in voluminous histories or in the condensed pages of a guide book, but to visit it and see its real life, to wander amid its old associations, and ask, when necessary, intelligent questions, which are everywhere courteously answered. The view north seen in a summer evening, is one long to be remembered. In such an hour the writer's idea of the Hudson as an open book with granite pages and crystal book-mark is most completely realized as indicated in the Highland section of his poem, "The Hudson":

> *On either side these mountain glens*
> *Lie open like a massive book,*
> *Whose words were graved with iron pens,*
> *And lead into the eternal rock:*

Which evermore shall here retain
The annals time cannot erase,
And while these granite leaves remain
This crystal ribbon marks the place.

PART II

Mythology

The Hudson River from Crow's Nest. Storm King mountain on left, Break Neck Mountain on right. Photographic print, c. 1922.

O waters of Pocantico!
Wild rivulet of wood and glen!
May thy glad laughter, sweet and low,
Long, long outlive the sighs of men.

—S. H. Thayer

The Indian Falls

Of grottoes in the far dim woods,

Of pools moss-rimmed and deep,

From whose embrace the little rills

In daring venture creep.

—E. A. Lente

CHAPTER 6

Indian Legends

Catskill Gnomes—Behind the New Grand Hotel, in the Catskills, is an amphitheatre of mountain that is held to be the place of which the Mohicans spoke when they told of people there who worked in metals, and had bushy beards and eyes like pigs. From the smoke of their forges, in autumn, came the haze of Indian summer; and when the moon was full, it was their custom to assemble on the edge of a precipice above the hollow and dance and caper until the night was nigh worn away. They brewed a liquor that had the effect of shortening the bodies and swelling the heads of all who drank it, and when Hudson and his crew visited the mountains, the pygmies held a carouse in his honor and invited him to drink their liquor. The crew went away, shrunken and distorted by the magic distillation, and thus it was that Rip Van Winkle found them on the eve of his famous sleep.

The Catskill Witch—When the Dutch gave the name of Katzbergs to the mountains west of the Hudson, by reason of the wild-cats and panthers that ranged there, they obliterated the beautiful Indian Ontiora, "mountains of the sky." In one tradition of the red men these hills were bones of a monster that fed on human beings until the Great Spirit turned it into stone as it was floundering toward the ocean to bathe. The two lakes near the summit were its eyes. These peaks were the home of an Indian witch, who adjusted the weather for the Hudson Valley with the certainty of a signal service bureau. It was she who let out the day and night in blessed alternation, holding back the one when the other was at large, for fear of conflict. Old moons she cut into stars as soon as she had hung new ones in the sky, and she was often seen perched on Round Top and North Mountain, spinning clouds and flinging them to the winds. Woe betide the valley residents if they showed irreverence, for then the clouds were black and heavy, and through them she poured floods of rain and launched the lightnings, causing disastrous freshets in the streams and blasting the wigwams of the mockers. In a frolic humor she would take the form of a bear or deer and lead the Indian hunters anything but a merry dance, exposing them to tire and peril, and vanishing or assuming some terrible shape when they had overtaken her. Sometimes she would lead them to the cloves and would leap into the air with a mocking "Ho, ho!" just as they stopped with a shudder at the brink of an abyss. Garden Rock was a spot where she was often found, and at its foot a lake once spread. This was held in such awe that an Indian would never wittingly pursue his quarry there; but once a hunter lost his way and emerged from the forest at the edge of the pond. Seeing a number of gourds in crotches of the trees he took one, but fearing the spirit he turned to leave so quickly that he stumbled and it fell. As it broke, a spring welled from it in such volume that the unhappy man was gulfed in its waters, swept to the edge of Kaaterskill clove and dashed on the rocks two hundred and sixty feet below. Nor did the water ever cease to run, and in these times the stream born of the witch's revenge is known as Catskill Creek.

<hr />

The Revenge of Shandaken—On the rock platform where the Catskill Mountain House now stands, commanding one of the fairest views in the world, old chief Shandaken set his wig-wam,—for it is a mistake to suppose that barbarians are indifferent to beauty,—and there his daughter, Lotowana, was sought in marriage by his braves. She, however, kept faith to an early vow exchanged with a young chief of the Mohawks. A suitor who was particularly troublesome was Norsereddin, proud, morose, dark-featured, a stranger to the red man, a descendant, so he claimed, from Egyptian kings, and who lived by himself on Kaaterskill Creek, appearing among white settlements but rarely.

On one of his visits to Catskill, a tavern-lounging Dutchman wagered him a thousand golden crowns that he could not win Lotowana, and, stung by avarice as well as inflamed by passion, Norsereddin laid new siege to her heart. Still the girl refused to listen, and Shandaken counselled him to be content with the smiles of others, thereby so angering the Egyptian that he assailed the chief and was driven from the camp with blows; but on the day of Lotowana's wedding with the Mohawk he returned, and in a honeyed speech asked leave to give a jewel to the bride to show that he had stifled jealousy and ill will. The girl took the handsome box he gave her and drew the cover, when a spring flew forward, driving into her hand the poisoned tooth of a snake that had been affixed to it. The venom was strong, and in a few minutes Lotowana lay dead at her husband's feet.

Though the Egyptian had disappeared into the forest directly on the acceptance of his treacherous gift, twenty braves set off in pursuit, and overtaking him on the Kalkberg, they dragged him back to the rock where father and husband were bewailing the maid's untimely fate. A pile of fagots was heaped within a few feet of the precipice edge, and tying their captive on them, they applied the torch, dancing about with cries of exultation as the shrieks of the wretch echoed from the cliffs. The dead girl was buried by the mourning tribe, while the ashes of Norsereddin were left to be blown abroad. On the day of his revenge Shandaken left his ancient dwelling-place, and his camp-fires never glimmered afterward on the front of Ontiora.

Big Indian—Intermarriages between white people and red ones in this country were not uncommon in the days when our ancestors led as rude a life as the natives, and several places in the Catskills commemorate this fact. Mount Utsayantha, for example, is named for an Indian woman whose life, with that of her baby and her white husband, was lost there. For the white men early found friends among these mountains. As far back as 1663 they spared Catherine Dubois and her three children, after some rash spirits had abducted them and carried them to a place on the upper Walkill, to do them to death; for the captives raised a Huguenot hymn and the hearts of their captors were softened.

In Esopus Valley lived Winnisook, whose height was seven feet, and who was known among the white settlers as "the big Indian." He loved a white girl of the neighborhood, one Gertrude Molyneux, and had asked for her hand; but while she was willing, the objections of her family were too strong to be overcome, and she was teased into marriage with Joseph Bundy, of her own race, instead. She liked the Indian all the better after that, however, because Bundy proved to be a bad fellow, and believing that she could be happier among barbarians than among a people that approved such marriages, she eloped with Winnisook. For a long time all trace of the runaway couple was lost, but one day the man having gone down to the plain to steal cattle, it was alleged, was discovered by some farmers who knew him, and who gave hot chase, coming up with him at the place now called Big Indian.

Foremost in the chase was Bundy. As he came near to the enemy of his peace he exclaimed, "I think the best way to civilize that yellow serpent is to let daylight into his heart," and, drawing his rifle to his shoulder, he fired. Mortally wounded, yet instinctively seeking refuge, the giant staggered into the hollow of a pine-tree, where the farmers lost sight of him. There, however, he was found by Gertrude, bolt upright, yet dead. The unwedded widow brought her dusky children to the place and spent the remainder of her days near his grave. Until a few years ago the tree was still pointed out, but a railroad company has now covered it with an embankment.

∾

The Devil's Dance-Chamber—Most storied of our New World rivers is the Hudson. Historic scenes have been enacted on its shores, and Indian, Dutchman, Briton, and American have invested it with romance. It had its source, in the red man's fancy, in a spring of eternal youth; giants and spirits dwelt in its woods and hills, and before the river-Shatemuc, king of streams, the red men called it—had broken through the highlands, those mountains were a pent for spirits who had rebelled against the

Manitou. After the waters had forced a passage to the sea these evil ones sought shelter in the glens and valleys that open to right and left along its course, but in time of tempest, when they hear Manitou riding down the ravine on wings of storm, dashing thunderbolts against the cliffs, it is the fear that he will recapture them and force them into lightless caverns to expiate their revolt, that sends them huddling among the rocks and makes the hills resound with roars and howls.

At the Devil's Dance-Chamber, a slight plateau on the west bank, between Newburg and Crom Elbow, the red men performed semi-religious rites as a preface to their hunting and fishing trips or ventures on the war-path. They built a fire, painted themselves, and in that frenzy into which savages are so readily lashed, and that is so like to the action of mobs in trousers, they tumbled, leaped, danced, yelled, sang, grimaced, and gesticulated until the Manitou disclosed himself, either as a harmless animal or a beast of prey. If he came in the former shape the augury was favorable, but if he showed himself as a bear or panther, it was a warning of evil that they seldom dared to disregard.

The crew of Hudson's ship, the Half Moon, having chanced on one of these orgies, were so impressed by the fantastic spectacle that they gave the name Duyvels Dans-Kamer to the spot. Years afterwards, when Stuyvesant ascended the river, his doughty retainers were horrified, on landing below the Dans-Kamer, to discover hundreds of painted figures frisking there in the firelight. A few surmised that they were but a new generation of savages holding a powwow, but most of the sailors fancied that the assemblage was demoniac, and that the figures were spirits of bad Indians repeating a scalp-dance and revelling in the mysterious fire-water that they had brought down from the river source in jars and skins. The spot was at least once profaned with blood, for a young Dutchman and his wife, of Albany, were captured here by an angry Indian, and although the young man succeeded in stabbing his captor to death, he was burned alive on the rock by the friends of the Indian whose wrath he had provoked. The wife, after being kept in captivity for a time, was ransomed.

Pokepsie—The name of this town has forty-two spellings in old records, and with singular pertinacity in ill-doing, the inhabitants have fastened on it the longest and clumsiest of all. It comes from the Mohegan words Apo-keep-sink, meaning a safe, pleasant harbor. Harbor it might be for canoes, but for nothing bigger, for it was only the little cove that was so called between Call Rock and Adder Cliff,—the former indicating where settlers awaiting passage hailed the masters of vessels from its top, and the latter taking its name from the snakes that abounded there.

Hither came a band of Delawares with Pequot captives, among them a young chief to whom had been offered not only life but leadership if he would renounce his tribe, receive the mark of the turtle on his breast, and become a Delaware. On his refusal, he was bound to a tree, and was about to undergo the torture, when a girl among the listeners sprang to his side. She, too, was a Pequot, but the turtle totem was on her bosom, and when she begged his life, because they had been betrothed, the captors paused to talk of it. She had chosen well the time to interfere, for a band of Hurons was approaching, and even as the talk went on their yell was heard in the wood. Instant measures for defence were taken, and in the fight that followed both chief and maiden were forgotten; but though she cut the cords that bound him, they were separated in the confusion, he disappearing, she falling captive to the Hurons, who, sated with blood, retired from the field. In the fantastic disguise of a wizard the young Pequot entered their camp soon after, and on being asked to try his enchantments for the cure of a young woman, he entered her tent, showing no surprise at finding her to be the maiden of his choice, who was suffering from nothing worse than nerves, due to the excitement of the battle. Left alone with his patient, he disclosed his identity, and planned a way of escape that proved effective on that very night, for, though pursued by the angry Hurons, the couple reached "safe harbor," thence making a way to their own country in the east, where they were married.

〰️

Chief Croton—Between the island of Manhattoes and the Catskills the Hudson shores were plagued with spooks, and even as late as the nineteenth century Hans Anderson, a man who tilled a farm back of Peekskill, was worried into his grave by the leaden-face likeness of a British spy whom he had hanged on

General Putnam's orders. "Old Put" doubtless enjoyed immunity from this vexatious creature, because he was born with few nerves. A region especially afflicted was the confluence of the Croton and the Hudson, for the Kitchawan burying-ground was here, and the red people being disturbed by the tramping of white men over their graves, "the walking sachems of Teller's Point" were nightly to be met on their errands of protest.

These Indians had built a palisade on Croton Point, and here they made their last stand against their enemies from the north. Throughout the fight old chief Croton stood on the wall with arrows showering around him, and directed the resistance with the utmost calm. Not until every one of his men was dead and the fort was going up in flame about him did he confess defeat. Then standing amid the charring timbers, he used his last breath in calling down the curse of the Great Spirit against the foe. As the victorious enemy rushed into the enclosure to secure the scalps of the dead he fell lifeless into the fire, and their jubilant yell was lost upon his ears. Yet, he could not rest nor bear to leave his ancient home, even after death, and often his form, in musing attitude, was seen moving through the woods. When a manor was built on the ruins of his fort, he appeared to the master of it, to urge him into the Continental army, and having seen this behest obeyed and laid a solemn injointure to keep the freedom of the land forever, he vanished, and never appeared again.

෴

The Retreat From Mahopac—After the English had secured the city of New Amsterdam and had begun to extend their settlements along the Hudson, the Indians congregated in large numbers about Lake Mahopac, and rejected all overtures for the purchase of that region. In their resolution they were sustained by their young chief Omoyao, who refused to abandon on any terms the country where his fathers had so long hunted, fished, and built their lodges. A half-breed, one Joliper, a member of this tribe, was secretly in the pay of the English, but the allurements and insinuations that he put forth on their behalf were as futile as the breathing of wind in the leaves. At last the white men grew angry. Have the land they would, by evil course if good ways were refused, and commissioning Joliper to act for them in a decisive manner, they guaranteed to supply him with forces if his negotiations fell through. This man never thought it needful to negotiate. He knew the temper of his tribe and he was too jealous of his chief to go to him for favors, because he loved Maya, the chosen one of Omoyao.

At the door of Maya's tent he entreated her to go with him to the white settlements, and on her refusal he broke into angry threats, declaring, in the self-forgetfulness of passion, that he would kill her lover and lead the English against the tribe. Unknown to both Omoyao had overheard this interview, and he immediately sent runners to tell all warriors of his people to meet him at once on the island in the lake. Though the runners were cautioned to keep their errand secret, it is probable that Joliper suspected that the alarm had gone forth, and he resolved to strike at once; so he summoned his renegades, stole into camp next evening and made toward Maya's wigwam, intending to take her to a place of safety. Seeing the chief at the door, he shot an arrow at him, but the shaft went wide and slew the girl's father. Realizing, upon this assault, that he was outwitted and that his people were outnumbered, the chief called to Maya to meet him at the island, and plunged into the brush, after seeing that she had taken flight in an opposite direction. The vengeful Joliper was close behind him with his renegades, and the chief was captured; then, that he might not communicate with his people or delay the operations against them, it was resolved to put him to death.

He was tied to a tree, the surrounding wood was set on fire, and he was abandoned to his fate, his enemies leaving him to destruction in their haste to reach the place of the council and slay or capture all who were there. Hardly were they out of hearing ere the plash of a paddle sounded through the roar of flame and Maya sprang upon the bank, cut her lover's bonds, and with him made toward the island, which they reached by a protected way before the assailants had arrived. They told the story of Joliper's cruelty and treason, and when his boats were seen coming in to shore they had eyes and hands only for Joliper. He was the first to land. Hardly had he touched the strand before he was surrounded by a frenzied crowd and had fallen bleeding from a hundred gashes.

The Indians were overpowered after a brief and bloody resistance. They took safety in flight. Omoyao and Maya, climbing upon the rock above their "council chamber," found that while most of their people had escaped their own retreat was cut off, and that it would be impossible to reach any of the canoes. They preferred death to torture and captivity, so, hand in hand, they leaped together down the cliff, and the English claimed the land next day.

◠◡

Niagara—The cataract of Niagara (properly pronounced *Nee-ah-gah-rah*), or Oniahgarah, is as fatal as it is fascinating, beautiful, sublime, and the casualties occurring there justify the tradition that "the Thundering Water asks two victims every year." It was reputed, before white men looked for the first time on these falls—and what thumping yarns they told about them!—that two lives were lost here annually, and this average has been kept up by men and women who fall into the flood through accident, recklessness or despair, while bloody battles have been fought on the shores, and vessels have been hurled over the brink, to be dashed to splinters on the rocks.

The sound of the cataract was declared to be the voice of a mighty spirit that dwelt in the waters, and in former centuries the Indians offered to it a yearly sacrifice. This sacrifice was a maiden of the tribe, who was sent over in a white canoe, decorated with fruit and flowers, and the girls contended for this honor, for the brides of Manitou were objects of a special grace in the happy hunting-grounds. The last recorded sacrifice was in 1679, when

Lelawala, the daughter of chief Eagle Eye, was chosen, in spite of the urgings and protests of the chevalier La Salle, who had been trying to restrain the people from their idolatries by an exposition of the Christian dogma. To his protests he received the unexpected answer, "Your words witness against you. Christ, you say, set us an example. We will follow it. Why should one death be great, while our sacrifice is horrible?" So the tribe gathered at the bank to watch the sailing of the white canoe. The chief watched the embarkation with the stoicism usual to the Indian when he is observed by others, but when the little bark swung out into the current his affection mastered him, and he leaped into his own canoe and tried to overtake his daughter. In a moment both were beyond the power of rescue. After their death they were changed into spirits of pure strength and goodness, and live in a crystal heaven so far beneath the fall that its roaring is a music to them: she, the maid of the mist; he, the ruler of the cataract. Another version of the legend makes a lover and his mistress the chief actors. Some years later a patriarch of the tribe and all his sons went over the fall when the white men had seized their lands, preferring death to flight or war.

In about the year 200 the Stone Giants waded across the river below the falls on their northward march. These beings were descended from an ancient family, and being separated from their stock in the year 150 by the breaking of a vine bridge across the Mississippi, they left that region. Indian Pass, in the Adirondacks, bore the names of Otneyarheh, Stony Giants; Ganosgwah, Giants Clothed in Stone; and Dayohjegago, Place

Where the Storm Clouds Fight the Great Serpent. Giants and serpents were held to be harmful inventions of the Evil Spirit, and the Lightning god, catching up clouds as he stood on the crags, broke them open, tore their lightnings out and hurled them against the monsters. These cannibals had almost exterminated the Iroquois, for they were of immense size and had made themselves almost invincible by rolling daily in the sand until their flesh was like stone. The Holder of the Heavens, viewing their evil actions from on high, came down disguised as one of their number—he used often to meditate on Manitou Rock, at the Whirlpool—and leading them to a valley near Onondaga, on pretence of guiding them to a fairer country, he stood on a hill above them and hurled rocks upon their heads until all, save one, who fled into the north, were dead. Yet, in the fulness of time, new children of the Stone Giants (mail-clad Europeans?) entered the region again and were destroyed by the Great Spirit,—oddly enough where the famous fraud known as the Cardiff giant was alleged to have been found. The Onondagas believed this statue to be one of their ancient foes.

∽

Old Indian Face—On Lower Ausable Pond is a large, ruddy rock showing a huge profile, with another, resembling a pappoose, below it. When the Tahawi ruled this region their sachem lived here at "the Dark Cup," as they called this lake, a man renowned for virtue and remarkable, in his age, for gentleness.

When his children had died and his manly grandson, who was the old man's hope, had followed them to the land of the cloud mountains, Adota's heart withered within him, and standing beneath this rock, he addressed his people, recounting what he had done for them, how he had swept their enemies from the Lakes of the Clustered Stars (the Lower Saranac) and Silver Sky (Upper Saranac) to the Lake of Wandah, gaining a land where they might hunt and fish in peace. The little one, the Star, had been ravished away to crown the brow of the thunder god, who, even now, was advancing across the peaks, bending the woods and lighting the valleys with his jagged torches.

Life was nothing to him longer; he resigned it.

As he spoke these words he fell back, and the breath passed out of him. Then came the thunder god, and with an appalling burst of fire sent the people cowering. The roar that followed seemed to shake the earth, but the medicine-man of the tribe stood still, listening to the speech of the god in the clouds. "Tribe of the Tahawi," he translated, "Adota treads the star-path to the happy hunting-grounds, and the sun is shining on his heart. He will never walk among you again, but the god loves both him and you, and he will set his face on the mountains. Look!" And, raising their eyes, they beheld the likeness of Adota and of his beloved child, the Star, graven by lightning-stroke on the cliff. There they buried the body of Adota and held their solemn festivals until the white men drove them out of the country.

࿇

The Division of the Saranacs—In the middle of the last century a large body of Saranac Indians occupied the forests of the Upper Saranac through which ran the Indian carrying-place, called by them the Eagle Nest Trail. Whenever they raided the Tahawi on the slopes of Mount Tahawus (Sky-splitter), there was a pleasing rivalry between two young athletes, called the Wolf and the Eagle, as to which would carry off the more scalps, and the tribe was divided in admiration of them. There was one who did not share this liking: an old sachem, one of the wizards who had escaped when the Great Spirit locked these workers of evil in the hollow trees that stood beside the trail. In their struggles to escape the less fortunate ones thrust

Winter Fishing

their arms through the closing bark, and they are seen there, as withered trunks and branches, to this day. Oquarah had not been softened by this exhibition of danger nor the qualification of mercy that allowed him still to exist. Rather he was more bitter when he saw, as he fancied, that the tribe thought more of the daring and powerful warriors than it did of the bent and malignant-minded counsellor.

It was in the moon of green leaves that the two young men set off to hunt the moose, and on the next day the Wolf returned alone. He explained that in the hunt they had been separated; he had called for hours for his friend, and had searched so long that he concluded he must have returned ahead of him. But he was not at the camp. Up rose the sachem with visage dark. "I hear a forked tongue," he cried. "The Wolf was jealous of the Eagle and his teeth have cut into his heart."

"The Wolf cannot lie," answered the young man.

"Where is the Eagle?" angrily shouted the sachem, clutching his hatchet.

"The Wolf has said," replied the other.

The old sachem advanced upon him, but as he raised his axe to strike, the wife of the Wolf threw herself before her husband, and the steel sank into her brain. The sachem fell an instant later with the Wolf's knife in his heart, and instantly the camp was in turmoil. Before the day had passed it had been broken up, and the people were divided into factions, for it was no longer possible to hold it together in peace. The Wolf, with half of the people, went down the Sounding River to new hunting-grounds, and the earth that separated the families was reddened whenever one side met the other.

Years had passed when, one morning, the upper tribe saw a canoe advancing across the Lake of the Silver Sky. An old man stepped from it: he was the Eagle. After the Wolf had left him he had fallen into a cleft in a rock, and had lain helpless until found by hunters who were on their way to Canada. He had joined the British against the French, had married a northern squaw, but had returned to die among the people of his early love. Deep was his sorrow that his friend should have been accused of doing him an injury, and that the once happy tribe should have been divided by that allegation. The warriors and sachems of both branches were summoned to a council, and in his presence they swore a peace, so that in the fulness of time he was able to die content. That peace was always kept.

ᘒᓚ

An Event in Indian Park—It was during the years when the Saranacs were divided that Howling Wind, one of the young men of Indian Carry, saw and fell in love with a girl of the family on Tupper Lake. He quickly found a way to tell his liking, and the couple met often in the woods and on the shore. He made bold to row her around the quieter bays, and one moonlight evening he took her to Devil's Rock, or Devil's Pulpit, where he told her the story of the place. This was to the effect that the fiend had paddled, on timbers, by means of his tail, to that rock, and had assembled fish and game about him in large numbers by telling them that he was going to preach to them, instead of which moral procedure he pounced upon and ate all that were within his grasp.

As so often happened in Indian history, the return of these lovers was seen by a disappointed rival, who had hurried back to camp and secured the aid of half a dozen men to arrest the favored one as soon as he should land. The capture was made after a struggle, and Howling Wind was dragged to the chief's tent for sentence. That sentence was death, and with a refinement of cruelty that was rare even among the Indians, the girl was ordered to execute it. She begged and wept to no avail. An axe was put into her hands, and she was ordered to despatch the prisoner. She took the weapon; her face grew stern and the tears dried on her cheeks; her lover, bound to a tree, gazed at her in amazement; his rival watched, almost in glee. Slowly the girl crossed the open space to her lover. She raised the tomahawk and at a blow severed the thongs that held him, then, like a flash, she leaped upon his rival, who had sprung forward to interfere, and clove his skull with a single stroke. The lovers fled as only those can fly who run for life. Happily for them, they met a party from the Carry coming to rescue Howling Wind from the danger to which his courtship had exposed him, and it was even said that this party entered the village and by presenting knives and arrows at the breast of the chief obtained his now superfluous consent to the union of the fugitives. The pair reached the Carry in safety and lived a long and happy life together.

The Indian Plume—The brightest flower that grows beside the brooks is the scarlet blossom of the Indian plume: the blood of Lenawee. Hundreds of years ago she lived happily among her brother and sister Saranacs beside Stony Creek, the Stream of the Snake, and was soon to marry the comely youth who, for the speed of his foot, was called the Arrow. But one summer the Quick Death came on the people, and as the viewless devil stalked through the village young and old fell before him. The Arrow was the first to die. In vain the Prophet smoked the Great Calumet: its smoke ascending took no shape that he could read. In vain was the white dog killed to take aloft the people's sins. But at last the Great Spirit himself came down to the mountain called the Storm Darer, splendid in lightning, awful in his thunder voice and robe of cloud. "My wrath is against you for your sins," he cried, "and naught but human blood will appease it."

In the morning the Prophet told his message, and all sat silent for a time. Then Lenawee entered the circle. "Lenawee is a blighted flower," she sobbed. "Let her blood flow for her people." And catching a knife from the Prophet's belt, she ran with it to the stream on which she and the Arrow had so often floated in their canoe. In another moment her blood had bedewed the earth. "Lay me with the Arrow," she murmured, and, smiling in their sad faces, breathed her last. The demon of the quick death shrank from the spot, and the Great Spirit smiled once more on the tribe that could produce such heroism. Lenawee's body was placed beside her lover's, and next morning, where her blood had spilt, the ground was pure, and on it grew in slender spires a new flower,—the Indian plume: the transformed blood of sacrifice. The people loved that flower in all years after. They decked their hair and dresses with it and made a feast in its honor. When parents taught their children the beauty of unselfishness they used as its emblem a stalk of Indian plume.

Birth of the Water-lily—Back from his war against the Tahawi comes the Sun, chief of the Lower Saranacs,—back to the Lake of the Clustered Stars, afterward called, by dullards, Tupper's Lake. Tall and invincible he comes among his people, boasting of his victories, Indian fashion, and stirring the scalps that hang at his breast. "The Eagle screams," he cries. "He greets the chief, the Blazing Sun. Wayotah has made the Tahawi tremble. They fly from him. Hooh, hooh! He is the chief." Standing apart with wistful glance stands Oseetah, the Bird. She loves the strong young chief, but she knows that another has his promise, and she dares not hope; yet the chief loves her, and when the feasting is over he follows her footprints to the shore, where he sees her canoe turning the point of an island. He silently pursues and comes upon her as she sits waving and moaning. He tries to embrace her, but she draws apart. He asks her to sing to him; she bids him begone.

He takes a more imperious tone and orders her to listen to her chief. She moves away. He darts toward her. Turning on him a face of sorrow, she runs to the edge of a steep rock and waves him back. He hastens after. Then she springs and disappears in the deep water. The Sun plunges after her and swims with mad strength here and there. He calls. There is no answer. Slowly he returns to the village and tells the people what has happened. The Bird's parents are stricken and the Sun moans in his sleep. At noon a hunter comes in with strange tidings: flowers are growing on the water! The people go to their canoes and row to the Island of Elms. There, in a cove, the still water is enamelled with flowers, some as white as snow, filling the air with perfume, others strong and yellow, like the lake at sunset.

"Explain to us," they cry, turning to the old Medicine of his tribe, "for this was not so yesterday."

"It is our daughter," he answered. "These flowers are the form she takes. The white is her purity, the yellow her love. You shall see that her heart will close when the sun sets, and will reopen at his coming." And the young chief went apart and bowed his head.

Rip Van Winkle surrounded by villagers.
Pen and ink drawing, c. 1890–1938.

A slanting ray lingered on the woody crests of the preci-
pices that overhung the river, giving greater depth to
the dark-gray and purple of the rocky sides.

—Washington Irving

R ip Van Winkle—The story of Rip Van Winkle, told by Irving, dramatized by Boucicault, acted by Jefferson, pictured by Darley, set to music by Bristow, is the best known of American legends. Rip was a real personage, and the Van Winkles are a considerable family at this day. An idle, good-natured, happy-go-lucky fellow, he lived, presumably, in the village of Catskill, and began his long sleep in 1769. His wife was a shrew, and to escape her abuse Rip often took his dog and gun and roamed away to the Catskills, nine miles westward, where he lounged or hunted, as the humor seized him. It was on a September evening, during a jaunt on South Mountain, that he met a stubby, silent man, of goodly girth, his round head topped with a steeple hat, the skirts of his belted coat and flaps of his petticoat trousers meeting at the tops of heavy boots, and the face—ugh!—green and ghastly, with unmoving eyes that glimmered in the twilight like phosphorus. The dwarf carried a keg, and on receiving an intimation, in a sign, that he would like Rip to relieve him of it, that cheerful vagabond shouldered it and marched on up the mountain.

At nightfall they emerged on a little plateau where a score of men in the garb of long ago, with faces like that of Rip's guide, and equally still and speechless, were playing bowls with great solemnity, the balls sometimes rolling over the plateau's edge and rumbling down the rocks with a boom like thunder. A cloaked and snowy-bearded figure, watching aloof, turned like the others, and gazed uncomfortably at the visitor who now came blundering in among them. Rip was at first for making off, but the sinister glare in the circle of eyes took the run out of his legs, and he was not displeased when they signed to him to tap the keg and join in a draught of the ripest schnapps that ever he had tasted,—and he knew the flavor of every brand in Catskill. While these strange men grew no more genial with passing of the flagons, Rip was pervaded by a satisfying glow; then, overcome by sleepiness and resting his head on a stone, he stretched his tired legs out and fell to dreaming.

Morning. Sunlight and leaf shadow were dappled over the earth when he awoke, and rising stiffly from his bed, with compunctions in his bones, he reached for his gun. The already venerable implement was so far gone with rot and rust that it fell to pieces in his hand, and looking down at the fragments of it, he saw that his clothes were dropping from his body in rags and mould, while a white beard flowed over his breast. Puzzled and alarmed, shaking his head ruefully as he recalled the carouse of the silent, he hobbled down the mountain as fast as he might for the grip of the rheumatism on his knees and elbows, and entered his native village. What! Was this Catskill? Was this the place that he left yesterday? Had all these houses sprung up overnight, and these streets been pushed across the meadows in a day? The people, too: where were his friends? The children who had romped with him, the rotund topers whom he had left cooling their hot noses in pewter pots at the tavern door, the dogs that used to bark a welcome, recognizing in him a kindred spirit of vagrancy: where were they?

And his wife, whose athletic arm and agile tongue had half disposed him to linger in the mountains how happened it that she was not awaiting him at the gate? But gate there was none in the familiar place: an unfenced yard of weeds and ruined foundation wall were there. Rip's home was gone. The idlers jeered at his bent, lean form, his snarl of beard and hair, his disreputable dress, his look of grieved astonishment. He stopped, instinctively, at the tavern, for he knew that place in spite of its new sign: an officer in blue regimentals and a cocked hat replacing the crimson George III. of his recollection, and labelled "General Washington." There was a quick gathering of ne'er-do-weels, of tavern-haunters and gaping 'prentices, about him, and though their faces were strange and their manners rude, he made bold to ask if they knew such and such of his friends. "Nick Vedder? He's dead and gone these eighteen years." "Brom Dutcher? He joined the army and was killed at Stony Point." "Van Brummel? He, too, went to the war, and is in Congress now." "And Rip Van Winkle?"

"Yes, he's here. That's him yonder."

And to Rip's utter confusion he saw before him a counterpart of himself, as young, lazy, ragged, and easy-natured as he remembered himself to be, yesterday—or, was it yesterday?

Rip Van Winkle House, Sleepy Hollow, Catskill Mountains, N.Y., c. 1902.

"That's young Rip," continued his informer. "His father was Rip Van Winkle, too, but he went to the mountains twenty years ago and never came back. He probably fell over a cliff, or was carried off by Indians, or eaten by bears."

Twenty years ago! Truly, it was so. Rip had slept for twenty years without awaking. He had left a peaceful colonial village; he returned to a bustling republican town. How he eventually found, among the oldest inhabitants, some who admitted that they knew him; how he found a comfortable home with his married daughter and the son who took after him so kindly; how he recovered from the effect of the tidings that his wife had died of apoplexy, in a quarrel; how he resumed his seat at the tavern tap and smoked long pipes and told long yarns for the rest of his days, were matters of record up to the beginning of this century.

And a strange story Rip had to tell, for he had served as cup-bearer to the dead crew of the Half Moon. He had quaffed a cup of Hollands with no other than Henry Hudson himself. Some say that Hudson's spirit has made its home amid these hills, that it may look into the lovely valley that he discovered; but others hold that every twenty years he and his men assemble for a revel in the mountains that so charmed them when first seen swelling against the western heavens, and the liquor they drink on this night has the bane of throwing any mortal who lips it into a slumber whence nothing can arouse him until the day dawns when the crew shall meet again. As you climb the east front of the mountains by the old carriage road, you pass, half-way up the height, the stone that Rip Van Winkle slept on, and may see that it is slightly hollowed by his form. The ghostly revellers are due in the Catskills in 1909, and let all tourists who are among the mountains in September of that year beware of accepting liquor from strangers.

Condemned to the Noose—Ralph Sutherland, who, early in the last century, occupied a stone house a mile from Leeds, in the Catskills, was a man of morose and violent disposition, whose servant, a Scotch girl, was virtually a slave, inasmuch as she was bound to work for him without pay until she had refunded to him her passage-money to this country. Becoming weary of bondage and of the tempers of her master, the girl ran away. The man set off in a raging chase, and she had not gone far before Sutherland overtook her, tied her by the wrists to his horse's tail, and began the homeward journey. Afterward, he swore that the girl stumbled against the horse's legs, so frightening the animal that it rushed off madly, pitching him out of the saddle and dashing the servant to death on rocks and trees; yet, knowing how ugly-tempered he could be, his neighbors were better inclined to believe that he had driven the horse into a gallop, intending to drag the girl for a short distance, as a punishment, and to rein up before he had done serious mischief. On this supposition he was arrested, tried, and sentenced to die on the scaffold.

The tricks of circumstantial evidence, together with pleas advanced by influential relatives of the prisoner, induced the court to delay sentence until the culprit should be ninety-nine years old, but it was ordered that, while released on his own recognizance, in the interim, he should keep a hangman's noose about his neck and show himself before the judges in Catskill once every year, to prove that he wore his badge of infamy and kept his crime in mind. This sentence he obeyed, and there were people living recently who claimed to remember him as he went about with a silken cord knotted at his throat. He was always alone, he seldom spoke, his rough, imperious manner had departed. Only when children asked him what the rope was for were his lips seen to quiver, and then he would hurry away. After dark his house was avoided, for gossips said that a shrieking woman passed it nightly, tied at the tail of a giant horse with fiery eyes and smoking nostrils; that a skeleton in a winding sheet had been found there; that a curious thing, somewhat like a woman, had been known to sit on his garden wall, with lights shining from her finger-tips, uttering unearthly laughter; and that domestic animals reproached the man by groaning and howling beneath his windows.

These beliefs he knew, yet he neither grieved, nor scorned, nor answered when he was told of them. Years sped on. Every year deepened his reserve and loneliness, and some began to whisper that he would take his own way out of the world, though others answered that men who were born to be hanged would never be drowned; but a new republic was created; new laws were made; new judges sat to minister them; so, on Ralph Sutherland's ninety-ninth birthday anniversary, there were none who would accuse him or execute sentence. He lived yet another year, dying in 1801. But was it from habit, or was it in self-punishment and remorse, that he never took off the cord? for, when he drew his last breath, though it was in his own house, his throat was still encircled by the hangman's rope.

The Baker's Dozen—Baas [Boss] Volckert Jan Pietersen Van Amsterdam kept a bake-shop in Albany, and lives in history as the man who invented New Year cakes and made gingerbread babies in the likeness of his own fat offspring. Good churchman though he was, the bane of his life was a fear of being bewitched, and perhaps it was to keep out evil spirits, who might make one last effort to gain the mastery over him, ere he turned the customary leaf with the incoming year, that he had primed himself with an extra glass of spirits on the last night of 1654. His sales had been brisk, and as he sat in his little shop, meditating comfortably on the gains he would make when his harmless rivals—the knikkerbakkers (bakers of marbles)—sent for their usual supply of olie-koeks and mince-pies on the morrow, he was startled by a sharp rap, and an ugly old woman entered. "Give me a dozen New Year's cookies!" she cried, in a shrill voice.

"Vell, den, you needn' sbeak so loud. I aind teaf, den."

"A dozen!" she screamed. "Give me a dozen. Here are only twelve."

"Vell, den, dwalf is a dozen."

"One more! I want a dozen."

"Vell, den, if you vant anodder, go to de duyvil and ged it."

Did the hag take him at his word? She left the shop, and from that time it seemed as if poor Volckert was bewitched, indeed, for his cakes were stolen; his bread was so light that it went up the chimney, when it was not so heavy that it fell through the oven; invisible hands plucked bricks from that same oven and pelted him until he was blue; his wife became deaf, his children went unkempt, and his trade went elsewhere. Thrice the old woman reappeared, and each time was sent anew to the devil; but at last, in despair, the baker called on Saint Nicolaus to come and advise him. His call was answered with startling quickness, for, almost while he was making it, the venerable patron of Dutch feasts stood before him. The good soul advised the trembling man to be more generous in his dealings with his fellows, and after a lecture on charity he vanished, when, lo! the old woman was there in his place.

She repeated her demand for one more cake, and Volckert Jan Pietersen, etc., gave it, whereupon she exclaimed, "The spell is broken, and from this time a dozen is thirteen!" Taking from the counter a gingerbread effigy of Saint Nicolaus, she made the astonished Dutchman lay his hand upon it and swear to give more liberal measure in the future. So, until thirteen new States arose from the ruins of the colonies,—when the shrewd Yankees restored the original measure,—thirteen made a baker's dozen.

∽

Dunderberg—Dunderberg, "Thunder Mountain," at the southern gate of the Hudson Highlands, is a wooded eminence, chiefly populated by a crew of imps of stout circumference, whose leader, the Heer, is a bulbous goblin clad in the dress worn by Dutch colonists two centuries ago, and carrying a speaking-trumpet, through which he bawls his orders for the blowing of winds and the touching off of lightnings. These orders are given in Low Dutch, and are put into execution by the imps aforesaid, who troop into the air and tumble about in the mist, sometimes smiting the flag or topsail of a ship to ribbons, or laying the vessel over before the wind until she is in peril of going on beam ends. At one time a sloop passing the Dunderberg had nearly foundered, when the crew discovered the sugar-loaf hat of the Heer at the mast-head. None dared to climb for it, and it was not until she had driven past Pollopel's Island—the limit of the Heer's jurisdiction—that she righted. As she did so the little hat spun into the air like a top, creating a vortex that drew up the storm-clouds, and the sloop kept her way prosperously for the rest of the voyage. The captain had nailed a horse-shoe to the mast. The "Hat Rogue" of the Devil's Bridge in Switzerland must be a relative of this gamesome sprite, for his mischief is usually of a harmless sort; but, to be on the safe side, the Dutchmen who plied along the river lowered their peaks in homage to the keeper of the mountain, and for years this was a common practice. Mariners who paid this courtesy to the Heer of the Donder Berg were never molested by his imps, though skipper Ouselsticker, of Fishkill,—for all he had a parson on board,—was once beset by a heavy squall, and the goblin came out of the mist and sat astraddle of his bowsprit, seeming to guide his schooner straight toward the rocks. The dominie chanted the song of Saint Nicolaus, and the goblin, unable to endure either its spiritual potency or the worthy parson's singing, shot upward like a ball and rode off on the gale, carrying with him the nightcap of the parson's wife, which he hung on the weathercock of Esopus steeple, forty miles away.

ꙮ

Why Spuyten Duyvil Is So Named—The tide-water creek that forms the upper boundary of Manhattan Island is known to dwellers in tenements round about as "Spittin' Divvle." The proper name of it is Spuyten Duyvil, and this, in turn, is the compression of a celebrated boast by Anthony Van Corlaer. This redoubtable gentleman, famous for fat, long wind, and long whiskers, was trumpeter for the garrison at New Amsterdam, which his countrymen had just bought for twenty-four dollars, and he sounded the brass so sturdily that in the fight between the Dutch and Indians at the Dey Street peach orchard his blasts struck more terror into the red men's hearts than did the matchlocks of his comrades. William the Testy vowed that Anthony and his trumpet were garrison enough for all Manhattan Island, for he argued that no regiment of Yankees would approach near enough to be struck with lasting deafness, as must have happened if they came when Anthony was awake.

Peter Stuyvesant—Peter the Headstrong showed his appreciation of Anthony's worth by making him his esquire, and when he got news of an English expedition on its way to seize his unoffending colony, he at once ordered Anthony to rouse the villages along the Hudson with a trumpet call to war. The esquire took a hurried leave of six or eight ladies, each of whom delighted to believe that his affections were lavished on her alone, and bravely started northward, his trumpet hanging on one side, a stone bottle, much heavier, depending from the other. It was a stormy evening when he arrived at the upper end of the island, and there was no ferryman in sight, so, after fuming up and down the shore, he swallowed a mighty draught of Dutch courage,—for he was as accomplished a performer on the horn as on the trumpet,—and swore with ornate and voluminous oaths that he would swim the stream "in spite of the devil" [En spuyt den Duyvil].

He plunged in, and had gone half-way across when the Evil One, not to be spited, appeared as a huge moss-bunker, vomiting boiling water and lashing a fiery tail. This dreadful fish seized Anthony by the leg; but the trumpeter was game, for, raising his instrument to his lips, he exhaled his last breath through it in a defiant blast that rang through the woods for miles and made the devil himself let go for a moment. Then he was dragged below, his nose shining through the water more and more faintly, until, at last, all sight of him was lost. The failure of his mission resulted in the downfall of the Dutch in America, for, soon after, the English won a bloodless victory, and St. George's cross flaunted from the ramparts where Anthony had so often saluted the setting sun. But it was years, even then, before he was hushed, for in stormy weather it was claimed that the shrill of his trumpet could be heard near the creek that he had named, sounding above the deeper roar of the blast.

❧

The Vanderdecken of Tappan Zee—It is Saturday night; the swell of the Hudson lazily heaves against the shores of Tappan Zee, the cliff above Tarrytown where the white lady cries on winter nights is pale in starlight, and crickets chirp in the boskage. It is so still that the lap of oars can be heard coming across the water at least a mile away. Some small boat, evidently, but of heavy build, for it takes a vigorous hand to propel it, and now there is a grinding of oars on thole-pins. Strange that it is not yet seen, for the sound is near. Look! Is that a shadow crossing that wrinkle of starlight in the water? The oars have stopped, and there is no wind to make that sound of a sigh.

Ho, Rambout Van Dam! Is it you? Are you still expiating your oath to pull from Kakiat to Spuyten Duyvil before the dawn of Sabbath, if it takes you a month of Sundays? Better for you had you passed the night with your roistering friends at Kakiat, or started homeward earlier, for Sabbath-breaking is no sin now, and you, poor ghost, will find little sympathy for your plight. Grant that your month of Sundays, or your cycle of months of Sundays, be soon up, for it is sad to be reminded that we may be punished for offences many years forgotten. When the sun is high to-morrow a score of barges will vex the sea of Tappan, each crowded with men and maids from New Amsterdam, jigging to profane music and refreshing themselves with such liquors as you, Rambout, never even smelled—be thankful for that much. If your shade sits blinking at them from the wooded buttresses of the Palisades, you must repine, indeed, at the hardness of your fate.

The Galloping Hessian—In the flower-gemmed cemetery of Tarrytown, where gentle Irving sleeps, a Hessian soldier was interred after sustaining misfortune in the loss of his head in one of the Revolutionary battles. For a long time after he was buried it was the habit of this gentleman to crawl from his grave at unseemly hours and gallop about the country, sending shivers through the frames of many worthy people, who shrank under their blankets when they heard the rush of hoofs along the unlighted roads.

In later times there lived in Tarrytown—so named because of the tarrying habits of Dutch gossips on market days, though some hard-minded people insist that Tarwe-town means Wheattown—a gaunt schoolmaster, one Ichabod Crane, who cherished sweet sentiments for Katrina Van Tassell, the buxom daughter of a farmer, also a famous maker of pies and doughnuts. Ichabod had been calling late one evening, and, his way home being long, Katrina's father lent him a horse to make the journey; but even with this advantage the youth set out with misgivings, for he had to pass the graveyard.

As it was near the hour when the Hessian was to ride, he whistled feebly to keep his courage up, but when he came to the dreaded spot the whistle died in a gasp, for he heard the tread of a horse. On looking around, his hair bristled and his heart came up like a plug in his throat to hinder his breathing, for he saw a headless horseman coming over the ridge behind him, blackly defined against the starry sky. Setting spurs to his nag with a hope of being first to reach Sleepy Hollow bridge, which the specter never passed, the unhappy man made the best possible time in that direction, for his follower was surely overtaking him. Another minute and the bridge would be reached; but, to Ichabod's horror, the Hessian dashed alongside and, rising in his stirrups, flung his head full at the fugitive's back. With a squeal of fright the schoolmaster rolled into a mass of weeds by the wayside, and for some minutes he remained there, knowing and remembering nothing.

Next morning farmer Van Tassell's horse was found grazing in a field near Sleepy Hollow, and a man who lived some miles southward reported that he had seen Mr. Crane striding as rapidly along the road to New York as his lean legs could take him, and wearing a pale and serious face as he kept his march. There were yellow stains on the back of his coat, and the man who restored the horse found a smashed pumpkin in the broken bushes beside the road. Ichabod never returned to Tarrytown, and when Brom Bones, a stout young ploughman and taphaunter, married Katrina, people made bold to say that he knew more about the galloping Hessian than any one else, though they believed that he never had reason to be jealous of Ichabod Crane.

Storm Ship of the Hudson—It was noised about New Amsterdam, two hundred years ago, that a round and bulky ship flying Dutch colors from her lofty quarter was careering up the harbor in the teeth of a north wind, through the swift waters of an ebbing tide, and making for the Hudson. A signal from the Battery to heave to and account for herself being disregarded, a cannon was trained upon her, and a ball went whistling through her cloudy and imponderable mass, for timbers she had none. Some of the sailor-folk talked of mirages that rose into the air of northern coasts and seas, but the wise ones put their fingers beside their noses and called to memory the Flying Dutchman, that wanderer of the seas whose captain, having sworn that he would round Cape Horn in spite of heaven and hell, has been beating to and fro along the bleak Fuegian coast and elsewhere for centuries, being allowed to land but once in seven years, when he can break the curse if he finds a girl who will love him. Perhaps Captain Vanderdecken found this maiden of his hopes in some Dutch settlement on the Hudson, or perhaps he expiated his rashness by prayer and penitence; howbeit, he never came down again, unless he slipped away to sea in snow or fog so dense that watchers and boatmen saw nothing of his passing. A few old settlers declared the vessel to be the Half Moon, and there were some who testified to seeing that identical ship with Hudson and his specter crew on board making for the Catskills to hold carouse.

This fleeting vision has been confounded with the storm ship that lurks about the foot of the Palisades and Point-no-Point, cruising through Tappan Zee at night when a gale is coming up. The Hudson is four miles wide at Tappan, and squalls have space enough to gather force; hence, when old skippers saw the misty form of a ship steal out from the shadows of the western hills, then fly like a gull from shore to shore, catching the moonlight on her topsails, but showing no lanterns, they made to windward and dropped anchor, unless their craft were stanch and their pilot's brains unvexed with liquor. On summer nights, when falls that curious silence which is ominous of tempest, the storm ship is not only seen spinning across the mirror surface of the river, but the voices of the crew are heard as they chant at the braces and halyards in words devoid of meaning to the listeners.

Sir Henry Hudson entering New York Bay, Sept. 11, 1609, with Indian family watching on shore. Photomechanical print of painting by Edward Moran, c. 1898.

It *floweth deep and strong and wide*
This river of romance
Along whose banks on moonlight nights
The Highland fairies dance.

—E. A. Lente

CHAPTER 8

Wilderness Legends

M oodua Creek—Moodua is an evolution, through Murdy's and Moodna, from Murderer's Creek, its present inexpressive name having been given to it by N. P. Willis. One Murdock lived on its shore with his wife, two sons, and a daughter; and often in the evening Naoman, a warrior of a neighboring tribe, came to the cabin, caressed the children, and shared the woodman's hospitality. One day the little girl found in the forest an arrow wrapped in snake-skin and tipped with crow's feather; then the boy found a hatchet hanging by a hair from a bough above the door; then a glare of evil eyes was caught for an instant in a thicket. Naoman, when he came, was reserved and stern, finding voice only to warn the family to fly that night; so, when all was still, the threatened family made its way softly, but quickly, to the Hudson shore, and embarked for Fisher's Kill, across the river.

The wind lagged and their boat drew heavily, and when, from the shade of Pollopel's Island, a canoe swept out, propelled by twelve men, the hearts of the people in the boat sank in despair. The wife was about to leap over, but Murdock drew her back;

Confluence of the Hudson and Scarron

then, loading and firing as fast as possible, he laid six of his pursuers low; but the canoe was savagely urged forward, and in another minute every member of the family was a helpless captive. When the skiff had been dragged back, the prisoners were marched through the wood to an open spot where the principal members of the tribe sat in council.

The sachem arose, twisted his hands in the woman's golden hair, bared his knife, and cried, "Tell us what Indian warned you and betrayed his tribe, or you shall see husband and children bleed before your eyes." The woman answered never a word, but after a little Naoman arose and said, "Twas I;" then drew his blanket about him and knelt for execution. An axe cleft his skull. Drunk with the sight of blood, the Indians rushed upon the captives and slew them, one by one. The prisoners neither shrank nor cried for mercy, but met their end with hymns upon their lips, and, seeing that they could so meet death, one member of the band let fall his arm and straight became a Christian. The cabin was burned, the bodies flung into the stream, and the stain of blood was seen for many a year in Murderer's Creek.

A Trapper's Ghastly Vengeance—About a mile back from the Hudson, at Coxsackie, stood the cabin of Nick Wolsey, who, in the last century, was known to the river settlements as a hunter and trapper of correct aim, shrewdness, endurance, and taciturn habit. For many years he lived in this cabin alone, except for the company of his dog; but while visiting a camp of Indians in the wilderness he was struck with the engaging manner of one of the girls of the tribe; he repeated the visit; he found cause to go to the camp frequently; he made presents to the father of the maid, and at length won her consent to be his wife. The simple marriage ceremony of the tribe was performed, and Wolsey led Minamee to his home; but the wedding was interrupted in an almost tragic manner, for a surly fellow who had loved the girl, yet who never had found courage to declare himself, was wrought to such a jealous fury at the discovery of Wolsey's good fortune that he sprang at him with a knife, and would have despatched him on the spot had not the white man's faithful hound leaped at his throat and borne him to the ground.

Wolsey disarmed the fellow and kicked and cuffed him to the edge of the wood, while the whole company shouted with laughter at this ignominious punishment, and approved it. A year or more passed. Wolsey and his Indian wife were happy in their free and simple life; happy, too, in their little babe. Wolsey was seldom absent from his cabin for any considerable length of time, and usually returned to it before the night set in. One evening he noticed that the grass and twigs were bent near his house by some passing foot that, with the keen eye of the woodman, he saw was not his wife's.

"Some hunter," he said, "saw the house when he passed here, and as, belike, he never saw one before, he stopped to look in." For the trail led to his window, and diverged thence to the forest again. A few days later, as he was returning, he came on the footprints that were freshly made, and a shadow crossed his face. On nearing the door he stumbled on the body of his dog, lying rigid on the ground. "How did this happen, Minamee?" he cried, as he flung open the door. The wife answered, in a low voice, "O Hush! you'll wake the child."

Nick Wolsey entered the cabin and stood as one turned to marble. Minamee, his wife, sat on the gold hearth, her face and hands cut and blackened, her dress torn, her eyes glassy, a meaningless smile on her lips. In her arms she pressed the body of her infant, its dress soaked with blood, and the head of the little creature lay on the floor beside her. She crooned softly over the cold clay as if hushing it to sleep, and when Wolsey at length found words, she only whispered, "Hush! you will wake him." The night went heavily on; day dawned, and the crooning became lower and lower; still, through all that day the bereft woman rocked to and fro upon the floor, and the agonized husband hung about her, trying in vain to give comfort, to bind her wounds, to get some explanation of the mystery that confronted him. The second night set in, and it was evident that it would be the last for Minamee. Her strength failed until she allowed herself to be placed on a couch of skins, while the body of her child was gently lifted from her arms. Then, for a few brief minutes, her reason was restored, and she found words to tell her husband how the Indian whose murderous attack he had thwarted at the wedding had come to the cabin, shot the dog that had rushed out to defend the place, beat the woman back from the door, tore the baby from its bed, slashed its head off with a knife, and, flinging the little body into her lap, departed with the words, "This is my revenge. I am satisfied." Before the sun was in the east again Minamee was with her baby.

Wolsey sat for hours in the ruin of his happiness, his breathing alone proving that he was alive, and when at last he arose and went out of the house, there were neither tears nor outcry; he saddled his horse and rode off to the westward. At nightfall he came

"Indian Pass," at the source of the Hudson in the Adirondacks

to the Indian village where he had won his wife, and relating to the assembled tribe what had happened, he demanded that the murderer be given up to him. His demand was readily granted, whereupon the white man advanced on the cowering wretch, who had confidently expected the protection of his people, and with the quick fling and jerk of a raw-hide rope bound his arms to his side. Then casting a noose about his neck and tying the end of it to his saddle-bow, he set off for the Hudson. All that night he rode, the Indian walking and running at the horse's heels, and next day he reached his cabin. Tying his prisoner to a tree, the trapper cut a quantity of young willows, from which he fashioned a large cradle-like receptacle; in this he placed the culprit, face upward, and tied so stoutly that he could not move a finger; then going into his house, he emerged with the body of Minamee, and laid it, face downward, on the wretch, who could not repress a groan of horror as the awful burden sank on his breast. Wolsey bound together the living and the dead, and with a swing of his powerful arms he flung them on his horse's back, securing them there with so many turns of rope that nothing could displace them. Now he began to lash his horse until the poor beast trembled with anger and pain, when, flinging off the halter, he gave it a final lash, and the animal plunged, foaming and snorting, into the wilderness. When it had vanished and the hoof-beats were no longer heard, Nick Wolsey took his rifle on his arm and left his home forever. And tradition says that the horse never stopped in its mad career, but that on still nights it can be heard sweeping through the woods along the Hudson and along the Mohawk like a whirlwind, and that as the sound goes by a smothered voice breaks out in cursing, in appeal, then in harsh and dreadful laughter.

怀

The Ramapo Salamander—A curious tale of the Rosicrucians runs to the effect that more than two centuries ago a band of German colonists entered the Ramapo valley and put up houses of stone, like those they had left in the Hartz Mountains, and when the Indians saw how they made knives and other wonderful things out of metal, which they extracted from the rocks by fire, they believed them to be manitous and went away, not wishing to resist their possession of the land. There was treasure here, for High Tor, or Torn Mountain, had been the home of Amasis, youngest of the magi who had followed the star of Bethlehem. He had found his way, through Asia and Alaska, to this country, had taken to wife a native woman, by whom he had a child, and here on the summit he had built a temple. Having refused the sun worship, when the Indians demanded that he should take their faith, he was set upon, and would have been killed had not an earthquake torn the ground at his feet, opening a new channel for the Hudson and precipitating into it every one but the magus and his daughter. To him had been revealed in magic vision the secrets of wealth in the rocks.

The leader in the German colony, one Hugo, was a man of noble origin, who had a wife and two children: a boy, named after himself; a girl,—Mary. Though it had been the custom in the other country to let out the forge fires once in seven years, Hugo opposed that practice in the forge he had built as needless. But his men murmured and talked of the salamander that once in seven years attains its growth in unquenched flame and goes forth doing mischief. On the day when that period was ended the master entered his works and saw the men gazing into the furnace at a pale form that seemed made from flame, that was nodding and turning in the fire, occasionally darting its tongue at them or allowing its tail to fall out and lie along the stone floor. As he came

A stone house typical of many built by early colonists in the Ramapo valley

to the door he, too, was transfixed, and the fire seemed burning his vitals, until he felt water sprinkled on his face, and saw that his wife, whom he had left at home too ill to move, stood behind him and was casting holy water into the furnace, speaking an incantation as she did so. At that moment a storm arose, and a rain fell that put out the fire; but as the last glow faded the lady fell dead.

When her children were to be consecrated, seven years later, those who stood outside of the church during the ceremony saw a vivid flash, and the nurse turned from the boy in her fright. She took her hands from her eyes. The child was gone. Twice seven years had passed and the daughter remained unspotted by the world, for, on the night when her father had led her to the top of High Torn Mountain and shown her what Amasis had seen,— the earth spirits in their caves heaping jewels and offering to give them if Hugo would speak the word that binds the free to the earth forces and bars his future for a thousand years,—it was her prayer that brought him to his senses and made the scene below grow dim, though the baleful light of the salamander clinging to the rocks at the bottom of the cave sent a glow into the sky.

Many nights after that the glow was seen on the height and Hugo was missing from his home, but for lack of a pure soul to stand as interpreter he failed to read the words that burned in the triangle on the salamander's back, and returned in rage and jealousy. A knightly man had of late appeared in the settlement, and between him and Mary a tender feeling had arisen, that, however, was unexpressed until, after saving her from the attack of a panther, he had allowed her to fall into his arms. She would willingly then have declared her love for him, but he placed her gently and regretfully from him and said, "When you slept I came to you and put a crown of gems on your head: that was because I was in the power of the earth spirit. Then I had power only over the element of fire, that either consumes or hardens to stone; but now water and life are mine. Behold! Wear these, for thou art worthy." And touching the tears that had fallen from her eyes, they turned into lilies in his hands, and he put them on her brow.

"Shall we meet again?" asked the girl.

"I do not know," said he. "I tread the darkness of the universe alone, and I peril my redemption by yielding to this love of earth. Thou art redeemed already, but I must make my way back to God through obedience tested in trial. Know that I am one of those that left heaven for love of man. We were of that subtle element which is flame, burning and glowing with love,—and when thy mother came to me with the power of purity to cast me out of the furnace, I lost my shape of fire and took that of a human being,—a child. I have been with thee often, and was rushing to annihilation, because I could not withstand the ordeal of the senses. Had I yielded, or found thee other than thou art, I should have become again an earth spirit. I have been led away by wish for power, such as I have in my grasp, and forgot the mission to the suffering. I became a wanderer over the earth until I reached this land, the land that you call new. Here was to be my last trial and here I am to pass the gate of fire."

As he spoke voices arose from the settlement.

"They are coming," said he. The stout form of Hugo was in

advance. With a fierce oath he sprang on the young man. "He has ruined my household," he cried. "Fling him into the furnace!" The young man stood waiting, but his brow was serene. He was seized, and in a few moments had disappeared through the mouth of the burning pit. But Mary, looking up, saw a shape in robes of silvery light, and it drifted upward until it vanished in the darkness. The look of horror on her face died away, and a peace came to it that endured until the end.

The Deformed of Zoar—The valley of Zoar, in western New York, is so surrounded by hills that its discoverers—a religious people, who gave it a name from Scripture—said, "This is Zoar; it is impregnable. From her we will never go." And truly, for lack of roads, they found it so hard to get out, having got in, that they did not leave it. Among the early settlers here were people of a family named Wright, whose house became a sort of inn for the infrequent traveller, inasmuch as they were not troubled with piety, and had no scruples against the selling of drink and the playing of cards at late hours. A peddler passed through the valley on his way to Buffalo and stopped at the Wright house for a lodging, but before he went to bed he incautiously showed a number of golden trinkets from his pack and drew a considerable quantity of money out of his pocket when he paid the fee for his lodging. Hardly had he fallen asleep before his greedy hosts were in the room, searching for his money. Their lack of caution caused him to awake, and as he found them rifling his pockets and his pack he sprang up and showed fight.

A blow sent him to the bottom of the stairs, where his attempt to escape was intercepted, and the family closed around him and bound his arms and legs. They showed him the money they had taken and asked where he had concealed the rest. He vowed that it was all he had. They insisted that he had more, and seizing a knife from the table the elder Wright slashed off one of his toes "to make him confess." No result came from this, and six toes were cut off,—three from each foot; then, in disgust, the unhappy peddler was knocked on the head and flung through a trap-door into a shallow cellar. Presently he arose and tried to draw himself out, but with hatchet and knife they chopped away his fingers and he fell back. Even the women shared in this work, and leaned forward to gaze into the cellar to see if he might yet be dead. While listening, they heard the man invoke the curse of heaven on them: he asked that they should wear the mark of crime even to the fourth generation, by coming into the world deformed and mutilated as he was then. And it was so. The next child born in that house had round, hoof-like feet, with only two toes, and hands that tapered from the wrist into a single long finger. And in time there were twenty people so deformed in the valley: The "crab-clawed Zoarites" they were called.

ᘒᘐ

The Drop Star—A little maid of three years was missing from her home on the Genesee. She had gone to gather water-lilies and did not return. Her mother, almost crazed with grief, searched for days, weeks, months, before she could resign herself to the thought that her little one—Kayutah, the Drop Star, the Indians called her—had indeed been drowned. Years went by. The woman's home was secure against pillage, for it was no longer the one house of a white family in that region, and the Indians had retired farther and farther into the wilderness. One day a hunter came to the woman and said, "I have seen old Skenandoh,—the last of his tribe, thank God! who bade me say this to you: that the ice is broken, and he knows of a hill of snow where a red berry grows that shall be yours if you will claim it." When the meaning of this message came upon her the woman fainted, but on recovering speech she despatched her nephew to the hut of the aged chief and passed that night in prayer.

The young man set off at sunset, and by hard riding, over dim trails, with only stars for light, he came in the gray of dawn to an upright timber, colored red and hung with scalps, that had been cut from white men's heads at the massacre of Wyoming. The place they still call Painted Post. Without drawing rein he sped along the hills that hem Lake Seneca, then, striking deeper into the wilds, he reached a smaller lake, and almost fell from his saddle before a rude tent near the shore. A new grave had been dug close by, and he shuddered to think that perhaps he had come too late, but a wrinkled Indian stepped forth at that moment and waited his word.

"I come," cried the youth,—"to see the berry that springs from snow."

"You come in time," answered Skenandoh. "No, 'tis not in that grave. It is my own child that is buried there. She was as a sister to the one you seek, and she bade me restore the Drop Star to her mother,—the squaw that we know as the New Moon's Light."

Stepping into the wigwam, he emerged again, clasping the wrist of a girl of eighteen, whose robe he tore asunder at the throat, showing the white breast, and on it a red birth-mark; then, leading her to the young man, he said,—"And now I must go to the setting sun." He slung a pouch about him, loaded, not with arms and food, but stones, stepped into his canoe, and paddled out upon the water, singing as he went a melancholy chant—his deathsong. On gaining the middle of the lake he swung his tomahawk and clove the bottom of the frail boat, so that it filled in a moment and the chief sank from sight. The young man took his cousin to her overjoyed mother, helped to win her back to the ways of civilized life, and eventually married her. She took her Christian name again, but left to the lake on whose banks she had lived so long her Indian name of Drop Star—Kayutah.

◊◊

Hudson River scenery, c. 1878

The sun-touched mountains in some places were of a bright orange, and the shadows between them a deep neutral tint of blue. And the river apparently had stopped running to reflect.

—Susan Warner

CHAPTER 9

Colonial-era Legends

Rogers's Slide—The shores of Lakes George and Champlain were ravaged by war. Up and down those lovely waters swept the barges of French and English, and the green hills rang to the shrill of bugles, the boom of cannon, and the yell of savages. Fiction and history have been weft across the woods and the memory of deeds still echoes among the heights. It was at Glen's Falls, in the cave on the rock in the middle of the river, that the brave Uncas held the watch with Hawkeye. Bloody Defile and Bloody Pond, between there and Lake George, take their names from the "Bloody morning scout" sent out by Sir William Johnson on a September day in 1755 to check Dieskau until Fort William Henry could be completed. In the action that ensued, Colonel Williams, founder of Williams College, and Captain Grant, of the Connecticut line, great-grandfather of the President who bore that name, were killed. The victims, dead and wounded alike, having been flung into Bloody Pond, it was thick and red for days, and tradition said that in after years it resumed its hue of crimson at sunset and held it until dawn. The captured, who were delivered to the Indians, had little to hope, for their white allies could not stay their savagery. Blind Rock was so called because the Indians brought a white man there, and tearing his eyes out, flung them into embers at the foot of the stone. Captives were habitually tortured, blazing splinters of pine being thrust into their flesh, their nails torn out, and their bodies slashed with knives before they went to the stake. An English prisoner was allowed to run the gauntlet here. They had already begun to strike at him as he sped between the lines, when he seized a pappoose, flung it on a fire, and, in the instant of confusion that followed, snatched an axe, cut the bonds of a comrade who had been doomed to die, and both escaped.

But the best-known history of this region is that of Rogers's Rock, or Rogers's Slide, a lofty precipice at the lower end of Lake George. Major Rogers did not toboggan down this rock in leather trousers, but his escape was no less remarkable than if he had. On March 13, 1758, while reconnoitring near Ticonderoga with two hundred rangers, he was surprised by a force of French and Indians. But seventeen of his men escaped death or capture, and he was pursued nearly to the brink of this cliff. During a brief delay among the red men, arising from the loss of his trail, he had time to throw his pack down the slide, reverse his snow-shoes, and go back over his own track to the head of a ravine before they emerged from the woods, and, seeing that his shoe-marks led to the rock, while none pointed back, they concluded that he had flung himself off and committed suicide to avoid capture. Great was their disappointment when they saw the major on the frozen surface of the lake beneath going at a lively rate toward Fort William Henry. He had gained the ice by way of the cleft in the rocks, but the savages, believing that he had leaped over the precipice, attributed his preservation to the Great Spirit and forbore to fire on him. Unconsciously, he had chosen the best possible place to disappear from, for the Indians held it in superstitious regard, believing that spirits haunted the wood and hurled bad souls down the cliff, drowning them in the lake, instead of allowing them to go to the happy hunting grounds. The major reached his quarters in safety, and lived to take up arms against the land of his birth when the colonies revolted, seventeen years later.

The Falls at Cohoes—When Occuna, a young Seneca, fell in love with a girl whose cabin was near the present town of Cohoes, he behaved very much as Americans of a later date have done. He picked wild flowers for her; he played on the bone pipe and sang sentimental songs in the twilight; he roamed the hills with her, gathering the loose quartz crystals that the Indians believed to be the tears of stricken deer, save on Diamond Rock, in Lansingburgh, where they are the tears of Moneta, a bereaved mother and wife; and in fine weather they went boating on the Mohawk above the rapids. They liked to drift idly on the current, because it gave

View of Cohoes Falls

them time to gaze into each other's eyes, and to build air castles that they would live in in the future. They were suddenly called to a realization of danger one evening, for the stream had been subtly drawing them on and on until it had them in its power. The stroke of the paddle failed and the air castles fell in dismal ruin. Sitting erect they began their death-song in this wise:

Occuna: *"Daughter of a mighty warrior, the Manitou calls me hence. I hear the roaring of his voice; I see the lightning of his glance along the river; he walks in clouds and spray upon the waters."*

The Maiden: *"Thou art thyself a warrior, O Occuna. Hath not thine axe been often bathed in blood? Hath the deer ever escaped thine arrow or the beaver avoided thy chase? Thou wilt not fear to go into the presence of Manitou."*

Occuna: *"Manitou, indeed, respects the strong. When I chose thee from the women of our tribe I promised that we should live and die together. The Thunderer calls us now. Welcome, O ghost of Oriska, chief of the invincible Senecas! A warrior and the daughter of a warrior come to join you in the feast of the blessed!"*

The boat leaped over the falls, and Occuna, striking on the rocks below, was killed at once; but, as by a miracle, the girl fell clear of them and was whirled on the seething current to shoal water, where she made her escape. For his strength and his virtues the dead man was canonized. His tribe raised him above the regions of the moon, whence he looked down on the scenes of his youth with pleasure, and in times of war gave pleasant dreams and promises to his friends, while he confused the enemy with evil omens. Whenever his tribe passed the falls they halted and with brief ceremonials commemorated the death of Occuna.

Francis Woolcott's Night-riders—In Copake, New York, among the Berkshire Hills, less than a century ago, lived Francis Woolcott, a dark, tall man, with protruding teeth, whose sinister laugh used to give his neighbors a creep along their spines. He had no obvious trade or calling, but the farmers feared him so that he had no trouble in making levies: pork, flour, meal, cider, he could have what he chose for the asking, for had he not halted horses at the plow so that neither blows nor commands could move them for two hours? Had he not set farmer Raught's pigs to walking on their hind legs and trying to talk? When he shouted "Hup! hup! hup!" to farmer Williams's children, had they not leaped to the moulding of the parlor wainscot,—a yard above the floor and only an inch wide,—and walked around it, afterward skipping like birds from chair-back to chair-back, while the furniture stood as if nailed to the floor? And was he not the chief of thirteen night-riders, whose faces no man had seen, nor wanted to see, and whom he sent about the country on errands of mischief every night when the moon was growing old? As to moons, had he not found a mystic message from our satellite on Mount Riga, graven on a meteor?

Horses' tails were tied, hogs foamed at the mouth and walked like men, cows gave blood for milk. These night-riders met Woolcott in a grove of ash and chestnut trees, each furnished with a stolen bundle of oat straw, and these bundles Woolcott changed to black horses when the night had grown dark enough not to let the way of the change be seen. These horses could not cross streams of water, and on the stroke of midnight they fell to pieces and were oaten sheaves once more, but during their time of action they rushed through woods, bearing their riders safely, and tore like hurricanes across the fields, leaping bushes, fences, even trees, without effort. Never could traces be found of them the next day. At last the devil came to claim his own. Woolcott, who was ninety years old, lay sick and helpless in his cabin. Clergymen refused to see him, but two or three of his neighbors stifled their fears and went to the wizard's house to soothe his dying moments. With the night came storm, and with its outbreak the old man's face took on such a strange and horrible look that the watchers fell back in alarm. There was a burst of purple flame at the window, a frightful peal, a smell of sulphur, and Woolcott was dead. When the watchers went out the roads were dry, and none in the village had heard wind, rain, or thunder. It was the coming of the fiend.

Polly's Lover—In about the middle of this century a withered woman of ninety was buried from a now deserted house in White Plains, New York, Polly Carter the name of her, but "Crazy Polly" was what the neighbors called her, for she was eccentric and not fond of company. Among the belongings of her house was a tall clock, such as relic hunters prize, that ticked solemnly in a landing on the stairs.

For a time, during the Revolution, the house stood within the British lines, and as her father was a colonel in Washington's army she was left almost alone in it. The British officers respected her sex, but they had an unpleasant way of running in unannounced and demanding entertainment, in the king's name, which she felt forced to grant. One rainy afternoon the door was flung open, then locked on the inside, and she found herself in the arms of a stalwart, handsome lieutenant, who wore the blue. It was her cousin and fiance. Their glad talk had not been going long when there came a rousing summons at the door. Three English officers were awaiting admittance.

Perhaps they had seen Lawrence Carter go into the house, and if caught he would be killed as a spy. He must be hidden, but in some place where they would not think of looking. The clock! That was the place. With a laugh and a kiss the young man submitted to be shut in this narrow quarter, and throwing his coat and hat behind some furniture the girl admitted the officers, who were wet and surly and demanded dinner. They tramped about the best room in their muddy boots, talking loudly, and in order to break the effect of the chill weather they passed the brandy bottle freely. Polly served them with a dinner as quickly as possible, for she wanted to get them out of the house, but they were in no mood to go, and the bottle passed so often that before the dinner was over they were noisy and tipsy and were using language that drove Polly from the room.

At last, to her relief, she heard them preparing to leave the house, but as they were about to go the senior officer, looking up at the landing, now dim in the paling light, said to one of the others, "See what time it is." The officer addressed, who happened to be the drunkest of the party, staggered up the stair and exclaimed, "The d——-d thing's stopped." Then, as if he thought it a good joke, he added, "It'll never go again." Drawing his saber he gave the clock a careless cut and ran the blade through the panel of the door; after this the three passed out. When their voices had died in distant brawling, Polly ran to release her lover. Something thick and dark was creeping from beneath the clock-case. With trembling fingers she pulled open the door, and Lawrence, her lover, fell heavily forward into her arms, dead. The officer was right: the clock never went again.

Crosby, the Patriot Spy—It was at the Jay house, in Westchester, New York, that Enoch Crosby met Washington and offered his services to the patriot army. Crosby was a cobbler, and not a very thriving one, but after the outbreak of hostilities he took a peddler's outfit on his back and, as a non-combatant, of Tory sympathies, he obtained admission through the British lines. After his first visit to head quarters it is certain that he always carried Sir Henry Clinton's passport in the middle of his pack, and so sure were his neighbors that he was in the service of the British that they captured him and took him to General Washington, but while his case was up for debate he managed to slip his handcuffs, which were not secure, and made off. Clinton, on the other hand, was puzzled by the unaccountable foresight of the Americans, for every blow that he prepared to strike was met,

Gate's headquarters

and he lost time and chance and temper. As if the suspicion of both armies and the hatred of his neighbors were not enough to contend against, Crosby now became an object of interest to the Skinners and Cowboys, who were convinced that he was making money, somehow, and resolved to have it.

The Skinners were camp-followers of the American troops and the Cowboys a band of Tories and renegade British. Both factions were employed, ostensibly, in foraging for their respective armies, but, in reality, for themselves, and the farmers and citizens occupying the neutral belt north of Manhattan Island had reason to curse them both impartially. While these fellows were daring thieves, they occasionally got the worst of it, even in the encounters with the farmers, as on the Neperan, near Tarrytown, where the Cowboys chased a woman to death, but were afterward cut to pieces by the enraged neighbors. Hers is but one of the many ghosts that haunt the neutral ground, and the croaking of the birds of ill luck that nest at Raven rock is blended with the cries of her dim figure. Still, graceless as these fellows were, they affected a loyalty to their respective sides, and were usually willing to fight each other when they met, especially for the plunder that was to be got by fighting.

In October, 1780, Claudius Smith, "king of the Cowboys," and three scalawag sons came to the conclusion that it was time for Crosby's money to revert to the crown, and they set off toward his little house one evening, sure of finding him in, for his father was seriously ill. The Smiths arrived there to find that the Skinners had preceded them on the same errand, and they recognized through the windows, in the leader of the band, a noted brigand on whose head a price was laid. He was searching every crack and cranny of the room, while Crosby, stripped to shirt and trousers, stood before the empty fireplace and begged for that night to be left alone with his dying father.

"To hell with the old man!" roared the Skinner. "Give up your gold, or we'll put you to the torture," and he significantly whirled the end of a rope that he carried about his waist. At that moment the faint voice of the old man was heard calling from another room.

"Take all that I have and let me go!" cried Crosby, and turning up a brick in the fire-place he disclosed a handful of gold, his life savings. The leader still tried to oppose his exit, but Crosby flung him to the floor and rushed away to his father, while the brigand, deeming it well to delay rising, dug his fingers into the hollow and began to extract the sovereigns. At that instant four muskets were discharged from without: there was a crash of glass, a yell of pain, and four of the Skinners rolled bleeding on the floor; two others ran into the darkness and escaped; their leader, trying to follow, was met at the threshold by the Smiths, who clutched the gold out of his hand and pinioned his elbows in a twinkling.

"I thought ye'd like to know who's got ye," said old Smith, peering into the face of the astonished and crestfallen robber, "for I've told ye many a time to keep out of my way, and now ye've got to swing for getting into it."

Within five minutes of the time that he had got his clutch

on Crosby's money the bandit was choking to death at the end of his own rope, hung from the limb of an apple-tree, and, having secured the gold, the Cowboys went their way into the darkness. Crosby soon made his appearance in the ranks of the Continentals, and, though they looked askant at him for a time, they soon discovered the truth and hailed him as a hero, for the information he had carried to Washington from Clinton's camp had often saved them from disaster. He had survived attack in his own house through the falling out of rogues, and he survived the work and hazard of war through luck and a sturdy frame. Congress afterwards gave him a sum of money larger than had been taken from him, for his chief had commended him in these lines: "Circumstances of political importance, which involved the lives and fortunes of many, have hitherto kept secret what this paper now reveals. Enoch Crosby has for years been a faithful and unrequited servant of his country. Though man does not, God may reward him for his conduct. GEORGE WASHINGTON."

Associated with Crosby in his work of getting information from the enemy was a man named Gainos, who kept an inn on the neutral ground, that was often raided. Being assailed by Cowboys once, Gainos, with his tenant and stable-boys, fired at the bandits together, just as the latter had forced his front door, then stepping quickly forward he slashed off the head of the leader with a cutlass. The retreating crew dumped the body into a well on the premises, and there it sits on the crumbling curb o' nights looking disconsolately for its head.

It may also be mentioned that the Skinners had a chance to revenge themselves on the Cowboys for their defeat at the Crosby house. They fell upon the latter at the tent-shaped cave in Yonkers,—it is called Washington's Cave, because the general napped there on bivouac,—and not only routed them, but secured so much of their treasure that they were able to be honest for several years after.

The Lost Grave of Paine—Failure to mark the resting-places of great men and to indicate the scenes of their deeds has led to misunderstanding and confusion among those who discover a regard for history and tradition in this practical age. Robert Fulton, who made steam navigation possible, lies in an unmarked tomb in the yard of Trinity Church—the richest church in America. The stone erected to show where Andre was hanged was destroyed by a cheap patriot, who thought it represented a compliment to the spy. The spot where Alexander Hamilton was shot in the duel by Aaron Burr is known to few and will soon be forgotten. It was not until a century of obloquy had been heaped on the memory of Thomas Paine that his once enemies were brought to know him as a statesman of integrity, a philanthropist, and philosopher. His deistic religion, proclaimed in "The Age of Reason," is unfortunately no whit more independent than is preached in dozens of pulpits to-day. He died ripe in honors, despite his want of creed, and his mortal part was buried in New Rochelle, New York, under a large walnut-tree in a hay-field. Some years later his friends removed the body to a new grave in higher ground, and placed over it a monument that the opponents of his principles quickly hacked to pieces. Around the original grave there still remains a part of the old inclosure, and it was proposed to erect a suitable memorial—the Hudson and its Hills the spot, but the owner of the tract would neither give nor sell an inch of his land for the purpose of doing honor to the man. Some doubt has already been expressed as to whether the grave is beneath the monument or in the inclosure; and it is also asserted that Paine's ghost appears at intervals, hovering in the air between the two burial-places, or flitting back and forth from one to the other, lamenting the forgetfulness of men and wailing, "Where is my grave? I have lost my grave!"

~

The Rising of Gouverneur Morris—Gouverneur Morris, American minister to the court of Louis XVI, was considerably enriched, at the close of the reign of terror, by plate, jewels, furniture, paintings, coaches, and so on, left in his charge by members of the French nobility, that they might not be confiscated in the sack of the city by the "sans culottes"; for so many of the aristocracy were killed and so many went into exile or disguised their names, that it was impossible to find heirs or owners for these effects. Some of the people who found France a good country to be out of came to America, where adventurers had found prosperity and refugees found peace so many times before. Marshal Ney and Bernadotte are alleged to have served in the American army during the Revolution, and at Hogansburg, New York, the Reverend Eleazer Williams, an Episcopal missionary, who lies buried in the church-yard there, was declared to be the missing son of Louis XVI. The question, "Have we a Bourbon among us?" was frequently canvassed; but he avoided publicity and went quietly on with his pastoral work.

All property left in Mr. Morris's hands that had not been claimed was removed to his mansion at Port Morris, when he returned from his ministry, and he gained in the esteem and envy of his neighbors when the extent of these riches was seen. Once, at the wine, he touched glasses with his wife, and said that if she bore a male child that son should be heir to his wealth. Two relatives who sat at the table exchanged looks at this and cast a glance of no gentle regard on his lady. A year went by. The son was born, but Gouverneur Morris was dead.

It is the first night of the year 1817, the servants are asleep, and the widow sits late before the fire, her baby in her arms, listening betimes to the wind in the chimney, the beat of hail on the shutters, the brawling of the Bronx and the clash of moving ice upon it; yet thinking of her husband and the sinister look his promise had brought to the faces of his cousins, when a tramp of horses is heard without, and anon a summons at the door. The panels are beaten by loaded riding-whips, and a man's voice cries, "Anne Morris, fetch us our cousin's will, or we'll break into the house and take it." The woman clutches the infant to her breast, but makes no answer. Again the clatter of the whips; but now a mist is gathering in the room, and a strange enchantment comes over her, for are not the lions breathing on the coat of arms above the door, and are not the portraits stirring in their frames?

They are, indeed. There is a rustle of robes and clink of steel and one old warrior leaps down, his armor sounding as he alights, and striking thrice his sword and shield together he calls on Gouverneur Morris to come forth. Somebody moves in the room where Morris died; there is a measured footfall in the corridor, with the clank of a scabbard keeping time; the door is opened, and on the blast that enters the widow hears a cry, then a double gallop, passing swiftly into distance. As she gazes, her husband appears, apparelled as in life, and with a smile he takes a candelabrum from the mantel and, beckoning her to follow, moves from room to room. Then, for the first time, the widow knows to what wealth her baby has been born, for the ghost discloses secret drawers in escritoires where money, title deeds, and gems are hidden, turns pictures and wainscots on unsuspected hinges, revealing shelves heaped with fabrics, plate, and lace; then, returning to the fireside, he stoops as if to kiss his wife and boy, but a bell strikes the first hour of morning and he vanishes into his portrait on the wall.

Henry Hudson trading with Indians on the bank of the Hudson River, wood engraving, 1856.

How soothing is this solitude
With nature in her wildest mood,
Where Hudson deep, majestic, wide,
Pours to the sea his monarch tide.

—William Wilson

CHAPTER 10

Other Legends

A nthony's Nose—The Hudson Highlands are suggestively named Bear Mountain, Sugar Loaf, Cro' Nest, Storm King, called by the Dutch Boterberg, or Butter Hill, from its likeness to a pat of butter; Beacon Hill, where the fires blazed to tell the country that the Revolutionary war was over; Dunderberg, Mount Taurus, so called because a wild bull that had terrorized the Highlands was chased out of his haunts on this height, and was killed by falling from a cliff on an eminence to the northward, known, in consequence, as Breakneck Hill. These, with Anthony's Nose, are the principal points of interest in the lovely and impressive panorama that unfolds before the view as the boats fly onward.

Concerning the last-named elevation, the aquiline promontory that abuts on the Hudson opposite Dunderberg, it takes title from no resemblance to the human feature, but is so named because Anthony Van Corlaer, the trumpeter, who afterwards left a reason for calling the upper boundary of Manhattan Island Spuyten Duyvil Creek, killed the first sturgeon ever eaten at the foot of this mountain. It happened in this wise: By assiduous devotion to keg and flagon Anthony had begotten a nose that was the wonder and admiration of all who knew it, for its size was prodigious; in color it rivalled the carbuncle, and it shone like polished copper. As Anthony was lounging over the quarter of Peter Stuyvesant's galley one summer morning this nose caught a ray from the sun and reflected it hissing into the water, where it killed a sturgeon that was rising beside the vessel. The fish was pulled aboard, eaten, and declared good, though the singed place savored of brimstone, and in commemoration of the event Stuyvesant dubbed the mountain that rose above his vessel Anthony's Nose.

∽

Kayuta and Waneta—The Indians loved our lakes. They had eyes for their beauty, and to them they were abodes of gracious spirits. They used to say of Oneida Lake, that when the Great Spirit formed the world "his smile rested on its waters and Frenchman's Island rose to greet it; he laughed and Lotus Island came up to listen." So they built lodges on their shores and skimmed their waters in canoes. Much of their history relates to them, and this is a tale of the Senecas that was revived a few years ago by the discovery of a deer-skin near Lakes Waneta and Keuka, New York, on which some facts of the history were rudely drawn, for all Indians are artists.

Waneta, daughter of a chief, had plighted her troth to Kayuta, a hunter of a neighboring tribe with which her people were at war. Their tryst was held at twilight on the farther shore of the lake from her village, and it was her gayety and happiness, after these meetings had taken place, that roused the suspicion and jealousy of Weutha, who had marked her for his bride against the time when he should have won her father's consent by some act of bravery. Shadowing the girl as she stole into the forest one evening, he saw her enter her canoe and row to a densely wooded spot; he heard a call like the note of a quail, then an answer; then Kayuta emerged on the shore, lifted the maiden from her little bark, and the twain sat down beside the water to listen to the lap of its waves and watch the stars come out.

Hurrying back to camp, the spy reported that an enemy was near them, and although Waneta had regained her wigwam by another route before the company of warriors had reached the lake, Kayuta was seen, pursued, and only escaped with difficulty. Next evening, not knowing what had happened after her home-ward departure on the previous night—for the braves deemed it best to keep the knowledge of their military operations from the women—the girl crept away to the lake again and rowed to the accustomed place, but while waiting for the quail call a twig dropped on the water beside her. With a quick instinct that civilization has spoiled she realized this to be a warning, and remaining perfectly still, she allowed her boat to drift toward shore, presently discovering that her lover was standing waist-deep in the water. In a whisper he told her that they were watched, and bade her row to a dead pine that towered at the foot of the lake, where he would soon meet her. At that instant an arrow grazed his side and flew quivering into the canoe.

Pushing the boat on its course and telling her to hasten, Kayuta sprang ashore, sounded the warwhoop, and as Weutha rose into sight he clove his skull with a tomahawk. Two other braves now leaped forward, but, after a struggle, Kayuta left them dead or sense-less, too. He would have stayed to tear their scalps off had he not heard his name uttered in a shriek of agony from the end of the lake, and, tired and bleeding though he was, he bounded along its mar-gin like a deer, for the voice that he heard was Waneta's. He reached the blasted pine, gave one look, and sank to the earth. Presently other Indians came, who had heard the noise of fighting, and burst upon him with yells and brandished weapons, but something in his look restrained them from a close advance. His eyes were fixed on a string of beads that lay on the bottom of the lake, just off shore, and when the meaning of it came to them, the savages thought no more of killing, but moaned their grief; for Waneta, in stepping from her canoe to wade ashore, had been caught and swallowed by a quagmire. All night and all next day Kayuta sat there like a man of stone. Then, just as the hour fell when he was used to meet his love, his heart broke, and he joined her in the spiritland.

Horseheads—The feeling recently created by an attempt to fasten the stupid names of Fairport or of North Elmira on the village in central New York that, off and on for fifty years, had been called Horseheads, caused an inquiry as to how that singular name chanced to be adopted for a settlement. In 1779, when General Sullivan was retiring toward the base of his supplies after a destructive campaign against the Indians in Genesee County, he stopped near this place and rested his troops. The country was then rude, unbroken, and still beset with enemies, however, and when the march was resumed it was thought best to gain time over a part of the way by descending the Chemung River on rafts.

As there were no appliances for building large floats, and the depth of the water was not known, the general ordered a destruction of all impedimenta that could be got rid of, and commanded that the poor and superfluous horses should be killed. His order was obeyed. As soon as the troops had gone, the wolves, that were then abundant, came forth and devoured the carcasses of the steeds, so that the clean-picked bones were strewn widely over the camp-ground. When the Indians ventured back into this region, some of them piled the skulls of the horses into heaps, and these curious monuments were found by white settlers who came into the valley some years later, and who named their village Horseheads, in commemoration of these relics. The Indians were especially loth to leave this region, for their tradition was that it had been the land of the Senecas from immemorial time, the tribe being descended from a couple that had a home on a hill near Horseheads.

The Prophet of Palmyra—It was at Palmyra, New York, that the principles of Mormonism were first enunciated by Joseph Smith, who claimed to have found the golden plates of the Book of Mormon in a hill-side in neighboring Manchester,—the "Hill of Cumorah,"—to which he was led by angels. The plates were written in characters similar to the masonic cabala, and he translated them by divine aid, giving to the world the result of his discovery. The Hebrew prophet Mormon was the alleged author of the record, and his son Moroni buried it. The basis of Mormonism was, however, an unpublished novel, called "The Manuscript Found," that was read to Sidney Rigdon (afterwards a Mormon elder) by its author, a clergyman, and that formulated a creed for a hypothetical church. Smith had a slight local celebrity, for he and his father were operators with the divining-rod, and when he appropriated this creed a harmless and beneficent one, for polygamy was a later "inspiration" of Brigham Young—and began to preach it, in 1844, it gained many converts. His arrogation of the presidency of the "Church of Latter Day Saints" and other rash performances won for him the enmity of the Gentiles, who imprisoned and killed him at Carthage, Missouri, leaving Brigham Young to lead the people across the deserts to Salt Lake, where they prospered through thrift and industry.

It was claimed that in the van of this army, on the march to Utah, was often seen a venerable man with silver beard, who never spoke, but who would point the way whenever the pilgrims were faint or discouraged. When they reached the spot where the temple was afterwards built, he struck his staff into the earth and vanished.

At Hydesville, near Palmyra, spiritualism, as it is commonly called, came into being on March 31, 1849, when certain of the departed announced themselves by thumping on doors and tables in the house of the Fox family, the survivors of which confessed the fraud nearly forty years after. It is of interest to note that the ground whence these new religions sprang was peopled by the Onondagas, the sacerdotal class of the Algonquin tribe, who have preserved the ancient religious rites of that great family until this day.

A Villain's Cremation—Bramley's Mountain, near the present village of Bloomfield, New York, on the edge of the Catskill group, was the home of a young couple that had married with rejoicing and had taken up the duties and pleasures of housekeeping with enthusiasm. To be sure, in those days housekeeping was not a thing to be much afraid of, and the servant question had not come up for discussion. The housewives did the work themselves, and the husband had no valets. The domicile of this particular pair was merely a tent of skins stretched around a frame of poles, and their furniture consisted principally of furs strewn over the earth floor; but they loved each other truly. The girl was thankful to be taken from her home to live, because, up to the time of her marriage, she had been persecuted by a morose and ill-looking fellow of her tribe, who laid siege to her affection with such vehemence that the more he pleaded the greater was her dislike; and now she hoped that she had seen the last of him. But that was not to be. He lurked about the wigwam of the pair, torturing himself with the sight of their felicity, and awaiting his chance to prove his hate. This chance came when the husband had gone to Lake Delaware to fish, for he rowed after and gave battle in the middle of the pond. Taken by surprise, and being insufficiently armed, the husband was killed and his body flung into the water. Then, casting an affectionate leer at the wife who had watched this act of treachery and malice with speechless horror from the mountain-side, he drove his canoe ashore and set off in pursuit of her. She retreated so slowly as to allow him to keep her in sight, and when she entered a cave he pressed forward eagerly, believing that now her escape was impossible; but she had purposely trapped him there, for she had already explored a tortuous passage that led to the upper air, and by this she had left the cavern in safety while he was groping and calling in the dark. Returning to the entrance, she loosened, by a jar, a ledge that overhung it, so that the door was almost blocked; then, gathering light wood from the dry trees around her, she made a fire and hurled the burning sticks into the prison where the wretch was howling, until he was dead in smoke and flame. When his yells and curses had been silenced she told a friend what she had done, then going back to the lake, she sang her death-song and cast herself into the water, hoping thus to rejoin her husband.

The Monster Mosquitoe—They have some pretty big mosquitoes in New Jersey and on Long Island, but, if report of their ancestry is true, they have degenerated in size and voracity; for the grand-father of all mosquitoes used to live in the neighborhood of Fort Onondaga, New York, and sallying out whenever he was hungry, would eat an Indian or two and pick his teeth with their ribs. The red men had no arms that could prevail against it, but at last the Holder of the Heavens, hearing their cry for aid, came down and attacked the insect. Finding that it had met its match, the mosquito flew away so rapidly that its assailant could hardly keep it in sight. It flew around the great lake, then turned eastward again. It sought help vainly of the witches that brooded in the sink-holes, or Green Lakes (near Janesville, New York), and had reached the salt lake of Onondaga when its pursuer came up and killed it, the creature piling the sand into hills in its dying struggles.

As its blood poured upon the earth it became small mosqui-toes, that gathered about the Holder of the Heavens and stung him so sorely that he half repented the service that he had done to men. The Tuscaroras say that this was one of two monsters that stood on opposite banks of the Seneca River and slew all men that passed. Hiawatha killed the other one. On their reservation is a stone, marked by the form of the Sky Holder, that shows where he rested during the chase, while his tracks were until lately seen south of Syracuse, alternating with footprints of the mosquito, which were shaped like those of a bird, and twenty inches long. At Brighton, New York, where these marks appeared, they were rev-erentially renewed by the Indians for many years.

The Green Picture—In a cellar in Green Street, Schenectady, there appeared, some years ago, the silhouette of a human form, painted on the floor in mould. It was swept and scrubbed away, but presently it was there again, and month by month, after each removal, it returned: a mass of fluffy mould, always in the shape of a recumbent man. When it was found that the house stood on the site of the old Dutch burial ground, the gossips fitted this and that together and concluded that the mould was planted by a spirit whose mortal part was put to rest a century and more ago, on the spot covered by the house, and that the spirit took this way of apprising people that they were trespassing on its grave. Others held that foul play had been done, and that a corpse, hastily and shallowly buried, was yielding itself back to the damp cellar in vegetable form, before its resolution into simpler elements. But a darker meaning was that it was the outline of a vampire that vainly strove to leave its grave, and could not because a virtuous spell had been worked about the place.

A vampire is a dead man who walks about seeking for those whose blood he can suck, for only by supplying new life to its cold limbs can he keep the privilege of moving about the earth. He fights his way from his coffin, and those who meet his gray and stiffened shape, with fishy eyes and blackened mouth, lurking by open windows, biding his time to steal in and drink up a human life, fly from him in terror and disgust. In northern Rhode Island those who die of consumption are believed to be victims of vampires who work by charm, draining the blood by slow draughts as they lie in their graves. To lay this monster he must be taken up and burned; at least, his heart must be; and he must be disinterred in the daytime when he is asleep and unaware. If he died with blood in his heart he has this power of nightly resurrection. As late as 1892 the ceremony of heart-burning was performed at Exeter, Rhode Island, to save the family of a dead woman that was threatened with the same disease that removed her, namely, consumption. But the Schenectady vampire has yielded up all his substance, and the green picture is no more.

The Nuns of Carthage—At Carthage, New York, where the Black River bends gracefully about a point, there was a stanch old house, built in the colonial fashion and designed for the occupancy of some family of hospitality and wealth, but the family died out or moved away, and for some years it remained deserted. During the war of 1812 the village gossips were excited by the appearance of carpenters, painters and upholsterers, and it was evident that the place was to be restored to its manorial dignities; but their curiosity was deepened instead of satisfied when, after the house had been put in order and high walls built around it, the occupants presented themselves as four young women in the garb of nuns. Were they daughters of the family? Were they English sympathizers in disguise, seeking asylum in the days of trouble? Had they registered a vow of celibacy until their lovers should return from the war? Were they on a secret and diplomatic errand? None ever knew, at least in Carthage. The nuns lived in great privacy, but in a luxury before unequalled in that part of the country. They kept a gardener, they received from New York wines and delicacies that others could not afford, and when they took the air, still veiled, it was behind a splendid pair of bays.

One afternoon, just after the close of the war, a couple of young American officers went to the convent, and, contrary to all precedent, were admitted. They remained within all that day, and no one saw them leave, but a sound of wheels passed through the street that evening. Next day there were no signs of life about the place, nor the day following, nor the next. The savage dog was quiet and the garden walks had gone unswept. Some neighbors climbed over the wall and reported that the place had been deserted. Why and by whom no one ever knew, but a cloud remained upon its title until a recent day, for it was thought that at some time the nuns might return.

☙

The Skull in the Wall—A skull is built into the wall above the door of the court-house at Goshen, New York. It was taken from a coffin unearthed in 1842, when the foundation of the building was laid. People said there was no doubt about it, only Claudius Smith could have worn that skull, and he deserved to be publicly pilloried in that manner. Before the Revolutionary war Smith was a farmer in Monroe, New York, and being prosperous enough to feel the king's taxes no burden, to say nothing of his jealousy of the advantage that an independent government would be to the hopes of his poorer neighbors, he declared for the king. After the declaration of independence had been published, his sympathies were illustrated in an unpleasantly practical manner by gathering a troop of other Tories about him, and, emboldened by the absence of most of the men of his vicinage in the colonial army, he began to harass the country as grievously in foray as the redcoats were doing in open field.

He pillaged houses and barns, then burned them; he insulted women, he drove away cattle and horses, he killed several persons who had undertaken to defend their property. His "campaigns" were managed with such secrecy that nobody knew when or whence to look for him. His murder of Major Nathaniel Strong, of Blooming Grove, roused indignation to such a point that a united effort was made to catch him, a money reward for success acting as a stimulus to the vigilance of the hunters, and at last he was captured on Long Island. He was sent back to Goshen, tried, convicted, and on January 22, 1779, was hanged, with five of his band. The bodies of the culprits were buried in the jail-yard, on the spot where the court-house stands, and old residents identified Smith's skeleton, when it was accidentally exhumed, by its uncommon size. A farmer from an adjacent town made off with a thigh bone, and a mason clapped mortar into the empty skull and cemented it into the wall, where it long remained.

The Haunted Mill—Among the settlers in the Adirondacks, forty or fifty years ago, was Henry Clymer, from Brooklyn, who went up to Little Black Creek and tried to make a farm out of the gnarly, stumpy land; but being a green hand at that sort of thing, he soon gave it up and put up the place near Northwood, that is locally referred to as the haunted mill. When the first slab was cut, a big party was on hand to cheer and eat pie in honor of the Clymers, for Mr. Clymer, who was a dark, hearty, handsome fellow, and his bright young wife had been liberal in their hospitality. The couple had made some talk, they were so loving before folks—too loving to last; and, besides, it was evident that Mrs. Clymer was used to a better station in life than her husband. It was while the crowd was laughing and chattering at the picnic-table of new boards from the mill that Mrs. Clymer stole away to her modest little house, and a neighbor who had followed her was an accidental witness to a singular episode. Mrs. Clymer was kneeling beside her bed, crying over the picture of a child, when Clymer entered unexpectedly and attempted to take the picture from her.

She faced him defiantly. "You kept that because it looked like him, I reckon," he said. "You might run back to him. You know what he'd call you and where you'd stand with your aristocracy."

The woman pointed to the door, and the man left without another word, and so did the listener. Next morning the body of Mrs. Clymer was found hanging to a beam in the mill. At the inquest the husband owned that he had "had a few words" with her on the previous day, and thought that she must have suddenly become insane. The jury took this view. News of the suicide was printed in some of the city papers, and soon after that the gossips had another sensation, for a fair-haired man, also from Brooklyn, arrived at the place and asked where the woman was buried. When he found the grave he sat beside it for some time, his head resting on his hand; then he inquired for Clymer, but Clymer, deadly pale, had gone into the woods as soon as he heard that a stranger had arrived. The new-comer went to Trenton, where he ordered a gravestone bearing the single word "Estella" to be placed where the woman's body had been interred. Clymer quickly sold out and disappeared. The mill never prospered, and has long been in a ruinous condition. People of the neighborhood think that the ghost of Mrs. Clymer—was that her name?—still troubles it, and they pass the place with quickened steps.

PART III

Literature

View in Hudson's River of Pakepsey & the Catts-Kill Mountains, from Sophos Island, sketched by Governor Pownal; painted and engraved by Paul Sandy; etching by Thomas Jefferys, May 20, 1761.

The queenly Hudson circling at thy feet

Lingers to sing a song of joy and love,

Pouring her heart in rippling wavelets sweet,

Which sun-kissed glance up to thy throne above.

—Kenneth Bruce

J. R. Drake, 1795–1820. Engraved
by Thomas Kelly, c. 1820–1841.

*I like to watch the tows at night, with their twinkling
lamps, and hear the husky panting of the steamers;
or catch the sloops' and schooners' shadowy forms,
like phantoms, white, silent, indefinite, out there.
Then the Hudson of a clear moonlit night.*

—Walt Whitman

*J*oseph **Rodman Drake** (1795–1820) was born in New York City and educated at Columbia University. In 1816 he became a physician and married Sarah Eckford. In 1819, he and Fitz-Greene Halleck wrote a series of satirical verses for the *New York Evening Post*, which were published after his death under the penname "The Croakers." Drake died in 1820, of consumption, at the age of twenty-five. His best-known work, *The Culprit Fay and Other Poems*, was published posthumously by his daughter in 1835.

The Culprit Fay, and Other Poems. 1836.

The Culprit Fay.

"My visual orbs are purged from film, and lo!

"Instead of Anster's turnip-bearing vales

"I see old fairy land's miraculous show!

"Her trees of tinsel kissed by freakish gales,

"Her Ouphs that, cloaked in leaf-gold, skim the breeze,

"And fairies, swarming—"

—Tennant's Anster Fair.

I.

'Tis the middle watch of a summer's night—

The earth is dark, but the heavens are bright;

Nought is seen in the vault on high

But the moon, and the stars, and the cloudless sky,

And the flood which rolls its milky hue,

A river of light on the welkin blue.

The moon looks down on old Cronest,

She mellows the shades on his shaggy breast,

And seems his huge gray form to throw

In a sliver cone on the wave below;

His sides are broken by spots of shade,

By the walnut bough and the cedar made,

And through their clustering branches dark

Glimmers and dies the fire-fly's spark—

Like starry twinkles that momently break

Through the rifts of the gathering tempest's rack.

II.

The stars are on the moving stream,
And fling, as its ripples gently flow,
A burnished length of wavy beam
In an eel-like, spiral line below;
The winds are whist, and the owl is still,
The bat in the shelvy rock is hid,
And nought is heard on the lonely hill
But the cricket's chirp, and the answer shrill
Of the gauze-winged katy-did;
And the plaint of the wailing whip-poor-will,
Who moans unseen, and ceaseless sings,
Ever a note of wail and wo,
Till morning spreads her rosy wings,
And earth and sky in her glances glow.

III.

'Tis the hour of fairy ban and spell:
The wood-tick has kept the minutes well;
He has counted them all with click and stroke,
Deep in the heart of the mountain oak,
And he has awakened the sentry elve
Who sleeps with him in the haunted tree,
To bid him ring the hour of twelve,

And call the fays to their revelry;
Twelve small strokes on his tinkling bell—
('Twas made of the white snail's pearly shell:—)
"Midnight comes, and all is well!
Hither, hither, wing your way!
'Tis the dawn of the fairy day."

IV.

They come from beds of lichen green,
They creep from the mullen's velvet screen;
Some on the backs of beetles fly
From the silver tops of moon-touched trees,
Where they swung in their cobweb hammocks high,
And rock'd about in the evening breeze;
Some from the hum-bird's downy nest—
They had driven him out by elfin power,
And pillowed on plumes of his rainbow breast,
Had slumbered there till the charmed hour;
Some had lain in the scoop of the rock,
With glittering ising-stars inlaid;
And some had opened the four-o'clock,
And stole within its purple shade.
And now they throng the moonlight glade,
Above—below—on every side,
Their little minim forms arrayed
In the tricksy pomp of fairy pride!

V.

They come not now to print the lea,
In freak and dance around the tree,
Or at the mushroom board to sup,
And drink the dew from the buttercup;—
A scene of sorrow waits them now,
For an Ouphe has broken his vestal vow;
He has loved an earthly maid,
And left for her his woodland shade;
He has lain upon her lip of dew,
And sunned him in her eye of blue,
Fann'd her cheek with his wing of air,
Played in the ringlets of her hair,
And, nestling on her snowy breast,
Forgot the lily-king's behest.
For this the shadowy tribes of air
To the elfin court must haste away:—
And now they stand expectant there,
To hear the doom of the Culprit Fay.

VI.

The throne was reared upon the grass
Of spice-wood and of sassafras;
On pillars of mottled tortoise-shell
Hung the burnished canopy—
And o'er it gorgeous curtains fell
Of the tulip's crimson drapery.

The monarch sat on his judgment-seat,

On his brow the crown imperial shone,

The prisoner Fay was at his feet,

And his peers were ranged around the throne.

He waved his sceptre in the air,

He looked around and calmly spoke;

His brow was grave and his eye severe,

But his voice in a softened accent broke:

VII.

"Fairy! Fairy! list and mark,

Thou hast broke thine elfin chain,

Thy flame-wood lamp is quenched and dark,

And thy wings are dyed with a deadly stain—

Thou hast sullied thine elfin purity

In the glance of a mortal maiden's eye,

Thou hast scorned our dread decree,

And thou shouldst pay the forfeit high,

But well I know her sinless mind

Is pure as the angel forms above,

Gentle and meek, and chaste and kind,

Such as a spirit well might love;

Fairy! had she spot or taint,

Bitter had been thy punishment.

Tied to the hornet's shardy wings;

Tossed on the pricks of nettles' stings;

Or seven long ages doomed to dwell

With the lazy worm in the walnut-shell;
Or every night to writhe and bleed
Beneath the tread of the centipede;
Or bound in a cobweb dungeon dim,
Your jailer a spider huge and grim,
Amid the carrion bodies to lie,
Of the worm, and the bug, and the murdered fly:
These it had been your lot to bear,
Had a stain been found on the earthly fair.
Now list, and mark our mild decree—
Fairy, this your doom must be:

VIII.

"Thou shalt seek the beach of sand
Where the water bounds the elfin land,
Thou shalt watch the oozy brine
Till the sturgeon leaps in the bright moonshine,
Then dart the glistening arch below,
And catch a drop from his silver bow.
The water-sprites will wield their arms
And dash around, with roar and rave,
And vain are the woodland spirits' charms,
They are the imps that rule the wave.
Yet trust thee in thy single might,
If thy heart be pure and thy spirit right,
Thou shalt win the warlock fight.

IX.

"If the spray-bead gem be won,
The stain of thy wing is washed away,
But another errand must be done
Ere thy crime be lost for aye;
Thy flame-wood lamp is quenched and dark,
Thou must re-illume its spark.
Mount thy steed and spur him high
To the heaven's blue canopy;
And when thou seest a shooting star,
Follow it fast, and follow it far—
The last faint spark of its burning train
Shall light the elfin lamp again.
Thou hast heard our sentence, Fay;
Hence! to the water-side, away!"

X.

The goblin marked his monarch well;
He spake not, but he bowed him low,
Then plucked a crimson colen-bell,
And turned him round in act to go.
The way is long, he cannot fly,
His soiled wing has lost its power,
And he winds adown the mountain high,
For many a sore and weary hour.
Through dreary beds of tangled fern,
Through groves of nightshade dark and dern,

Over the grass and through the brake,
Where toils the ant and sleeps the snake;
Now o'er the violet's azure flush
He skips along in lightsome mood;
And now he thrids the bramble bush,
Till its points are dyed in fairy blood.
He has leapt the bog, he has pierced the briar,
He has swum the brook, and waded the mire,
Till his spirits sank, and his limbs grew weak,
And the red waxed fainter in his cheek.
He had fallen to the ground outright,
For rugged and dim was his onward track,
But there came a spotted toad in sight,
And he laughed as he jumped upon her back;
He bridled her mouth with a silk-weed twist;
He lashed her sides with an osier thong;
And now through evening's dewy mist,
With leap and spring they bound along,
Till the mountain's magic verge is past,
And the beach of sand is reached at last.

XI.

Soft and pale is the moony beam,
Moveless still the glassy stream,
The wave is clear, the beach is bright
With snowy shells and sparkling stones;
The shore-surge comes in ripples light,

In murmurings faint and distant moans;
And ever afar in the silence deep
Is heard the splash of the sturgeon's leap,
And the bend of his graceful bow is seen—
A glittering arch of silver sheen,
Spanning the wave of burnished blue,
And dripping with gems of the river dew.

XII.

The elfin cast a glance around,
As he lighted down from his courser toad,
Then round his breast his wings he wound,
And close to the river's brink he strode;
He sprang on a rock, he breathed a prayer,
Above his head his arms he threw,
Then tossed a tiny curve in air,
And headlong plunged in the waters blue.

XIII.

Up sprung the spirits of the waves,
From sea-silk beds in their coral caves,
With snail-plate armour snatched in haste,
They speed their way through the liquid waste;
Some are rapidly borne along
On the mailed shrimp or the prickly prong,
Some on the blood-red leeches glide,
Some on the stony star-fish ride,

Some on the back of the lancing squab,
Some on the sidelong soldier-crab;
And some on the jellied quarl, that flings
At once a thousand streamy stings—
They cut the wave with the living oar
And hurry on to the moonlight shore,
To guard their realms and chase away
The footsteps of the invading Fay.

XIV.

Fearlessly he skims along,
His hope is high, and his limbs are strong,
He spreads his arms like the swallow's wing,
And throws his feet with a frog-like fling;
His locks of gold on the waters shine,
At his breast the tiny foam-beads rise,
His back gleams bright above the brine,
And the wake-line foam behind him lies.
But the water-sprites are gathering near
To check his course along the tide;
Their warriors come in swift career
And hem him round on every side;
On his thigh the leech has fixed his hold,
The quarl's long arms are round him roll'd,
The prickly prong has pierced his skin,
And the squab has thrown his javelin,
The gritty star has rubbed him raw,

And the crab has struck with his giant claw;
He howls with rage, and he shrieks with pain,
He strikes around, but his blows are vain;
Hopeless is the unequal fight,
Fairy! nought is left but flight.

XV.

He turned him round and fled amain
With hurry and dash to the beach again;
He twisted over from side to side,
And laid his cheek to the cleaving tide.
The strokes of his plunging arms are fleet,
And with all his might he flings his feet,
But the water-sprites are round him still,
To cross his path and work him ill.
They bade the wave before him rise;
They flung the sea-fire in his eyes,
And they stunned his ears with the scallop stroke,
With the porpoise heave and the drum-fish croak.
Oh! but a weary wight was he
When he reached the foot of the dog-wood tree;
—Gashed and wounded, and stiff and sore,
He laid him down on the sandy shore;
He blessed the force of the charmed line,
And he banned the water-goblin's spite,
For he saw around in the sweet moonshine,
Their little wee faces above the brine,

Giggling and laughing with all their might
At the piteous hap of the Fairy wight.

XVI.

Soon he gathered the balsam dew
From the sorrel leaf and the henbane bud;
Over each wound the balm he drew,
And with cobweb lint he stanched the blood.
The mild west wind was soft and low,
It cooled the heat of his burning brow,
And he felt new life in his sinews shoot,
As he drank the juice of the cal'mus root;
And now he treads the fatal shore,
As fresh and vigorous as before.

XVII.

Wrapped in musing stands the sprite:
'Tis the middle wane of night,
His task is hard, his way is far,
But he must do his errand right
Ere dawning mounts her beamy car,
And rolls her chariot wheels of light;
And vain are the spells of fairy-land,
He must work with a human hand.

XVIII.

He cast a saddened look around,

But he felt new joy his bosom swell,

When, glittering on the shadowed ground,

He saw a purple muscle shell;

Thither he ran, and he bent him low,

He heaved at the stern and he heaved at the bow,

And he pushed her over the yielding sand,

Till he came to the verge of the haunted land.

She was as lovely a pleasure boat

As ever fairy had paddled in,

For she glowed with purple paint without,

And shone with silvery pearl within;

A sculler's notch in the stern he made,

An oar he shaped of the bootle blade;

Then spung to his seat with a lightsome leap,

And launched afar on the calm blue deep.

XIX.

The imps of the river yell and rave;

They had no power above the wave,

But they heaved the billow before the prow,

And they dashed the surge against her side,

And they struck her keel with jerk and blow,

Till the gunwale bent to the rocking tide.

She wimpled about in the pale moonbeam,

Like a feather that floats on a wind tossed-stream;

And momently athwart her track
The quarl upreared his island back,
And the fluttering scallop behind would float,
And patter the water about the boat;
But he bailed her out with his colen-bell,
And he kept her trimmed with a wary tread,
While on every side like lightening fell
  The heavy strokes of his bootle-blade.

XX.

Onward still he held his way,
Till he came where the column of moonshine lay,
And saw beneath the surface dim
The brown-backed sturgeon slowly swim:
Around him were the goblin train—
But he sculled with all his might and main,
And followed wherever the sturgeon led,
Till he saw him upward point his head;
Then he dropped his paddle blade,
And held his colen goblet up
To catch the drop in its crimson cup.

XXI.

With sweeping tail and quivering fin,
Through the wave the sturgeon flew,
And, like the heaven-shot javelin,
He sprung above the waters blue.

Instant as the star-fall light,
He plunged him in the deep again,
But left an arch of silver bright
The rainbow of the moony main.
It was a strange and lovely sight
To see the puny goblin there;
He seemed an angel form of light,
With azure wing and sunny hair,
Throned on a cloud of purple fair,
Circled with blue and edged with white,
And sitting at the fall of even
Beneath the bow of summer heaven.

XXII.

A moment and its lustre fell,
But ere it met the billow blue,
He caught within his crimson bell,
A droplet of its sparkling dew—
Joy to thee, Fay! thy task is done,
Thy wings are pure, for the gem is won—
Cheerly ply thy dripping oar,
And haste away to the elfin shore.

XXIII.

He turns, and lo! on either side
The ripples on his path divide;
And the track o'er which his boat must pass

Is smooth as a sheet of polished glass.
Around, their limbs the sea-nymphs lave,
With snowy arms half swelling out,
While on the glossed and gleamy wave
Their sea-green ringlets loosely float;
They swim around with smile and song;
They press the bark with pearly hand,
And gently urge her course along,
Toward the beach of speckled sand;
And, as he lightly leapt to land,
They bade adieu with nod and bow,
Then gayly kissed each little hand,
And dropped in the crystal deep below.

XXIV.

A moment staied the fairy there;
He kissed the beach and breathed a prayer,
Then spread his wings of gilded blue,
And on to the elfin court he flew;
As ever ye saw a bubble rise,
And shine with a thousand changing dyes,
Till lessening far through ether driven,
It mingles with the hues of heaven:
As, at the glimpse of morning pale,
The lance-fly spreads his silken sail,
And gleams with blendings soft and bright,
Till lost in the shades of fading night;

So rose from earth the lovely Fay—
So vanished, far in heaven away!

Up, Fairy! quit thy chick-weed bower,
The cricket has called the second hour,
Twice again, and the lark will rise
To kiss the streaking of the skies—
Up! thy charmed armour don,
Thou'lt need it ere the night be gone.

XXV.

He put his acorn helmet on;
It was plumed of the silk of the thistle down:
The corslet plate that guarded his breast
Was once the wild bee's golden vest;
His cloak, of a thousand mingled dyes,
Was formed of the wings of butterflies;
His shield was the shell of a lady-bug queen,
Studs of gold on a ground of green;
And the quivering lance which he brandished bright,
Was the sting of a wasp he had slain in fight.
Swift he bestrode his fire-fly steed;
He bared his blade of the bent grass blue;
He drove his spurs of the cockle seed,
And away like a glance of thought he flew,
To skim the heavens and follow far
The fiery trail of the rocket-star.

XXVI.

The moth-fly, as he shot in air,
Crept under the leaf, and hid her there;
The katy-did forgot its lay,
The prowling gnat fled fast away,
The fell mosqueto checked his drone
And folded his wings till the Fay was gone,
And the wily beetle dropped his head,
And fell on the ground as if he were dead;
They crouched them close in the darksome shade,
They quaked all o'er with awe and fear,
For they had felt the blue-bent blade,
And writhed at the prick of the elfin spear;
Many a time on a summer's night,
When the sky was clear and the moon was bright,
They had been roused from the haunted ground,
By the yelp and bay of the fairy hound;
They had heard the tiny bugle horn,
They had heard of twang of the maize-silk string,
When the vine-twig bows were tightly drawn,
And the nettle-shaft through the air was borne,
Feathered with down the hum-bird's wing.
And now they deemed the courier ouphe,
Some hunter sprite of the elfin ground;
And they watched till they saw him mount the roof
That canopies the world around;
Then glad they left their covert lair,
And freaked about in the midnight air.

XXVII.

Up to the vaulted firmament
His path the fire-fly courser bent,
And at every gallop on the wind,
He flung a glittering spark behind;
He flies like a feather in the blast
Till the first light cloud in heaven is past,
But the shapes of air have begun their work,
And a drizzly mist is round him cast,
He cannot see through the mantle murk,
He shivers with cold, but he urges fast,
Through storm and darkness, sleet and shade,
He lashes his steed and spurs amain,
For shadowy hands have twitched the rein,
And flame-shot tongues around him played,
And near him many a fiendish eye
Glared with a fell malignity,
And yells of rage, and shrieks of fear,
Came screaming on his startled ear.

XXVIII.

His wings are wet around his breast,
The plume hangs dripping from his crest,
His eyes are blur'd with the lightning's glare,
And his ears are stunned with the thunder's blare,
But he gave a shout, and his blade he drew,
He thrust before and he struck behind,

Till he pierced their cloudy bodies through,
And gashed their shadowy limbs of wind;
Howling the misty spectres flew,
They rend the air with frightful cries,
For he has gained the welkin blue,
And the land of clouds beneath him lies.

XXIX.

Up to the cope careering swift
In breathless motion fast,
Fleet as the swallow cuts the drift,
Or the sea-roc rides the blast,
The sapphire sheet of eve is shot,
The sphered moon is past,
The earth but seems a tiny blot
On a sheet of azure cast.
O! it was sweet in the clear moonlight,
To tread the starry plain of even,
To meet the thousand eyes of night,
And feel the cooling breath of heaven!
But the Elfin made no stop or stay
Till he came to the bank of the milky-way,
Then he checked his courser's foot,
And watched for the glimpse of the planet-shoot.

XXX.

Sudden along the snowy tide
That swelled to meet their footstep's fall,
The sylphs of heaven were seen to glide,
Attired in sunset's crimson pall;
Around the Fay they weave the dance,
They skip before him on the plain,
And one has taken his wasp-sting lance,
And one upholds his bridle rein;
With warblings wild they lead him on
To where through clouds of amber seen,
Studded with stars, resplendent shone
The palace of the sylphid queen.
Its spiral columns gleaming bright
Were streamers of the northern light;
Its curtain's light and lovely flush
Was of the morning's rosy blush,
And the ceiling fair that rose aboon
The white and feathery fleece of noon.

XXXI.

But oh! how fair the shape that lay
Beneath a rainbow bending bright,
She seemed to the entranced Fay
The loveliest of the forms of light;
Her mantle was the purple rolled
At twilight in the west afar;

'Twas tied with threads of dawning gold,
And buttoned with a sparkling star.
Her face was like the lily roon
That veils the vestal planet's hue;
Her eyes, two beamlets from the moon,
Set floating in the welkin blue.
Her hair is like the sunny beam,
And the diamond gems which round it gleam
Are the pure drops of dewy even
That ne'er have left their native heaven.

XXXII.

She raised her eyes to the wondering sprite,
And they leapt with smiles, for well I ween
Never before in the bowers of light
Had the form of an earthly Fay been seen.
Long she looked in his tiny face;
Long with his butterfly cloak she played;
She smoothed his wings of azure lace,
And handled the tassel of his blade;
And as he told in accents low
The story of his love and wo,
She felt new pains in her bosom rise,
And the tear-drop started in her eyes.
And 'O sweet spirit of earth,' she cried,
'Return no more to your woodland height,
But ever here with me abide

In the land of everlasting light!
Within the fleecy drift we'll lie,
We'll hang upon the rainbow's rim;
And all the jewels of the sky
Around thy brow shall brightly beam!
And thou shalt bathe thee in the stream
That rolls its whitening foam aboon,
And ride upon the lightning's gleam,
And dance upon the orbed moon!
We'll sit within the Pleiad ring,
We'll rest on Orion's starry belt,
And I will bid my sylphs to sing
The song that makes the dew-mist melt;
Their harps are of the umber shade,
That hides the blush of waking day,
And every gleamy string is made
Of silvery moonshine's lengthened ray;
And thou shalt pillow on my breast,
While heavenly breathings float around,
And, with the sylphs of ether blest,
Forget the joys of fairy ground.'

XXXIII.

She was lovely and fair to see
And the elfin's heart beat fitfully;
But lovelier far, and still more fair,
The earthly form imprinted there;

Nought he saw in the heavens above
Was half so dear as his mortal love,
For he thought upon her looks so meek,
And he thought of the light flush on her cheek;
Never again might he bask and lie
On that sweet cheek and moonlight eye,
But in his dreams her form to see,
To clasp her in his reverie,
To think upon his virgin bride,
Was worth all heaven and earth beside.

XXXIV.

'Lady,' he cried, 'I have sworn to-night,
On the word of a fairy knight,
To do my sentence-task aright;
My honour scarce is free from stain,
I may not soil its snows again;
Betide me weal, betide me wo,
Its mandate must be answered now.'
Her bosom heaved with many a sigh,
The tear was in her drooping eye;
But she led him to the palace gate,
And called the sylphs who hovered there,
And bade them fly and bring him straight
Of clouds condensed a sable car.
With charm and spell she blessed it there,
From all the fiends of upper air;

Then round him cast the shadowy shroud,
And tied his steed behind the cloud;
And pressed his hand as she bade him fly
Far to the verge of the northern sky,
For by its wane and wavering light
There was a star would fall to-night.

XXXV.

Borne after on the wings of the blast,
Northward away, he speeds him fast,
And his courser follows the cloudy wain
Till the hoof-strokes fall like pattering rain.
The clouds roll backward as he flies,
Each flickering star behind him lies,
And he has reached the northern plain,
And backed his fire-fly steed again,
Ready to follow in its flight
The streaming of the rocket-light.

XXXVI.

The star is yet in the vault of heaven,
But its rocks in the summer gale;
And now 'tis fitful and uneven,
And now 'tis deadly pale;
And now 'tis wrapp'd in sulphur smoke,
And quenched is its rayless beam,
And now with a rattling thunder-stroke

It bursts in flash and flame.
As swift as the glance of the arrowy lance
That the storm-spirit flings from high,
The star-shot flew o'er the welkin blue,
As it fell from the sheeted sky.
As swift as the wind in its trail behind
The elfin gallops along,
The fiends of the clouds are bellowing loud,
But the sylphid charm is strong;
He gallops unhurt in the shower of fire,
While the cloud-fiends fly from the blaze;
He watches each flake till its sparks expire,
And rides in the light of its rays.
But he drove his steed to the lightning's speed,
And caught a glimmering spark;
Then wheeled around to the fairy ground,
And sped through the midnight dark.

Ouphe and goblin! imp and sprite!
Elf of eve! and starry Fay!
Ye that love the moon's soft light,
Hither—hither wend your way;
Twine ye in the jocund ring,
Sing and trip it merrily,
Hand to hand, and wing to wing,
Round the wild witch-hazel tree.

Hail the wanderer again,
With dance and song, and lute and lyre,
Pure his wing and strong his chain,
And doubly bright his fairy fire.
Twine ye in an airy round,
Brush the dew and print the lea;
Skip and gambol, hop and bound,
Round the wild witch-hazel tree.

The beetle guards our holy ground,
He flies about the haunted place,
And if mortal there be found,
He hums in his ears and flaps his face;
The leaf-harp sounds our roundelay,
The owlet's eyes our lanterns be;
Thus we sing, and dance and play,
Round the wild witch-hazel tree.

But hark! from tower on tree-top high,
The sentry elf his call has made,
A streak is in the eastern sky,
Shapes of moonlight! flit and fade!
The hill-tops gleam in morning's spring,
The sky-lark shakes his dappled wing,
The day-glimpse glimmers on the lawn,
The cock has crowed, the Fays are gone.

To a Friend.

"You damn me with faint praise."

I.

Yes, faint was my applause and cold my praise,
Though soul was glowing in each polished line;
But nobler subjects claim the poet's lays,
A brighter glory waits a muse like thine.
Let amorous fools in love-sick measure pine;
Let Strangford whimper on, in fancied pain,
And leave to Moore his rose leaves and his vine;
Be thine the task a higher crown to gain,
The envied wreath that decks the patriot's holy strain.

II.

Yet not in proud triumphal song alone,
Or martial ode, or sad sepulchral dirge,
There needs no voice to make our glories known;
There needs no voice the warrior's soul to urge
To tread the bounds of nature's stormy verge;
Columbia still shall win the battle's prize;
But be it thine to bid her mind emerge
To strike her harp, until its soul arise
From the neglected shade, where low in dust it lies.

III.

Are there no scenes to touch the poet's soul?
No deeds of arms to wake the lordly strain?
Shall Hudson's billows unregarded roll?
Has Warren fought, Montgomery died in vain?
Shame! that while every mountain stream and plain
Hath theme for truth's proud voice or fancy's wand,
No native bard the patriot harp hath ta'en,
But left to minstrels of a foreign strand
To sing the beauteous scenes of nature's loveliest land.

IV.

Oh! for a seat on Appalachia's brow,
That I might scan the glorious prospect round,
Wild waving woods, and rolling floods below,
Smooth level glades and fields with grain embrown'd,
High heaving hills, with tufted forests crown'd,
Rearing their tall tops to the heaven's blue dome,
And emerald isles, like banners green unwound,
Floating along the lake, while round them roam
Bright helms of billowy blue and plumes of dancing foam.

V.

'Tis true no fairies haunt our verdant meads,
No grinning imps deform our blazing hearth;
Beneath the kelpie's fang no traveller bleeds,
Nor gory vampyre taints our holy earth,

Nor spectres stalk to frighten harmless mirth,

Nor tortured demon howls adown the gale;

Fair reason checks these monsters in their birth.

Yet have we lay of love and horrid tale

Would dim the manliest eye and make the bravest pale.

VI.

Where is the stony eye that hath not shed

Compassion's heart-drops o'er the sweet Mc Rea?

Through midnight's wilds by savage bandits led,

"Her heart is sad—her love is far away!"

Elate that lover waits the promised day

When he shall clasp his blooming bride again—

Shine on, sweet visions! dreams of rapture, play!

Soon the cold corse of her he loved in vain

Shall blight his withered heart and fire his frenzied brain.

VII.

Romantic Wyoming! could none be found

Of all that rove thy Eden groves among,

To wake a native harp's untutored sound,

And give thy tale of wo the voice of song?

Oh! if description's cold and nerveless tongue

From stranger harps such hallowed strains could call,

How doubly sweet the descant wild had rung,

From one who, lingering round thy ruined wall,

Had plucked thy mourning flowers and wept thy timeless fall.

VIII.

The Huron chief escaped from foemen nigh,
His frail bark launches on Niagara's tides,
"Pride in his port, defiance in his eye,"
Singing his song of death the warrior glides;
In vain they yell along the river sides,
In vain the arrow from its sheaf is torn,
Calm to his doom the willing victim rides,
And, till adown the roaring torrent borne,
Mocks them with gesture proud, and laughs their rage to scorn.

IX.

But if the charms of daisied hill and vale,
And rolling flood, and towering rock sublime,
If warrior deed or peasant's lowly tale
Of love or wo should fail to wake the rhyme,
If to the wildest heights of song you climb,
(Tho' some who know you less, might cry, beware!)
Onward! I say—your strains shall conquer time;
Give your bright genius wing, and hope to share
Imagination's worlds—the ocean, earth, and air.

X.

Arouse, my friend—let vivid fancy soar,
Look with creative eye on nature's face,
Bid airy sprites in wild Niagara roar,
And view in every field a fairy race.

Spur thy good Pacolet to speed apace,

And spread a train of nymphs on every shore;

Or if thy muse would woo a ruder grace,

The Indian's evil Manitou's explore,

And rear the wondrous tale of legendary lore.

XI.

Away! to Susquehannah's utmost springs,

Where, throned in mountain mist, Areouski reigns,

Shrouding in lurid clouds his plumeless wings,

And sternly sorrowing o'er his tribes remains;

His was the arm, like comet ere it wanes

That tore the streamy lightnings from the skies,

And smote the mammoth of the southern plains;

Wild with dismay the Creek affrighted flies,

While in triumphant pride Kanawa's eagles rise.

XII.

Or westward far, where dark Miami wends,

Seek that fair spot as yet to fame unknown;

Where, when the vesper dew of heaven descends,

Soft music breathes in many a melting tone,

At times so sadly sweet it seems the moan

Of some poor Ariel penanced in the rock;

Anon a louder burst—a scream! a groan!

And now amid the tempest's reeling shock,

Gibber, and shriek, and wail—and fiend-like laugh and mock.

XIII.

Or climb the Pallisado's lofty brows,
Were dark Omana waged the war of hell,
Till, waked to wrath, the mighty spirit rose
And pent the demons in their prison cell;
Full on their head the uprooted mountain fell,
Enclosing all within its horrid womb
Straight from the teeming earth the waters swell,
And pillared rocks arise in cheerless gloom
Around the drear abode—their last eternal tomb!

XIV.

Be these your future themes—no more resign
The soul of song to laud your lady's eyes;
Go! kneel a worshipper at nature's shrine!
For you her fields are green, and fair her skies!
For you her rivers flow, her hills arise!
And will you scorn them all, to pour forth tame
And heartless lays of feigned or fancied sighs?
Still will you cloud the muse? nor blush for shame
To cast away renown, and hide your head from fame?

Washington Irving, photographed
by Mathew Brady, c. 1861.

The majestic Hudson is on my left,
The Catskills rise in my dream;
The cataracts leap from the mountain cleft
And the brooks in the sunlight gleam.

—*Minot J. Savage*

CHAPTER 12

Washington Irving

Washington Irving (April 3, 1783—November 28, 1859) was an American author of the early 19th century. In 1802, the nineteen-year-old Irving began writing letters to *The Morning Chronicle*. In 1809 Irving's *A History of New York* became an immediate bestseller. After the War of 1812, he left for Europe, where he remained for the next seventeen years. In 1819–1820 he published *The Sketch Book of Geoffrey Crayon*, which includes his best-known stories, "The Legend of Sleepy Hollow" and "Rip Van Winkle." It was a tremendous success, which he followed in 1824 with *Tales of a Traveller.*

Irving went to Madrid in early 1826 and published *The Life and Voyages of Christopher Columbus* in 1828, the *Conquest of Granada* in 1829, and the *Voyages of the Companions of Columbus* in 1831.

Irving returned to the United States in 1832 and traveled extensively in the West, which inspired *A Tour on the Prairies* (1835), *Astoria* (1836), and *The Adventures of Captain Bonneville* (1837).

In 1842, President John Tyler appointed Irving as Minister to Spain. Returning from Spain in 1845, Irving took up residence at Sunnyside. Between 1855 and 1859, Irving wrote additional works, including *Wolfert's Roost*, and a five-volume biography of George Washington.

On the evening of November 28, 1859, Washington Irving died of a heart attack in his bedroom at Sunnyside at the age of 76. He was buried at Sleepy Hollow cemetery on December 1, 1859.

⚭

Sunnyside—Irving aptly describes it in one of his stories as "made up of gable-ends, and full of angles and corners as an old cocked hat. It is said, in fact, to have been modeled after the hat of Peter the Headstrong, as the Escurial of Spain was fashioned after the gridiron of the blessed St. Lawrence." Wolfert's Roost, as it was once styled (Roost signifying Rest), took its name from Wolfert Acker, a former owner. It consisted originally of ten acres when purchased by Irving in 1835, but eight acres were afterwards added. With great humor Irving put above the porch entrance

"George Harvey, Boum'r," Boumeister being an old Dutch word for architect. A storm-worn weather-cock, "which once battled with the wind on the top of the Stadt House of New Amsterdam in the time of Peter Stuyvesant, erects his crest on the gable, and a gilded horse in full gallop, once the weather-cock of the great Van der Heyden palace of Albany, glitters in the sunshine, veering with every breeze, on the peaked turret over the portal."

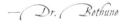

Irving chose his residence in the valley, not amid the mountains; by the fields and meadows of the broad Tappan Zee, rather than the Highlands; in a congenial region suited to his temperament.

—Dr. Bethune

About 100 years ago, a cutting of Walter Scott's favorite ivy at Melrose Abbey was transported across the Atlantic, and trained over the porch of "Sunnyside," by the hand of Mrs. Renwick, daughter of Rev. Andrew Jeffrey of Lochmaben, known in girlhood as the "Bonnie Jessie" of Annandale, or the "Blue-eyed Lassie" of Robert Burns:—a graceful tribute, from the shrine of Waverley to the nest of Knickerbocker:

A token of friendship immortal
With Washington Irving returns:—

Scott's ivy entwined o'er his portal
By the Blue-eyed Lassie of Burns.

Scott's cordial greeting at Abbotsford, and his persistence in getting Murray to reconsider the publication of the "Sketch Book," which he had previously declined, were never forgotten by Irving. It was during a critical period of his literary career, and the kindness of the Great Magician, in directing early attention to his genius, is still cherished by every reader of the "Sketch Book" from Manhattan to San Francisco. The hearty grasp of the Minstrel at the gateway of Abbotsford was in reality a warm handshake to a wider brotherhood beyond the sea.

჻

In purple tints woven together
The Hudson shakes hands with the Tweed,
Commingling with Abbotsford's heather
The clover of Sunnyside's mead.

—Wallace Bruce

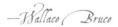

჻

While he was building "Sunnyside," a letter came from Daniel Webster, then Secretary of State, appointing him minister to Spain. It was unexpected and unsolicited, and Webster

Sunnyside, home of Washington Irving, Tarrytown, N.Y., c. 1945.

remarked that day to a friend: "Washington Irving to-day will be the most surprised man in America." Irving had already shown diplomatic ability in London in promoting the settlement of the "North Western Boundary," and his appointment was received with universal favor. Then as now Sunnyside was already a Mecca for travelers, and, among many well-known to fame, was a young man, afterwards Napoleon the Third. Referring to his visit, Irving wrote in 1853: "Napoleon and Eugenie, Emperor and Empress! The one I have had as a guest at my cottage, the other I have held as a pet child upon my knee in Granada. The last I saw of Eugenie Montijo, she was one of the reigning belles of Madrid; now, she is upon the throne, launched from a return-less shore, upon a dangerous sea, infamous for its tremendous shipwrecks. Am I to live to see the catastrophe of her career, and the end of this suddenly conjured up empire, which seems to be of such stuff as dreams are made of? I confess my personal acquaintance with the individuals in this historical romance gives me uncommon interest in it; but I consider it stamped with danger and instability, and as liable to extravagant vicissitudes as one of Dumas' novels." A wonderful prophecy completely fulfilled in the short space of seventeen years.

How many such men as Washington Irving are there in America.
God don't send many such spirits into this world.

—Lord Byron

The aggregate sale of Irving's works when he received his portfolio to Spain was already more than half a million copies, with an equal popularity achieved in Britain. No writer was ever more truly loved on both sides of the Atlantic, and his name is cherished to-day in England as fondly as it is in our own country. It has been the good fortune of the writer to spend many a delightful day in the very center of Merrie England, in the quiet town of Stratford-on-Avon, and feel the gentle companionship of Irving. Of all writers who have brought to Stratford their heart homage Irving stands the acknowledged chief. The sitting-room in the "Red Horse Hotel," where he was disturbed in his midnight reverie, is still called Irving's room, and the walls are hung with portraits taken at different periods of his life. Mine host said that visitors from every land were as much interested in this room as in Shakespeare's birth-place. The remark may have been intensified to flatter an American visitor, but there are few names dearer to the Anglo-Saxon race than that on the plain headstone in the burial-yard of Sleepy Hollow.

Sunnyside is scarcely visible. A little gleam of color here and there amid the trees, close to the river bank, near a small boat-house, merely indicates its location; and the traveler by train has only a hurried glimpse, as it is within one hundred feet of the New York Central Railroad. Tappan Zee, at this point, is a little more than two miles wide and over the beautiful expanse Irving has thrown a wondrous charm. There is, in fact, "magic in the web" of all his works. A few modern critics, lacking appreciation alike for humor and genius, may regard his essays as a thing of the past, but as long as the Mahicanituk, the ever-flowing Hudson, pours its waters to the sea, as long as Rip Van Winkle sleeps in the blue Catskills, or the "Headless Horseman" rides at midnight along the Old Post Road en route for Teller's Point, so long will the writings of Washington Irving be remembered and cherished. We somehow feel the reality of every legend he has given us. The spring bubbling up near his cottage was brought over, as he gravely tells us, in a churn from Holland by one of the old time settlers, and we are half inclined to believe it; and no one ever thinks of doubting that the "Flying Dutchman,"

Mynheer Van Dam, has been rowing for two hundred years and never made a port. It is in fact still said by the old inhabitants, that often in the soft twilight of summer evenings, when the sea is like glass and the opposite hills throw their shadows across it, that the low vigorous pull of oars is heard but no boat is seen.

◎

Here was no castle in the air, but a realized day-dream. Irving was there, as genial, humorous and imaginative as if he had never wandered from the primal haunts of his childhood and his fame.

—*Henry T. Tuckerman*

◎

According to Irving "Sunnyside" was once the property of old Baltus Van Tassel, and here lived the fair Katrina, beloved by all the youths of the neighborhood, but more especially by Ichabod Crane, the country school-master, and a reckless youth by the name of Van Brunt. Irving tells us that he thought out the story one morning on London Bridge, and went home and completed it in thirty-six hours. The character of Ichabod Crane was a sketch of a young man whom he met at Kinderhook when writing his Knickerbocker history. It will be remembered that Ichabod Crane went to a quilting-bee at the home of Mynheer Van Tassel, and, after the repast, was regaled with various ghost stories peculiar to the locality. When the "party" was over he lingered for a time with the fair Katrina, but sallied out soon after with an air quite desolate and chop-fallen. The night grew darker and darker. He had never before felt so lonesome and miserable. As he passed the fatal tree where Arnold was captured, there started up before him the identical "Headless Horseman" to whom he had been introduced by the story of Brom Bones. Nay, not entirely headless; for the head which "should have rested upon his shoulders was carried before him on the pommel of the saddle. His terror rose to desperation. He rode for death and life. The strange horseman sped beside him at an equal pace. He fell into a walk. The strange horseman did the same. He endeavored to sing a psalm-tune, but his tongue clove to the roof of his mouth. If he could but reach the bridge Ichabod thought he would be safe. Away then he flew in rapid flight. He reached the bridge, he thundered over the resounding planks. Then he saw the goblin rising in his stirrups, and in the very act of launching his head at him. It encountered his cranium with a tremendous crash. He was tumbled headlong into the dirt, and the black steed and the spectral rider passed by like a whirlwind. The next day tracks of horses deeply dented in the road were traced to the bridge, beyond which, on the bank of a broad part of the brook, where the water ran deep and black, was found the hat of the unfortunate Ichabod, and close beside it a shattered pumpkin." All honor to him who fills this working-day world with humor, romance and beauty!

I beg you will have the kindness to let me know when Mr. Irving

takes pen in hand again; for assuredly I shall expect a very great

treat which I may chance never to hear of but through

your kindness.

—Sir Walter Scott

The Legend of Sleepy Hollow: Found Among the Papers of the Late Diedrich Knickerbocker. 1819.

A pleasing land of drowsy head it was,
Of dreams that wave before the half-shut eye;
And of gay castles in the clouds that pass,
Forever flushing round a summer sky.
—Castle of Indolence.

In the bosom of one of those spacious coves which indent the eastern shore of the Hudson, at that broad expansion of the river denominated by the ancient Dutch navigators the Tappan Zee, and where they always prudently shortened sail and implored the protection of St. Nicholas when they crossed, there lies a small market town or rural port, which by some is called Greensburgh, but which is more generally and properly known by the name of Tarry Town. This name was given, we are told, in former days, by the good housewives of the adjacent country, from the invet-

View at Katz-Kill Landing

erate propensity of their husbands to linger about the village tavern on market days. Be that as it may, I do not vouch for the fact,
but merely advert to it, for the sake of being precise and authentic. Not far from this village, perhaps about two miles, there is a
little valley or rather lap of land among high hills, which is one
of the quietest places in the whole world. A small brook glides
through it, with just murmur enough to lull one to repose; and
the occasional whistle of a quail or tapping of a woodpecker is
almost the only sound that ever breaks in upon the uniform
tranquillity.

I recollect that, when a stripling, my first exploit in squirrel-
shooting was in a grove of tall walnut-trees that shades one side

of the valley. I had wandered into it at noontime, when all nature is peculiarly quiet, and was startled by the roar of my own gun, as it broke the Sabbath stillness around and was prolonged and reverberated by the angry echoes. If ever I should wish for a retreat whither I might steal from the world and its distractions, and dream quietly away the remnant of a troubled life, I know of none more promising than this little valley.

From the listless repose of the place, and the peculiar character of its inhabitants, who are descendants from the original Dutch settlers, this sequestered glen has long been known by the name of SLEEPY HOLLOW, and its rustic lads are called the Sleepy Hollow Boys throughout all the neighboring country. A drowsy, dreamy influence seems to hang over the land, and to pervade the very atmosphere. Some say that the place was bewitched by a High German doctor, during the early days of the settlement; others, that an old Indian chief, the prophet or wizard of his tribe, held his powwows there before the country was discovered by Master Hendrick Hudson. Certain it is, the place still continues under the sway of some witching power, that holds a spell over the minds of the good people, causing them to walk in a continual reverie. They are given to all kinds of marvellous beliefs, are subject to trances and visions, and frequently see strange sights, and hear music and voices in the air. The whole neighborhood abounds with local tales, haunted spots, and twilight superstitions; stars shoot and meteors glare oftener across the valley than in any other part of the country, and the nightmare, with her whole ninefold, seems to make it the favorite scene of her gambols.

The dominant spirit, however, that haunts this enchanted region, and seems to be commander-in-chief of all the powers of the air, is the apparition of a figure on horseback, without a head. It is said by some to be the ghost of a Hessian trooper, whose head had been carried away by a cannon-ball, in some nameless battle during the Revolutionary War, and who is ever and anon seen by the country folk hurrying along in the gloom of night, as if on the wings of the wind. His haunts are not confined to the valley, but extend at times to the adjacent roads, and especially to the vicinity of a church at no great distance. Indeed, certain of the most authentic historians of those parts, who have been careful in collecting and collating the floating facts concerning this spectre, allege that the body of the trooper having been buried in the churchyard, the ghost rides forth to the scene of battle in nightly quest of his head, and that the rushing speed with which he sometimes passes along the Hollow, like a midnight blast, is owing to his being belated, and in a hurry to get back to the churchyard before daybreak.

Such is the general purport of this legendary superstition, which has furnished materials for many a wild story in that region of shadows; and the specter is known at all the country firesides, by the name of the Headless Horseman of Sleepy Hollow.

It is remarkable that the visionary propensity I have mentioned is not confined to the native inhabitants of the valley, but is unconsciously imbibed by every one who resides there for a time. However wide awake they may have been before they entered that sleepy region, they are sure, in a little time, to inhale the witching influence of the air, and begin to grow imaginative, to dream dreams, and see apparitions.

I mention this peaceful spot with all possible laud, for it is in such little retired Dutch valleys, found here and there embosomed in the great State of New York, that population, manners, and customs remain fixed, while the great torrent of migration and improvement, which is making such incessant changes in other parts of this restless country, sweeps by them unobserved. They are like those little nooks of still water, which border a rapid stream, where we may see the straw and bubble riding quietly at anchor, or slowly revolving in their mimic harbor, undisturbed by the rush of the passing current. Though many years have elapsed since I trod the drowsy shades of Sleepy Hollow, yet I question whether I should not still find the same trees and the same families vegetating in its sheltered bosom.

In this by-place of nature there abode, in a remote period of American history, that is to say, some thirty years since, a worthy wight of the name of Ichabod Crane, who sojourned, or, as he expressed it, "tarried," in Sleepy Hollow, for the purpose of instructing the children of the vicinity. He was a native of Connecticut, a State which supplies the Union with pioneers for the mind as well as for the forest, and sends forth yearly its legions of frontier woodmen and country schoolmasters. The cognomen of Crane was not inapplicable to his person. He was tall, but exceedingly lank, with narrow shoulders, long arms and legs, hands that dangled a mile out of his sleeves, feet that might have served for shovels, and his whole frame most loosely hung together. His head was small, and flat at top, with huge ears, large green glassy eyes, and a long snipe nose, so that it looked like a weather-cock perched upon his spindle neck to tell which way the wind blew. To see him striding along the profile of a hill on a windy day, with his clothes bagging and fluttering about him, one might have mistaken him for the genius of famine descending upon the earth, or some scarecrow eloped from a cornfield.

His schoolhouse was a low building of one large room, rudely constructed of logs; the windows partly glazed, and partly patched with leaves of old copybooks. It was most ingeniously secured at vacant hours, by a withe twisted in the handle of the door, and stakes set against the window shutters; so that though a thief might get in with perfect ease, he would find some embarrassment in getting out,—an idea most probably borrowed by the architect, Yost Van Houten, from the mystery of an eelpot. The schoolhouse stood in a rather lonely but pleasant situation, just at the foot of a woody hill, with a brook running close by, and a formidable birch-tree growing at one end of it. From hence the low murmur of his pupils' voices, conning over their lessons, might be heard in a drowsy summer's day, like the hum of a bee-hive; interrupted now and then by the authoritative voice of the master, in the tone of menace or command, or, peradventure, by the appalling sound of the birch, as he urged some tardy loiterer along the flowery path of knowledge. Truth to say, he was a conscientious man, and ever bore in mind the golden maxim, "Spare the rod and spoil the child." Ichabod Crane's scholars certainly were not spoiled.

I would not have it imagined, however, that he was one of those cruel potentates of the school who joy in the smart of their subjects; on the contrary, he administered justice with discrimination rather than severity; taking the burden off the backs of the weak, and laying it on those of the strong. Your mere puny stripling, that winced at the least flourish of the rod, was passed by with indulgence; but the claims of justice were satisfied by inflicting a double portion on some little tough wrong-headed, broad-skirted Dutch urchin, who sulked and swelled and grew dogged and sullen beneath the birch. All this he called "doing his duty by their parents;" and he never inflicted a chastisement without following it by the assurance, so consolatory to the smarting urchin, that "he would remember it and thank him for it the longest day he had to live."

When school hours were over, he was even the companion and playmate of the larger boys; and on holiday afternoons would convoy some of the smaller ones home, who happened to have pretty sisters, or good housewives for mothers, noted for the comforts of the cupboard. Indeed, it behooved him to keep on good terms with his pupils. The revenue arising from his school was small, and would have been scarcely sufficient to furnish him with daily bread, for he was a huge feeder, and, though lank, had the dilating powers of an anaconda; but to help out his maintenance, he was, according to country custom in those parts, boarded and lodged at the houses of the farmers whose children he instructed. With these he lived successively a week at a time, thus going the rounds of the neighborhood, with all his worldly effects tied up in a cotton handkerchief.

That all this might not be too onerous on the purses of his rustic patrons, who are apt to consider the costs of schooling a grievous burden, and schoolmasters as mere drones, he had various ways of rendering himself both useful and agreeable. He assisted the farmers occasionally in the lighter labors of their farms, helped to make hay, mended the fences, took the horses to water, drove the cows from pasture, and cut wood for the winter fire. He laid aside, too, all the dominant dignity and absolute sway with which he lorded it in his little empire, the school, and became wonderfully gentle and ingratiating. He found favor in the eyes of the mothers by petting the children, particularly the youngest; and like the lion bold, which whilom so magnanimously the lamb did hold, he would sit with a child on one knee, and rock a cradle with his foot for whole hours together.

In addition to his other vocations, he was the singing-master of the neighborhood, and picked up many bright shillings by instructing the young folks in psalmody. It was a matter of no little vanity to him on Sundays, to take his station in front of the church gallery, with a band of chosen singers; where, in his own mind, he completely carried away the palm from the parson. Certain it is, his voice resounded far above all the rest of the congregation; and there are peculiar quavers still to be heard in that church, and which may even be heard half a mile off, quite to the opposite side of the millpond, on a still Sunday morning, which are said to be legitimately descended from the nose of Ichabod Crane. Thus, by divers little makeshifts, in that ingenious way which is commonly denominated "by hook and by crook," the worthy pedagogue got on tolerably enough, and was thought, by all who understood nothing of the labor of headwork, to have a wonderfully easy life of it.

The schoolmaster is generally a man of some importance in the female circle of a rural neighborhood; being considered a kind of idle, gentlemanlike personage, of vastly superior taste and accomplishments to the rough country swains, and, indeed, inferior in learning only to the parson. His appearance, therefore, is apt to occasion some little stir at the tea-table of a farmhouse, and the addition of a supernumerary dish of cakes or sweetmeats, or, peradventure, the parade of a silver teapot. Our man of letters, therefore, was peculiarly happy in the smiles of all the country damsels. How he would figure among them in the churchyard, between services on Sundays; gathering grapes for them from the wild vines that overran the surrounding trees; reciting for their amusement all the epitaphs on the tombstones; or sauntering, with a whole bevy of them, along the banks of the adjacent millpond; while the more bashful country bumpkins hung sheepishly back, envying his superior elegance and address.

From his half-itinerant life, also, he was a kind of travelling gazette, carrying the whole budget of local gossip from house to house, so that his appearance was always greeted with satisfaction. He was, moreover, esteemed by the women as a man of great erudition, for he had read several books quite through, and was a perfect master of Cotton Mather's "History of New England Witchcraft," in which, by the way, he most firmly and potently believed.

He was, in fact, an odd mixture of small shrewdness and simple credulity. His appetite for the marvellous, and his powers of digesting it, were equally extraordinary; and both had been increased by his residence in this spell-bound region. No tale was too gross or monstrous for his capacious swallow. It was often his delight, after his school was dismissed in the afternoon, to stretch himself on the rich bed of clover bordering the little brook that whimpered by his schoolhouse, and there con over old Mather's direful tales, until the gathering dusk of evening made the printed page a mere mist before his eyes. Then, as he wended his way by swamp and stream and awful woodland, to the farmhouse where he happened to be quartered, every sound of nature, at that witching hour, fluttered his excited imagination,—the moan of the whip-poor-will from the hillside, the boding cry of the tree toad, that harbinger of storm, the dreary hooting of the screech owl, or the sudden rustling in the thicket of birds frightened from their roost. The fireflies, too, which sparkled most vividly in the darkest places, now and then startled him, as one of uncommon brightness would stream across his path; and if, by chance, a huge blockhead of a beetle came winging his blundering flight against him, the poor varlet was ready to give up the ghost, with the idea that he was struck with a witch's token. His only resource on such occasions, either to drown thought or drive away evil spirits, was to sing psalm tunes and the good people of Sleepy Hollow, as they sat by their doors of an evening, were often filled with awe at hearing his nasal melody, "in linked sweetness long drawn out," floating from the distant hill, or along the dusky road.

Another of his sources of fearful pleasure was to pass long winter evenings with the old Dutch wives, as they sat spinning by the fire, with a row of apples roasting and spluttering along the hearth, and listen to their marvellous tales of ghosts and goblins, and haunted fields, and haunted brooks, and haunted bridges, and haunted houses, and particularly of the headless horseman, or Galloping Hessian of the Hollow, as they some-times called him. He would delight them equally by his anec-dotes of witchcraft, and of the direful omens and portentous sights and sounds in the air, which prevailed in the earlier times of Connecticut; and would frighten them woefully with specu-lations upon comets and shooting stars; and with the alarming fact that the world did absolutely turn round, and that they were half the time topsy-turvy!

But if there was a pleasure in all this, while snugly cuddling in the chimney corner of a chamber that was all of a ruddy glow from the crackling wood fire, and where, of course, no specter dared to show its face, it was dearly purchased by the terrors of his subsequent walk homewards. What fearful shapes and shad-ows beset his path, amidst the dim and ghastly glare of a snowy night! With what wistful look did he eye every trembling ray of light streaming across the waste fields from some distant window! How often was he appalled by some shrub covered with snow, which, like a sheeted specter, beset his very path! How often did he shrink with curdling awe at the sound of his own steps on the frosty crust beneath his feet; and dread to look over his shoulder, lest he should behold some uncouth being tramping close behind him! And how often was he thrown into complete dismay by some rushing blast, howling among the trees, in the idea that it was the Galloping Hessian on one of his nightly scourings!

All these, however, were mere terrors of the night, phantoms of the mind that walk in darkness; and though he had seen many specters in his time, and been more than once beset by Satan in divers shapes, in his lonely perambulations, yet daylight put an end to all these evils; and he would have passed a pleasant life of it, in despite of the Devil and all his works, if his path had not been crossed by a being that causes more perplexity to mortal man than ghosts, goblins, and the whole race of witches put together, and that was—a woman.

Among the musical disciples who assembled, one evening in each week, to receive his instructions in psalmody, was Katrina Van Tassel, the daughter and only child of a substantial Dutch farmer. She was a blooming lass of fresh eighteen; plump as a partridge; ripe and melting and rosy-cheeked as one of her father's peaches, and universally famed, not merely for her beauty, but her vast expectations. She was withal a little of a coquette, as might be perceived even in her dress, which was a mixture of ancient and modern fashions, as most suited to set off her charms. She wore the ornaments of pure yellow gold, which her great-great-grandmother had brought over from Saardam; the tempting stomacher of the olden time, and withal a provokingly short petticoat, to display the prettiest foot and ankle in the country round.

Ichabod Crane had a soft and foolish heart towards the sex; and it is not to be wondered at that so tempting a morsel soon found favor in his eyes, more especially after he had visited her in her paternal mansion. Old Baltus Van Tassel was a perfect picture of a thriving, contented, liberal-hearted farmer. He seldom, it is true, sent either his eyes or his thoughts beyond the boundaries of his own farm; but within those everything was snug, happy and well-conditioned. He was satisfied with his wealth, but not proud of it; and piqued himself upon the hearty abundance, rather than the style in which he lived. His stronghold was situated on the banks of the Hudson, in one of those green, sheltered, fertile nooks in which the Dutch farmers are so fond of nestling. A great elm tree spread its broad branches over it, at the foot of which bubbled up a spring of the softest and sweetest water, in a little well formed of a barrel; and then stole sparkling away through the grass, to a neighboring brook, that babbled along among alders and dwarf willows. Hard by the farmhouse was a vast barn, that might have served for a church; every window and crevice of which seemed bursting forth with the treasures of the farm; the flail was busily resounding within it from morning to night; swallows and martins skimmed twittering about the eaves; and rows of pigeons, some with one eye turned up, as if watching the weather, some with their heads under their wings or buried in their bosoms, and others swelling, and cooing, and bowing about their dames, were enjoying the sunshine on the roof. Sleek unwieldy porkers were grunting in the repose and abundance of their pens, from whence sallied forth, now and then, troops of sucking pigs, as if to snuff the air. A stately squadron of snowy geese were riding in an adjoining pond, convoying whole fleets of ducks; regiments of turkeys were gobbling through the farmyard, and Guinea fowls fretting about it, like ill-tempered housewives, with their peevish, discontented cry. Before the barn door strutted the gallant cock, that pattern of a husband, a warrior and a fine gentleman, clapping his burnished wings and crowing in the pride and gladness of his heart,—sometimes tearing up the earth with his feet, and then generously calling his ever-hungry family of wives and children to enjoy the rich morsel which he had discovered.

The pedagogue's mouth watered as he looked upon this sumptuous promise of luxurious winter fare. In his devouring mind's eye, he pictured to himself every roasting-pig running about with a pudding in his belly, and an apple in his mouth; the pigeons were snugly put to bed in a comfortable pie, and tucked in with a coverlet of crust; the geese were swimming in their own gravy; and the ducks pairing cosily in dishes, like snug married couples, with a decent competency of onion sauce. In the porkers he saw carved out the future sleek side of bacon, and juicy relishing ham; not a turkey but he beheld daintily trussed up, with its gizzard under its wing, and, peradventure, a necklace of savory sausages; and even bright chanticleer himself lay sprawling on his back, in a side dish, with uplifted claws, as if craving that quarter which his chivalrous spirit disdained to ask while living.

As the enraptured Ichabod fancied all this, and as he rolled his great green eyes over the fat meadow lands, the rich fields of wheat, of rye, of buckwheat, and Indian corn, and the orchards burdened with ruddy fruit, which surrounded the warm tenement of Van Tassel, his heart yearned after the damsel who was to inherit these domains, and his imagination expanded with the idea, how they might be readily turned into cash, and the money invested in immense tracts of wild land, and shingle palaces in the wilderness. Nay, his busy fancy already realized his hopes, and presented to him the blooming Katrina, with a whole family of children, mounted on the top of a wagon loaded with household trumpery, with pots and kettles dangling beneath; and he beheld himself bestriding a pacing mare, with a colt at her heels, setting out for Kentucky, Tennessee,—or the Lord knows where!

When he entered the house, the conquest of his heart was complete. It was one of those spacious farmhouses, with high-ridged but lowly sloping roofs, built in the style handed down from the first Dutch settlers; the low projecting eaves forming a piazza along the front, capable of being closed up in bad weather. Under this were hung flails, harness, various utensils of husbandry, and nets for fishing in the neighboring river. Benches were built along the sides for summer use; and a great spinning-wheel at one end, and a churn at the other, showed the various uses to which this important porch might be devoted. From this piazza the wondering Ichabod entered the hall, which formed the center of the mansion, and the place of usual residence. Here rows of resplendent pewter, ranged on a long dresser, dazzled his eyes. In one corner stood a huge bag of wool, ready to be spun; in another, a quantity of linsey-woolsey just from the loom; ears of Indian corn, and strings of dried apples and peaches, hung in gay festoons along the walls, mingled with the gaud of red peppers; and a door left ajar gave him a peep into the best parlor, where the claw-footed chairs and dark mahogany tables shone like mirrors; andirons, with their accompanying shovel and tongs, glistened from their covert of asparagus tops; mock-oranges and conch-shells decorated the mantelpiece; strings of various-colored birds eggs were suspended above it; a great ostrich egg was hung from the center of the room, and a corner cupboard, knowingly left open, displayed immense treasures of old silver and well-mended china.

From the moment Ichabod laid his eyes upon these regions of delight, the peace of his mind was at an end, and his only study was how to gain the affections of the peerless daughter of Van Tassel. In this enterprise, however, he had more real difficulties than generally fell to the lot of a knight-errant of yore, who seldom had anything but giants, enchanters, fiery dragons, and such like easily conquered adversaries, to contend with and had to make his way merely through gates of iron and brass, and walls of adamant to the castle keep, where the lady of his heart was confined; all which he achieved as easily as a man would carve his way to the center of a Christmas pie; and then the lady gave him her hand as a matter of course. Ichabod, on the contrary, had to win his way to the heart of a country coquette, beset with a labyrinth of whims and caprices, which were forever presenting new difficulties and impediments; and he had to encounter a host of fearful adversaries of real flesh and blood, the numerous rustic admirers, who beset every portal to her heart, keeping a watchful and angry eye upon each other, but ready to fly out in the common cause against any new competitor.

Among these, the most formidable was a burly, roaring, roystering blade, of the name of Abraham, or, according to the Dutch abbreviation, Brom Van Brunt, the hero of the country round, which rang with his feats of strength and hardihood. He was broad-shouldered and double-jointed, with short curly black hair, and a bluff but not unpleasant countenance, having a mingled air of fun and arrogance. From his Herculean frame and great powers of limb he had received the nickname of BROM BONES, by which he was universally known. He was famed for great knowledge and skill in horsemanship, being as dexterous on horseback as a Tartar. He was foremost at all races and cock fights; and, with the ascendancy which bodily strength always acquires in rustic life, was the umpire in all disputes, setting his hat on one side, and giving his decisions with an air and tone that admitted of no gainsay or appeal. He was always ready for either a fight or a frolic; but had more mischief than ill-will in his composition; and with all his overbearing roughness, there was a strong dash of waggish good humor at bottom. He had three or four boon companions, who regarded him as their model, and at the head of whom he scoured the country, attending every scene of feud or merriment for miles round. In cold weather he was distinguished by a fur cap, surmounted with a flaunting fox's tail; and when the folks at a country gathering descried this well-known crest at a distance, whisking about among a squad of hard riders, they always stood by for a squall. Sometimes his crew would be heard dashing along past the farmhouses at midnight, with whoop and halloo, like a troop of Don Cossacks; and the old dames, startled out of their sleep, would listen for a moment till the hurry-scurry had clattered by, and then exclaim, "Ay, there goes Brom Bones and his gang!" The neighbors looked upon him with a mixture of awe, admiration, and good-will; and, when any madcap prank or rustic brawl occurred in the vicinity, always shook their heads, and warranted Brom Bones was at the bottom of it.

This rantipole hero had for some time singled out the blooming Katrina for the object of his uncouth gallantries, and though his amorous toyings were something like the gentle caresses and endearments of a bear, yet it was whispered that she did not altogether discourage his hopes. Certain it is, his advances were signals for rival candidates to retire, who felt no inclination to cross a lion in his amours; insomuch, that when his horse was seen tied to Van Tassel's paling, on a Sunday night, a sure sign that his master was courting, or, as it is termed, "sparking," within, all other suitors passed by in despair, and carried the war into other quarters.

Such was the formidable rival with whom Ichabod Crane had to contend, and, considering all things, a stouter man than he would have shrunk from the competition, and a wiser man would have despaired. He had, however, a happy mixture of pliability and perseverance in his nature; he was in form and spirit like a supple-jack—yielding, but tough; though he bent, he never broke; and though he bowed beneath the slightest pressure, yet, the moment it was away—jerk!—he was as erect, and carried his head as high as ever.

To have taken the field openly against his rival would have been madness; for he was not a man to be thwarted in his amours, any more than that stormy lover, Achilles. Ichabod, therefore, made his advances in a quiet and gently insinuating manner. Under cover of his character of singing-master, he made frequent visits at the farmhouse; not that he had anything to apprehend from the meddlesome interference of parents, which is so often a stumbling-block in the path of lovers. Balt Van Tassel was an easy indulgent soul; he loved his daughter better even than his pipe, and, like a reasonable man and an excellent father, let her have her way in everything. His notable little wife, too, had enough to do to attend to her housekeeping and manage her poultry; for, as she sagely observed, ducks and geese are foolish things, and must be looked after, but girls can take care of themselves. Thus, while the busy dame bustled about the house, or plied her spinning-wheel at one end of the piazza, honest Balt would sit smoking his evening pipe at the other, watching the achievements of a little wooden warrior, who, armed with a sword in each hand, was most valiantly fighting the wind on the pinnacle of the barn. In the mean time, Ichabod would carry on his suit with the daughter by the side of the spring under the great elm, or sauntering along in the twilight, that hour so favorable to the lover's eloquence.

I profess not to know how women's hearts are wooed and won. To me they have always been matters of riddle and admiration. Some seem to have but one vulnerable point, or door of access; while others have a thousand avenues, and may be captured in a thousand different ways. It is a great triumph of skill to gain the former, but a still greater proof of generalship to maintain possession of the latter, for man must battle for his fortress at every door and window. He who wins a thousand common hearts is therefore entitled to some renown; but he who keeps undisputed sway over the heart of a coquette is indeed a hero. Certain it is, this was not the case with the redoubtable Brom Bones; and from the moment Ichabod Crane made his advances, the interests of the former evidently declined: his horse was no longer seen tied to the palings on Sunday nights, and a deadly feud gradually arose between him and the preceptor of Sleepy Hollow.

Brom, who had a degree of rough chivalry in his nature, would fain have carried matters to open warfare and have settled their pretensions to the lady, according to the mode of those most concise and simple reasoners, the knights-errant of yore,— by single combat; but Ichabod was too conscious of the superior might of his adversary to enter the lists against him; he had overheard a boast of Bones, that he would "double the schoolmaster up, and lay him on a shelf of his own schoolhouse;" and he was too wary to give him an opportunity. There was something extremely provoking in this obstinately pacific system; it left Brom no alternative but to draw upon the funds of rustic waggery in his disposition, and to play off boorish practical jokes upon his rival. Ichabod became the object of whimsical persecution to Bones and his gang of rough riders. They harried his hitherto peaceful domains; smoked out his singing school by stopping up the chimney; broke into the schoolhouse at night, in spite of its formidable fastenings of withe and window stakes, and turned everything topsy-turvy, so that the poor schoolmaster began to think all the witches in the country held their meetings there. But what was still more annoying, Brom took all opportunities of turning him into ridicule in presence of his mistress, and had a scoundrel dog whom he taught to whine in the most ludicrous manner, and introduced as a rival of Ichabod's, to instruct her in psalmody.

In this way matters went on for some time, without producing any material effect on the relative situations of the contending powers. On a fine autumnal afternoon, Ichabod, in pensive mood, sat enthroned on the lofty stool from whence he usually watched all the concerns of his little literary realm. In his hand he swayed a ferule, that scepter of despotic power; the birch of justice reposed on three nails behind the throne, a constant terror to evil doers, while on the desk before him might be seen sundry contraband articles and prohibited weapons, detected upon the persons of idle urchins, such as half-munched apples, popguns, whirligigs, fly-cages, and whole legions of rampant little paper gamecocks. Apparently there had been some appalling act of justice recently inflicted, for his scholars were all busily intent upon their books, or slyly whispering behind them with one eye kept upon the master; and a kind of buzzing stillness reigned throughout the schoolroom. It was suddenly interrupted by the appearance of a negro in tow-cloth jacket and trowsers, a round-crowned fragment of a hat, like the cap of Mercury, and mounted on the back of a ragged, wild, half-broken colt, which he managed with a rope by way of halter. He came clattering up to the school door with an invitation to Ichabod to attend a merry-making or "quilting frolic," to be held that evening at Mynheer Van Tassel's; and having delivered his message with that air of importance, and effort at fine language, which a negro is apt to display on petty embassies of the kind, he dashed over the brook, and was seen scampering away up the hollow, full of the importance and hurry of his mission.

All was now bustle and hubbub in the late quiet schoolroom. The scholars were hurried through their lessons without stopping at trifles; those who were nimble skipped over half with impunity, and those who were tardy had a smart application now and then in the rear, to quicken their speed or help them over a tall word. Books were flung aside without being put away on the shelves, inkstands were overturned, benches thrown down, and the whole school was turned loose an hour before the usual time, bursting forth like a legion of young imps, yelping and racketing about the green in joy at their early emancipation.

The gallant Ichabod now spent at least an extra half hour at his toilet, brushing and furbishing up his best, and indeed only suit of rusty black, and arranging his locks by a bit of broken looking-glass that hung up in the schoolhouse. That he might make his appearance before his mistress in the true style of a cavalier, he borrowed a horse from the farmer with whom he was domiciliated, a choleric old Dutchman of the name of Hans Van Ripper, and, thus gallantly mounted, issued forth like a knight-errant in quest of adventures. But it is meet I should, in the true spirit of romantic story, give some account of the looks and equipments of my hero and his steed. The animal he bestrode was a broken-down plow-horse, that had outlived almost every-thing but its viciousness. He was gaunt and shagged, with a ewe neck, and a head like a hammer; his rusty mane and tail were tangled and knotted with burs; one eye had lost its pupil, and was glaring and spectral, but the other had the gleam of a genu-ine devil in it. Still he must have had fire and mettle in his day, if we may judge from the name he bore of Gunpowder. He had, in fact, been a favorite steed of his master's, the choleric Van Ripper, who was a furious rider, and had infused, very probably, some of his own spirit into the animal; for, old and broken-down as he looked, there was more of the lurking devil in him than in any young filly in the country.

Ichabod was a suitable figure for such a steed. He rode with short stirrups, which brought his knees nearly up to the pom-mel of the saddle; his sharp elbows stuck out like grasshoppers'; he carried his whip perpendicularly in his hand, like a scepter, and as his horse jogged on, the motion of his arms was not unlike the flapping of a pair of wings. A small wool hat rested on the top of his nose, for so his scanty strip of forehead might be called, and the skirts of his black coat fluttered out almost to the horses tail. Such was the appearance of Ichabod and his steed as they shambled out of the gate of Hans Van Ripper, and it was altogether such an apparition as is seldom to be met with in broad daylight.

It was, as I have said, a fine autumnal day; the sky was clear and serene, and nature wore that rich and golden livery which we always associate with the idea of abundance. The forests had put on their sober brown and yellow, while some trees of the tenderer kind had been nipped by the frosts into brilliant dyes of orange, purple, and scarlet. Streaming files of wild ducks began to make their appearance high in the air; the bark of the squirrel might be heard from the groves of beech and hickory- nuts, and the pensive whistle of the quail at intervals from the neighboring stubble field.

The small birds were taking their farewell banquets. In the fullness of their revelry, they fluttered, chirping and frolicking from bush to bush, and tree to tree, capricious from the very profusion and variety around them. There was the honest cock robin, the favorite game of stripling sportsmen, with its loud querulous note; and the twittering blackbirds flying in sable clouds; and the golden-winged woodpecker with his crimson crest, his broad black gorget, and splendid plumage; and the cedar bird, with its red-tipt wings and yellow-tipt tail and its little monteiro cap of feathers; and the blue jay, that noisy coxcomb, in his gay light blue coat and white underclothes, screaming and chattering, nodding and bobbing and bowing, and pretending to be on good terms with every songster of the grove.

As Ichabod jogged slowly on his way, his eye, ever open to every symptom of culinary abundance, ranged with delight over the treasures of jolly autumn. On all sides he beheld vast store of apples; some hanging in oppressive opulence on the trees; some gathered into baskets and barrels for the market; others heaped up in rich piles for the cider-press. Farther on he beheld great fields of Indian corn, with its golden ears peeping from their leafy coverts, and holding out the promise of cakes and hasty-pudding; and the yellow pumpkins lying beneath them, turning up their fair round bellies to the sun, and giving ample prospects of the most luxurious of pies; and anon he passed the fragrant buckwheat fields breathing the odor of the beehive, and as he beheld them, soft anticipations stole over his mind of dainty slapjacks, well buttered, and garnished with honey or treacle, by the delicate little dimpled hand of Katrina Van Tassel.

Thus feeding his mind with many sweet thoughts and "sugared suppositions," he journeyed along the sides of a range of hills which look out upon some of the goodliest scenes of the mighty Hudson. The sun gradually wheeled his broad disk down in the west. The wide bosom of the Tappan Zee lay motionless and glassy, excepting that here and there a gentle undulation waved and prolonged the blue shadow of the distant mountain. A few amber clouds floated in the sky, without a breath of air to move them. The horizon was of a fine golden tint, changing gradually into a pure apple green, and from that into the deep blue of the mid-heaven. A slanting ray lingered on the woody crests of the precipices that overhung some parts of the river, giving greater depth to the dark gray and purple of their rocky sides. A sloop was loitering in the distance, dropping slowly down with the tide, her sail hanging uselessly against the mast; and as the reflection of the sky gleamed along the still water, it seemed as if the vessel was suspended in the air.

It was toward evening that Ichabod arrived at the castle of the Heer Van Tassel, which he found thronged with the pride and flower of the adjacent country. Old farmers, a spare leathern-faced race, in homespun coats and breeches, blue stockings, huge shoes, and magnificent pewter buckles. Their brisk, withered little dames, in close-crimped caps, long-waisted short gowns, homespun petticoats, with scissors and pincushions, and gay calico pockets hanging on the outside. Buxom lasses, almost as antiquated as their mothers, excepting where a straw hat, a fine ribbon, or perhaps a white frock, gave symptoms of city innovation. The sons, in short square-skirted coats, with rows of stupendous brass buttons, and their hair generally queued in the fashion of the times, especially if they could procure an eel-skin for the purpose, it being esteemed throughout the country as a potent nourisher and strengthener of the hair.

Brom Bones, however, was the hero of the scene, having come to the gathering on his favorite steed Daredevil, a creature, like himself, full of mettle and mischief, and which no one but himself could manage. He was, in fact, noted for preferring vicious animals, given to all kinds of tricks which kept the rider in constant risk of his neck, for he held a tractable, well-broken horse as unworthy of a lad of spirit.

Fain would I pause to dwell upon the world of charms that burst upon the enraptured gaze of my hero, as he entered the state parlor of Van Tassel's mansion. Not those of the bevy of buxom lasses, with their luxurious display of red and white; but the ample charms of a genuine Dutch country tea-table, in the sumptuous time of autumn. Such heaped up platters of cakes of various and almost indescribable kinds, known only to experienced Dutch housewives! There was the doughty doughnut, the tender oly koek, and the crisp and crumbling cruller; sweet cakes and short cakes, ginger cakes and honey cakes, and the whole family of cakes. And then there were apple pies, and peach pies, and pumpkin pies; besides slices of ham and smoked beef; and moreover delectable dishes of preserved plums, and peaches, and pears, and quinces; not to mention broiled shad and roasted chickens; together with bowls of milk and cream, all mingled higgledy-piggledy, pretty much as I have enumerated them, with the motherly teapot sending up its clouds of vapor from the midst—Heaven bless the mark! I want breath and time to discuss this banquet as it deserves, and am too eager to get on with my story. Happily, Ichabod Crane was not in so great a hurry as his historian, but did ample justice to every dainty.

He was a kind and thankful creature, whose heart dilated in proportion as his skin was filled with good cheer, and whose spirits rose with eating, as some men's do with drink. He could not help, too, rolling his large eyes round him as he ate, and chuckling with the possibility that he might one day be lord of all this scene of almost unimaginable luxury and splendor. Then, he thought, how soon he'd turn his back upon the old school-house; snap his fingers in the face of Hans Van Ripper, and every other niggardly patron, and kick any itinerant pedagogue out of doors that should dare to call him comrade!

Old Baltus Van Tassel moved about among his guests with a face dilated with content and good humor, round and jolly as the harvest moon. His hospitable attentions were brief, but expressive, being confined to a shake of the hand, a slap on the shoulder, a loud laugh, and a pressing invitation to "fall to, and help themselves."

And now the sound of the music from the common room, or hall, summoned to the dance. The musician was an old gray-headed negro, who had been the itinerant orchestra of the neigh-borhood for more than half a century. His instrument was as old and battered as himself. The greater part of the time he scraped on two or three strings, accompanying every movement of the bow with a motion of the head; bowing almost to the ground, and stamping with his foot whenever a fresh couple were to start.

Ichabod prided himself upon his dancing as much as upon his vocal powers. Not a limb, not a fiber about him was idle; and to have seen his loosely hung frame in full motion, and clatter-ing about the room, you would have thought St. Vitus himself, that blessed patron of the dance, was figuring before you in person. He was the admiration of all the negroes; who, having gathered, of all ages and sizes, from the farm and the neighborhood, stood forming a pyramid of shining black faces at every door and window, gazing with delight at the scene, rolling their white eyeballs, and showing grinning rows of ivory from ear to ear. How could the flogger of urchins be otherwise than animated and joyous? The lady of his heart was his partner in the dance, and smiling graciously in reply to all his amorous oglings; while Brom Bones, sorely smitten with love and jealousy, sat brooding by himself in one corner.

When the dance was at an end, Ichabod was attracted to a knot of the sager folks, who, with Old Van Tassel, sat smoking at one end of the piazza, gossiping over former times, and drawing out long stories about the war.

This neighborhood, at the time of which I am speaking, was one of those highly favored places which abound with chronicle and great men. The British and American line had run near it during the war; it had, therefore, been the scene of marauding and infested with refugees, cowboys, and all kinds of border chivalry. Just sufficient time had elapsed to enable each storyteller to dress up his tale with a little becoming fiction, and, in the indistinctness of his recollection, to make himself the hero of every exploit.

There was the story of Doffue Martling, a large blue-bearded Dutchman, who had nearly taken a British frigate with an old iron nine-pounder from a mud breastwork, only that his gun burst at the sixth discharge. And there was an old gentleman who shall be nameless, being too rich a mynheer to be lightly mentioned, who, in the battle of White Plains, being an excellent master of defence, parried a musket-ball with a small sword, insomuch that he absolutely felt it whiz round the blade, and glance off at the hilt; in proof of which he was ready at any time to show the sword, with the hilt a little bent. There were several more that had been equally great in the field, not one of whom but was persuaded that he had a considerable hand in bringing the war to a happy termination.

But all these were nothing to the tales of ghosts and apparitions that succeeded. The neighborhood is rich in legendary treasures of the kind. Local tales and superstitions thrive best in these sheltered, long-settled retreats; but are trampled under foot by the shifting throng that forms the population of most of our country places. Besides, there is no encouragement for ghosts in most of our villages, for they have scarcely had time to finish their first nap and turn themselves in their graves, before their surviving friends have travelled away from the neighborhood; so that when they turn out at night to walk their rounds, they have no acquaintance left to call upon. This is perhaps the reason why we so seldom hear of ghosts except in our long-established Dutch communities.

The immediate cause, however, of the prevalence of supernatural stories in these parts, was doubtless owing to the vicinity of Sleepy Hollow. There was a contagion in the very air that blew from that haunted region; it breathed forth an atmosphere of dreams and fancies infecting all the land. Several of the Sleepy

Hollow people were present at Van Tassel's, and, as usual, were doling out their wild and wonderful legends. Many dismal tales were told about funeral trains, and mourning cries and wailings heard and seen about the great tree where the unfortunate Major André was taken, and which stood in the neighborhood. Some mention was made also of the woman in white, that haunted the dark glen at Raven Rock, and was often heard to shriek on winter nights before a storm, having perished there in the snow. The chief part of the stories, however, turned upon the favorite specter of Sleepy Hollow, the Headless Horseman, who had been heard several times of late, patrolling the country; and, it was said, tethered his horse nightly among the graves in the churchyard.

The sequestered situation of this church seems always to have made it a favorite haunt of troubled spirits. It stands on a knoll, surrounded by locust-trees and lofty elms, from among which its decent, whitewashed walls shine modestly forth, like Christian purity beaming through the shades of retirement. A gentle slope descends from it to a silver sheet of water, bordered by high trees, between which, peeps may be caught at the blue hills of the Hudson. To look upon its grass-grown yard, where the sunbeams seem to sleep so quietly, one would think that there at least the dead might rest in peace. On one side of the church extends a wide woody dell, along which raves a large brook among broken rocks and trunks of fallen trees. Over a deep black part of the stream, not far from the church, was formerly thrown a wooden bridge; the road that led to it, and the bridge itself, were thickly shaded by overhanging trees, which cast a gloom about it, even in the daytime; but occasioned a fearful darkness at night. Such was one of the favorite haunts of the Headless Horseman, and the place where he was most frequently encountered. The tale was told of old Brouwer, a most heretical disbeliever in ghosts, how he met the Horseman returning from his foray into Sleepy Hollow, and was obliged to get up behind him; how they galloped over bush and brake, over hill and swamp, until they reached the bridge; when the Horseman suddenly turned into a skeleton, threw old Brouwer into the brook, and sprang away over the tree-tops with a clap of thunder.

This story was immediately matched by a thrice marvellous adventure of Brom Bones, who made light of the Galloping Hessian as an arrant jockey. He affirmed that on returning one night from the neighboring village of Sing Sing, he had been overtaken by this midnight trooper; that he had offered to race with him for a bowl of punch, and should have won it too, for Daredevil beat the goblin horse all hollow, but just as they came to the church bridge, the Hessian bolted, and vanished in a flash of fire.

All these tales, told in that drowsy undertone with which men talk in the dark, the countenances of the listeners only now and then receiving a casual gleam from the glare of a pipe, sank deep in the mind of Ichabod. He repaid them in kind with large extracts from his invaluable author, Cotton Mather, and added many marvellous events that had taken place in his native State of Connecticut, and fearful sights which he had seen in his nightly walks about Sleepy Hollow.

The revel now gradually broke up. The old farmers gathered together their families in their wagons, and were heard for some time rattling along the hollow roads, and over the distant hills. Some of the damsels mounted on pillions behind their favorite swains, and their light-hearted laughter, mingling with the clatter of hoofs, echoed along the silent woodlands, sounding fainter and fainter, until they gradually died away,—and the late scene of noise and frolic was all silent and deserted. Ichabod only lingered behind, according to the custom of country lovers, to have a tête-à-tête with the heiress; fully convinced that he was now on the high road to success. What passed at this interview I will not pretend to say, for in fact I do not know. Something, however, I fear me, must have gone wrong, for he certainly sallied forth, after no very great interval, with an air quite desolate and chapfallen. Oh, these women! these women! Could that girl have been playing off any of her coquettish tricks? Was her encouragement of the poor pedagogue all a mere sham to secure her conquest of his rival? Heaven only knows, not I! Let it suffice to say, Ichabod stole forth with the air of one who had been sacking a henroost, rather than a fair lady's heart. Without looking to the right or left to notice the scene of rural wealth, on which he had so often gloated, he went straight to the stable, and with several hearty cuffs and kicks roused his steed most uncourteously from the comfortable quarters in which he was soundly sleeping, dreaming of mountains of corn and oats, and whole valleys of timothy and clover.

It was the very witching time of night that Ichabod, heavy-hearted and crestfallen, pursued his travels homewards, along the sides of the lofty hills which rise above Tarry Town, and which he had traversed so cheerily in the afternoon. The hour was as dismal as himself. Far below him the Tappan Zee spread its dusky and indistinct waste of waters, with here and there the tall mast of a sloop, riding quietly at anchor under the land. In the dead hush of midnight, he could even hear the barking of the watchdog from the opposite shore of the Hudson; but it was so vague and faint as only to give an idea of his distance from this faithful companion of man. Now and then, too, the long-drawn crowing of a cock, accidentally awakened, would sound far, far off, from some farmhouse away among the hills—but it was like a dreaming sound in his ear. No signs of life occurred near him, but occasionally the melancholy chirp of a cricket, or perhaps the guttural twang of a bullfrog from a neighboring marsh, as if sleeping uncomfortably and turning suddenly in his bed.

All the stories of ghosts and goblins that he had heard in the afternoon now came crowding upon his recollection. The night grew darker and darker; the stars seemed to sink deeper in the sky, and driving clouds occasionally hid them from his sight. He had never felt so lonely and dismal. He was, moreover, approaching the very place where many of the scenes of the ghost stories had been laid. In the center of the road stood an enormous tulip-tree, which towered like a giant above all the other trees of the neighborhood, and formed a kind of landmark. Its limbs were gnarled and fantastic, large enough to form trunks for ordinary trees, twisting down almost to the earth, and rising again into the air. It was connected with the tragical story of the unfortunate André, who had been taken prisoner hard by; and was universally known by the name of Major André's tree. The common people regarded it with a mixture of respect and superstition, partly out of sympathy for the fate of its ill-starred namesake, and partly from the tales of strange sights, and doleful lamentations, told concerning it.

As Ichabod approached this fearful tree, he began to whistle; he thought his whistle was answered; it was but a blast sweeping sharply through the dry branches. As he approached a little nearer, he thought he saw something white, hanging in the midst of the tree: he paused and ceased whistling but, on looking more narrowly, perceived that it was a place where the tree had been scathed by lightning, and the white wood laid bare. Suddenly he heard a groan—his teeth chattered, and his knees smote against the saddle: it was but the rubbing of one huge bough upon another, as they were swayed about by the breeze. He passed the tree in safety, but new perils lay before him.

About two hundred yards from the tree, a small brook crossed the road, and ran into a marshy and thickly-wooded glen, known by the name of Wiley's Swamp. A few rough logs, laid side by side, served for a bridge over this stream. On that side of the road where the brook entered the wood, a group of oaks and chestnuts, matted thick with wild grape-vines, threw a cavernous gloom over it. To pass this bridge was the severest trial. It was at this identical spot that the unfortunate André was captured, and under the covert of those chestnuts and vines were the sturdy yeomen concealed who surprised him. This has ever since been considered a haunted stream, and fearful are the feelings of the schoolboy who has to pass it alone after dark.

As he approached the stream, his heart began to thump; he summoned up, however, all his resolution, gave his horse half a score of kicks in the ribs, and attempted to dash briskly across the bridge; but instead of starting forward, the perverse old animal made a lateral movement, and ran broadside against the fence. Ichabod, whose fears increased with the delay, jerked the reins on the other side, and kicked lustily with the contrary foot: it was all in vain; his steed started, it is true, but it was only to plunge to the opposite side of the road into a thicket of brambles and alder bushes. The schoolmaster now bestowed both whip and heel upon the starveling ribs of old Gunpowder, who dashed forward, snuffling and snorting, but came to a stand just by the bridge, with a suddenness that had nearly sent his rider sprawling over his head. Just at this moment a plashy tramp by the side of the bridge caught the sensitive ear of Ichabod. In the dark shadow of the grove, on the margin of the brook, he beheld something huge, misshapen and towering. It stirred not, but seemed gathered up in the gloom, like some gigantic monster ready to spring upon the traveller.

The hair of the affrighted pedagogue rose upon his head with terror. What was to be done? To turn and fly was now too late; and besides, what chance was there of escaping ghost or goblin, if such it was, which could ride upon the wings of the wind? Summoning up, therefore, a show of courage, he demanded in stammering accents, "Who are you?" He received no reply. He repeated his demand in a still more agitated voice. Still there was no answer. Once more he cudgelled the sides of the inflexible Gunpowder, and, shutting his eyes, broke forth with involuntary fervor into a psalm tune. Just then the shadowy object of alarm put itself in motion, and with a scramble and a bound stood at once in the middle of the road. Though the night was dark and dismal, yet the form of the unknown might now in some degree be ascertained. He appeared to be a horseman of large dimensions, and mounted on a black horse of powerful frame. He made no offer of molestation or sociability, but kept aloof on one side of the road, jogging along on the blind side of old Gunpowder, who had now got over his fright and waywardness.

Ichabod, who had no relish for this strange midnight companion, and bethought himself of the adventure of Brom Bones with the Galloping Hessian, now quickened his steed in hopes of leaving him behind. The stranger, however, quickened his horse to an equal pace. Ichabod pulled up, and fell into a walk, thinking to lag behind,—the other did the same. His heart began to sink within him; he endeavored to resume his psalm tune, but his parched tongue clove to the roof of his mouth, and he could not utter a stave. There was something in the moody and dogged silence of this pertinacious companion that was mysterious and appalling. It was soon fearfully accounted for. On mounting a rising ground, which brought the figure of his fellow-traveller in relief against the sky, gigantic in height, and muffled in a cloak, Ichabod was horror-struck on perceiving that he was headless!—but his horror was still more increased on observing that the head, which should have rested on his shoulders, was carried before him on the pommel of his saddle! His terror rose to desperation; he rained a shower of kicks and blows upon Gunpowder, hoping by a sudden movement to give his companion the slip; but the specter started full jump with him. Away, then, they dashed through thick and thin; stones flying and sparks flashing at every bound. Ichabod's flimsy garments fluttered in the air, as he stretched his long lank body away over his horse's head, in the eagerness of his flight.

They had now reached the road which turns off to Sleepy Hollow; but Gunpowder, who seemed possessed with a demon, instead of keeping up it, made an opposite turn, and plunged headlong downhill to the left. This road leads through a sandy hollow shaded by trees for about a quarter of a mile, where it crosses the bridge famous in goblin story; and just beyond swells the green knoll on which stands the whitewashed church.

As yet the panic of the steed had given his unskilful rider an apparent advantage in the chase, but just as he had got half way through the hollow, the girths of the saddle gave way, and he felt it slipping from under him. He seized it by the pommel, and endeavored to hold it firm, but in vain; and had just time to save himself by clasping old Gunpowder round the neck, when the saddle fell to the earth, and he heard it trampled under foot by his pursuer. For a moment the terror of Hans Van Ripper's wrath passed across his mind,—for it was his Sunday saddle; but this was no time for petty fears; the goblin was hard on his haunches;

and (unskilful rider that he was!) he had much ado to maintain his seat; sometimes slipping on one side, sometimes on another, and sometimes jolted on the high ridge of his horse's backbone, with a violence that he verily feared would cleave him asunder.

An opening in the trees now cheered him with the hopes that the church bridge was at hand. The wavering reflection of a silver star in the bosom of the brook told him that he was not mistaken. He saw the walls of the church dimly glaring under the trees beyond. He recollected the place where Brom Bones's ghostly competitor had disappeared. "If I can but reach that bridge," thought Ichabod, "I am safe." Just then he heard the black steed panting and blowing close behind him; he even fancied that he felt his hot breath. Another convulsive kick in the ribs, and old Gunpowder sprang upon the bridge; he thundered over the resounding planks; he gained the opposite side; and now Ichabod cast a look behind to see if his pursuer should vanish, according to rule, in a flash of fire and brimstone. Just then he saw the goblin rising in his stirrups, and in the very act of hurling his head at him. Ichabod endeavored to dodge the horrible missile, but too late. It encountered his cranium with a tremendous crash,—he was tumbled headlong into the dust, and Gunpowder, the black steed, and the goblin rider, passed by like a whirlwind.

The next morning the old horse was found without his saddle, and with the bridle under his feet, soberly cropping the grass at his master's gate. Ichabod did not make his appearance at breakfast; dinner-hour came, but no Ichabod. The boys assembled at the schoolhouse, and strolled idly about the banks of the brook; but no schoolmaster. Hans Van Ripper now began to feel some uneasiness about the fate of poor Ichabod, and his saddle. An inquiry was set on foot, and after diligent investigation they came upon his traces. In one part of the road leading to the church was found the saddle trampled in the dirt; the tracks of horses' hoofs deeply dented in the road, and evidently at furious speed, were traced to the bridge, beyond which, on the bank of a broad part of the brook, where the water ran deep and black, was found the hat of the unfortunate Ichabod, and close beside it a shattered pumpkin.

The brook was searched, but the body of the schoolmaster was not to be discovered. Hans Van Ripper as executor of his estate, examined the bundle which contained all his worldly effects. They consisted of two shirts and a half; two stocks for the neck; a pair or two of worsted stockings; an old pair of corduroy small-clothes; a rusty razor; a book of psalm tunes full of dog's-ears; and a broken pitch-pipe. As to the books and furniture of the schoolhouse, they belonged to the community, excepting Cotton Mather's "History of Witchcraft," a "New England Almanac," and a book of dreams and fortune-telling; in which last was a sheet of foolscap much scribbled and blotted in several fruitless attempts to make a copy of verses in honor of the heiress of Van Tassel. These magic books and the poetic scrawl were forthwith consigned to the flames by Hans Van Ripper; who, from that time forward, determined to send his children no more to school, observing that he never knew any good come of this same reading and writing. Whatever money the schoolmaster possessed, and he had received his quarter's pay but a day or two before, he must have had about his person at the time of his disappearance.

The mysterious event caused much speculation at the church on the following Sunday. Knots of gazers and gossips were collected in the churchyard, at the bridge, and at the spot where the hat and pumpkin had been found. The stories of Brouwer, of Bones, and a whole budget of others were called to mind; and when they had diligently considered them all, and compared them with the symptoms of the present case, they shook their heads, and came to the conclusion that Ichabod had been carried off by the Galloping Hessian. As he was a bachelor, and in nobody's debt, nobody troubled his head any more about him; the school was removed to a different quarter of the hollow, and another pedagogue reigned in his stead.

It is true, an old farmer, who had been down to New York on a visit several years after, and from whom this account of the ghostly adventure was received, brought home the intelligence that Ichabod Crane was still alive; that he had left the neighborhood partly through fear of the goblin and Hans Van Ripper, and partly in mortification at having been suddenly dismissed by the heiress; that he had changed his quarters to a distant part of the country; had kept school and studied law at the same time; had been admitted to the bar; turned politician; electioneered; written for the newspapers; and finally had been made a justice of the Ten Pound Court. Brom Bones, too, who, shortly after his rival's disappearance conducted the blooming Katrina in triumph to the altar, was observed to look exceedingly knowing whenever the story of Ichabod was related, and always burst into a hearty laugh at the mention of the pumpkin; which led some to suspect that he knew more about the matter than he chose to tell.

The old country wives, however, who are the best judges of these matters, maintain to this day that Ichabod was spirited away by supernatural means; and it is a favorite story often told about the neighborhood round the winter evening fire. The bridge became more than ever an object of superstitious awe; and that may be the reason why the road has been altered of late years, so as to approach the church by the border of the millpond. The schoolhouse being deserted soon fell to decay, and was reported to be haunted by the ghost of the unfortunate pedagogue and the plowboy, loitering homeward of a still summer evening, has often fancied his voice at a distance, chanting a melancholy psalm tune among the tranquil solitudes of Sleepy Hollow.

William Cullen Bryant, engraved
by G. Parker.

O legends full of life and health,
That live when records fail and die,
Ye are the Hudson's richest wealth,
The frondage of her history!

—Wallace Bruce

W illiam Cullen Bryant (November 3, 1794–June 12, 1878) was an American romantic poet associated with the Hudson River School of American artists, a journalist, and longtime editor of the *New York Evening Post*.

Born in the Berkshires of Massachusetts, Bryant attended Williams College for a year before studying law at Worthington and Bridgewater in Massachusetts. He was admitted to the bar in 1815.

Bryant developed an interest in poetry early in life. His most famous work, "Thanatopsis," dated variously to 1811 or 1813, was published in 1817 by the *North American Review*.

In 1821 he married Francis Fairchild and settled into practicing law in Great Barrington. He moved to New York City in 1826, where he was hired as Associate Editor of the *New-York Evening Post*, a newspaper founded by Alexander Hamilton. From 1829 until his death in 1878, he was Editor-in-Chief and a part owner. He was one of the major supporters of Abraham Lincoln, whom he introduced at Cooper Union.

In his later years, Bryant lectured and translated Homer's *The Iliad* and *The Odyssey*. Bryant died in 1878 of complications from an accidental fall. New York City's Bryant Park is named after him.

෬

Poems by William Cullen Bryant. 1854.

A Scene on the Banks of the Hudson.

Cool shades and dews are round my way,
And silence of the early day;
Mid the dark rocks that watch his bed,
Glitters the mighty Hudson spread,
Unrippled, save by drops that fall
From shrubs that fringe his mountain wall;
And o'er the clear still water swells
The music of the Sabbath bells.

All, save this little nook of land
Circled with trees, on which I stand;
All, save that line of hills which lie
Suspended in the mimic sky—
Seems a blue void, above, below,
Through which the white clouds come and go,
And from the green world's farthest steep
I gaze into the airy deep.

Loveliest of lovely things are they,
On earth, that soonest pass away.
The rose that lives its little hour
Is prized beyond the sculptured flower.
Even love, long tried and cherished long,
Becomes more tender and more strong,
At thought of that insatiate grave
From which its yearnings cannot save.

River! in this still hour thou hast
Too much of heaven on earth to last;
Nor long may thy still waters lie,
An image of the glorious sky.
Thy fate and mine are not repose,
And ere another evening close,
Thou to thy tides shalt turn again,
And I to seek the crowd of men.

Catterskill Falls.

Midst greens and shades the Catterskill leaps,
From cliffs where the wood-flower clings;
All summer he moistens his verdant steeps
With the sweet light spray of the mountain springs;
And he shakes the woods on the mountain side,
When they drip with the rains of autumn-tide.

But when, in the forest bare and old,
The blast of December calls,
He builds, in the starlight clear and cold,
A palace of ice where his torrent falls,
With turret, and arch, and fretwork fair,
And pillars blue as the summer air.

For whom are those glorious chambers wrought,
In the cold and cloudless night?
Is there neither spirit nor motion of thought
In forms so lovely, and hues so bright?
Hear what the gray-haired woodmen tell
Of this wild stream and its rocky dell.

'Twas hither a youth of dreamy mood,
A hundred winters ago,
Had wandered over the mighty wood,
When the panther's track was fresh on the snow,
And keen were the winds that came to stir

The long dark boughs of the hemlock fir.

Too gentle of mien he seemed and fair,
For a child of those rugged steeps;
His home lay low in the valley where
The kingly Hudson rolls to the deeps;
But he wore the hunter's frock that day,
And a slender gun on his shoulder lay.

And here he paused, and against the trunk
Of a tall gray linden leant,
When the broad clear orb of the sun had sunk
From his path in the frosty firmament,
And over the round dark edge of the hill
A cold green light was quivering still.

And the crescent moon, high over the green,
From a sky of crimson shone,
On that icy palace, whose towers were seen
To sparkle as if with stars of their own;
While the water fell with a hollow sound,
'Twixt the glistening pillars ranged around.

Is that a being of life, that moves
Where the crystal battlements rise?
A maiden watching the moon she loves,
At the twilight hour, with pensive eyes?

Was that a garment which seemed to gleam
Betwixt the eye and the falling stream?

'Tis only the torrent tumbling o'er,
In the midst of those glassy walls,
Gushing, and plunging, and beating the floor
Of the rocky basin in which it falls.
'Tis only the torrent—but why that start?
Why gazes the youth with a throbbing heart?

He thinks no more of his home afar,
Where his sire and sister wait.
He heeds no longer how star after star
Looks forth on the night as the hour grows late.
He heeds not the snow-wreaths, lifted and cast
From a thousand boughs, by the rising blast.

His thoughts are alone of those who dwell
In the halls of frost and snow,
Who pass where the crystal domes upswell
From the alabaster floors below,
Where the frost-trees shoot with leaf and spray,
And frost-gems scatter a silvery day.

"And oh that those glorious haunts were mine!"
He speaks, and throughout the glen
Thin shadows swim in the faint moonshine,

And take a ghastly likeness of men,
As if the slain by the wintry storms
Came forth to the air in their earthly forms.

There pass the chasers of seal and whale,
With their weapons quaint and grim,
And bands of warriors in glittering mail,
And herdsmen and hunters huge of limb.
There are naked arms, with bow and spear,
And furry gauntlets the carbine rear.

There are mothers—and oh how sadly their eyes
On their children's white brows rest!
There are youthful lovers—the maiden lies,
In a seeming sleep, on the chosen breast;
There are fair wan women with moonstruck air,
The snow stars flecking their long loose hair.

They eye him not as they pass along,
But his hair stands up with dread,
When he feels that he moves with that phantom throng,
Till those icy turrets are over his head,
And the torrent's roar as they enter seems
Like a drowsy murmur heard in dreams.

The glittering threshold is scarcely passed,
When there gathers and wraps him round

A thick white twilight, sullen and vast,
In which there is neither form nor sound;
The phantoms, the glory, vanish all,
With the dying voice of the waterfall.

Slow passes the darkness of that trance,
And the youth now faintly sees
Huge shadows and gushes of light that dance
On a rugged ceiling of unhewn trees,
And walls where the skins of beasts are hung,
And rifles glitter on antlers strung.

On a couch of shaggy skins he lies;
As he strives to raise his head,
Hard-featured woodmen, with kindly eyes,
Come round him and smooth his furry bed
And bid him rest, for the evening star
Is scarcely set and the day is far.

They had found at eve the dreaming one
By the base of that icy steep,
When over his stiffening limbs begun
The deadly slumber of frost to creep,
And they cherished the pale and breathless form,
Till the stagnant blood ran free and warm.

☙❧

Noon. From an Unfinished Poem.

'Tis noon. At noon the Hebrew bowed the knee
And worshipped, while the husbandmen withdrew
From the scorched field, and the wayfaring man
Grew faint, and turned aside by bubbling fount,
Or rested in the shadow of the palm.

I, too, amid the overflow of day,
Behold the power which wields and cherishes
The frame of Nature. From this brow of rock
That overlooks the Hudson's western marge,
I gaze upon the long array of groves,
The piles and gulfs of verdure drinking in
The grateful heats. They love the fiery sun;
Their broadening leaves grow glossier, and their sprays
Climb as he looks upon them. In the midst,
The swelling river, into his green gulfs,
Unshadowed save by passing sails above,
Takes the redundant glory, and enjoys
The summer in his chilly bed. Coy flowers,
That would not open in the early light,
Push back their plaited sheaths. The rivulet's pool,
That darkly quivered all the morning long
In the cool shade, now glimmers in the sun;
And o'er its surface shoots, and shoots again,
The glittering dragon-fly, and deep within
Run the brown water-beetles to and fro.

A silence, the brief sabbath of an hour,
Reigns o'er the fields; the laborer sits within
His dwelling; he has left his steers awhile,
Unyoked, to bite the herbage, and his dog
Sleeps stretched beside the door-stone in the shade.
Now the grey marmot, with uplifted paws,
No more sits listening by his den, but steals
Abroad, in safety, to the clover field,
And crops its juicy blossoms. All the while
A ceaseless murmur from the populous town
Swells o'er these solitudes: a mingled sound
Of jarring wheels, and iron hoofs that clash
Upon the stony ways, and hammer-clang,
And creak of engines lifting ponderous bulks,
And calls and cries, and tread of eager feet,
Innumerable, hurrying to and fro.
Noon, in that mighty mart of nations, brings
No pause to toil and care. With early day
Began the tumult, and shall only cease
When midnight, hushing one by one the sounds
Of bustle, gathers the tired brood to rest.

Thus, in this feverish time, when love of gain
And luxury possess the hearts of men,
Thus is it with the noon of human life.
We, in our fervid manhood, in our strength
Of reason, we, with hurry, noise, and care,

Plan, toil, and strife, and pause not to refresh
Our spirits with the calm and beautiful
Of God's harmonious universe, that won
Our youthful wonder; pause not to inquire
Why we are here; and what the reverence
Man owes to man, and what the mystery
That links us to the greater world, beside
Whose borders we but hover for a space.

James Fenimore Cooper, 1789–
1851. Engraved by O. Pelton from
a painting by M. Mirbel.

The Highlands and the Palisades
Mirror their beauty in the tide,
The history of whose forest shades
A nation reads with conscious pride.

—Wallace Bruce

CHAPTER 14

James Fenimore Cooper

James Fenimore Cooper (September 15, 1789–
September 14, 1851) was a popular American author
of the early 19th century. Born in Burlington, New
Jersey, his family moved to New York State, where
his father established a settlement that became
Cooperstown. He briefly attended Yale University,
then married Susan Augusta de Lancey on New
Year's Day, 1811.

Cooper moved to Scarsdale, New York, and published his first book, *Precaution* (1820). This was followed by *The Spy* (1821); *The Pioneers* (1823), the first of the *Leatherstocking* series; *The Pilot* (1824); *Lionel Lincoln* (1825); and *The Last of the Mohicans* (1826), which many consider his masterpiece.

Moving to Europe for seven years, Cooper published *The Prairie* (1826); *The Red Rover* (1828); *The Wept of Wish-Ton-Wish* (1829); *The Notions of a Traveling Bachelor* (1828); *The Waterwitch* (1830); *The Bravo* (1831); *The Heidenmauer* (1832); and *The Headsman: or The Abbaye of Vigneron* (1833).

In 1833 Cooper returned to America and published *A Letter to My Countrymen* (1834); *The Monikins* (1835); *The American Democrat* (1835); *England* (1837); *Homeward Bound* and *Home as Found* (1838); *A History of the Navy of the United States* (1839); *The Pathfinder* (1840); *Mercedes of Castile* (1840); *The Deerslayer* (1841); *The Two Admirals* and *Wing and Wing* (1842); *Wyandotte, The History of a Pocket Handkerchief; Ned Myers* (1843); *Afloat and Ashore, or the Adventures of Miles Wallingford* (1844); *Littlepage Manuscripts* (1845–1846); *Lives of Distinguished American Naval Officers* (1846); *The Crater, or Vulcan's Peak* (1847); *Oak Openings* and *Jack Tier* (1848); *The Sea Lions* (1849); and *The Ways of the Hour* (1850).

Cooper spent the last years of his life in Cooperstown. He died of dropsy on September 14, 1851, a day before his 62nd birthday.

Afloat and Ashore: A Sea Tale. 1844.

"Home-keeping youth have ever homely wits."

—Two Gentlemen of Verona

Preface

The writer has published so much truth which the world has insisted was fiction, and so much fiction which has been received as truth, that, in the present instance, he is resolved to say nothing on the subject. Each of his readers is at liberty to believe just as much, or as little, of the matter here laid before him, or her, as may suit his, or her notions, prejudices, knowledge of the world, or ignorance. If anybody is disposed to swear he knows precisely where Clawbonny is, that he was well acquainted with old Mr. Hardinge, nay, has often heard him preach—let him make his affidavit, in welcome. Should he get a little wide of the mark, it will not be the first document of that nature, which has possessed the same weakness.

It is possible that certain captious persons may be disposed to inquire into the "cui bono?" of such a book. The answer is this. Everything which can convey to the human mind distinct and accurate impressions of events, social facts, professional peculiarities, or past history, whether of the higher or more familiar character, is of use. All that is necessary is, that the pictures should be true to nature, if not absolutely drawn from living sitters. The knowledge we gain by our looser reading, often becomes service-able in modes and manners little anticipated in the moments when it is acquired.

Perhaps the greater portion of all our peculiar opinions have their foundation in prejudices. These prejudices are produced in consequence of its being out of the power of any one man to see, or know, every thing. The most favoured mortal must receive far more than half of all that he learns on his faith in others; and it may aid those who can never be placed in positions to judge for themselves of certain phases of men and things, to get pictures of the same, drawn in a way to give them nearer views than they might otherwise obtain. This is the greatest benefit of all light lit-erature in general, it being possible to render that which is purely fictitious even more useful than that which is strictly true, by avoiding extravagancies, by pourtraying with fidelity, and, as our friend Marble might say, by "generalizing" with discretion.

This country has undergone many important changes since the commencement of the present century. Some of these changes have been for the better; others, we think out of all question, for the worse. The last is a fact that can be known to the generation which is coming into life, by report only, and these pages may possibly throw some little light on both points, in representing things as they were. The population of the republic is probably something more than eighteen millions and a half to-day; in the year of our Lord one thousand eight hundred, it was but a little more than five millions. In 1800, the population of New-York was somewhat less than six hundred thousand souls; to-day it is probably a little less than two millions seven hundred thousand souls. In 1800, the town of New-York had sixty thousand inhabitants, whereas, including Brooklyn and Williamsburg, which then virtually had no existence, it must have at this moment quite four hundred thousand. These are prodigious numerical changes, that have produced changes of another sort. Although an increase of numbers does not necessarily infer an increase of high civilization, it reasonably leads to the expectation of great melioration in the commoner comforts. Such has been the result, and to those familiar with facts as they now exist, the difference will probably be apparent in these pages.

Although the moral changes in American society have not kept even pace with those that are purely physical, many that are essential have nevertheless occurred. Of all the British possessions on this continent, New-York, after its conquest from the Dutch, received most of the social organization of the mother country. Under the Dutch, even, it had some of these characteristic peculiarities, in its patroons; the lords of the manor of the New Netherlands. Some of the southern colonies, it is true, had their caciques and other semi-feudal, and semi-savage noblesse, but the system was of short continuance; the peculiarities of that section of the country, arising principally from the existence of domestic slavery, on an extended scale. With New-York it was different. A conquered colony, the mother country left the impression of its own institutions more deeply engraved than on any of the settlements that were commenced by grants to proprietors, or under charters from the crown. It was strictly a royal colony, and so continued to be, down to the hour of separation. The social consequences of this state of things were to be traced in her habits until the current of immigration became so strong, as to bring with it those that were conflicting, if not absolutely antagonist. The influence of these two sources of thought is still obvious to the reflecting, giving rise to a double set of social opinions; one of which bears all the characteristics of its New England and puritanical origin, while the other may be said to come of the usages and notions of the Middle States, proper.

This is said in anticipation of certain strictures that will be likely to follow some of the incidents of our story, it not being always deemed an essential in an American critic, that he should understand his subject. Too many of them, indeed, justify the retort of the man who derided the claims to knowledge of life, set up by a neighbour, that "had been to meetin' and had been to mill." We can all obtain some notions of the portion of a subject that is placed immediately before our eyes; the difficulty is to understand that which we have no means of studying.

On the subject of the nautical incidents of this book, we have endeavoured to be as exact as our authorities will allow. We are fully aware of the importance of writing what the world thinks, rather than what is true, and are not conscious of any very palpable errors of this nature.

It is no more than fair to apprize the reader, that our tale is not completed in the First Part, or the volumes that are now published. This, the plan of the book would not permit: but we can promise those who may feel any interest in the subject, that the season shall not pass away, so far as it may depend on ourselves, without bringing the narrative to a close. Poor Captain Wallingford is now in his sixty-fifth year, and is naturally desirous of not being hung up long on the tenter-hooks of expectation, so near the close of life. The old gentleman having seen much and suffered much, is entitled to end his days in peace. In this mutual frame of mind between the principal, and his editors, the public shall have no cause to complain of unnecessary delay, whatever may be its rights of the same nature on other subjects.

The author—perhaps editor would be the better word—does not feel himself responsible for all the notions advanced by the hero of this tale, and it may be as well to say as much. That one born in the Revolution should think differently from the men of the present day, in a hundred things, is to be expected. It is in just this difference of opinion, that the lessons of the book are to be found.

Chapter 3

"There's a youth in this city, it were a great pity
That he from our lasses should wander awa';
For he's bonny and braw, weel-favoured with a'.
And his hair has a natural buckle and a'.
His coat is the hue of his bonnet so blue;
His pocket is white as the new-driven snaw;
His hose they are blue, and his shoon like the slae,
And his clean siller buckles they dazzle us a'."

— *Burns.*

We had selected our time well, as respects the hour of departure. It was young ebb, and the boat floated swiftly down the creek, though the high banks of the latter would have prevented our feeling any wind, even if there were a breeze on the river. Our boat was of some size, sloop-rigged and half-decked; but Neb's vigorous arms made her move through the water with some rapidity, and, to own the truth, the lad sprang to his work like a true runaway negro. I was a skilful oarsman myself, having received many lessons from my father in early boyhood, and being in almost daily practice for seven mouths in the year. The excitement of the adventure, its romance, or what for a short time seemed to me to be romance, and the secret apprehension of being detected, which I believe accompanies every clandestine undertaking, soon set me in motion also. I took one of the oars, and, in less than twenty minutes, the Grace & Lucy, for so the boat was called, emerged from between two, high, steep banks, and entered on the broader bosom of the Hudson.

Neb gave a half-suppressed, negro-like cry of exultation, as we shot out from our cover, and ascertained that there was a pleasant and fair breeze blowing. In three minutes we had the jib and mainsail on the boat, the helm was up, the sheet was eased off, and we were gliding down-stream at the rate of something like five miles an hour. I took the helm, almost as a matter of course; Rupert being much too indolent to do anything unnecessarily, while Neb was far too humble to aspire to such an office while Master Miles was there, willing and ready. In that day, indeed, it was so much a matter of course for the skipper of a Hudson river craft to steer, that most of the people who lived on the banks of the stream imagined that Sir John Jervis, Lord Anson, and the other great English admirals of whom they had read and heard, usually amused themselves with that employment, out on the ocean. I remember the hearty laugh in which my unfortunate father indulged, when Mr. Hardinge once asked him how he could manage to get any sleep, on account of this very duty. But we were very green, up at Clawbonny, in most things that related to the world.

The hour that succeeded was one of the most painful I ever passed in my life. I recalled my father, his manly frankness, his liberal bequests in my favour, and his precepts of respect and obedience; all of which, it now seemed to me, I had openly dishonoured. Then came the image of my mother, with her love and sufferings, her prayers, and her mild but earnest exhortations to be good. I thought I could see both these parents regarding me with sorrowful, though not with reproachful countenances. They appeared to be soliciting my return, with a species of silent, but not the less eloquent, warnings of the consequences. Grace and Lucy, and their sobs, and admonitions, and entreaties to abandon my scheme, and to write, and not to remain away long, and all that tender interest had induced two warm-hearted girls to utter at our parting, came fresh and vividly to my mind. The recollection proved nearly too much for me. Nor did I forget Mr. Hardinge, and the distress he would certainly feel, when he discovered that he had not only lost his ward, but his only son. Then Clawbonny itself, the house, the orchards, the meadows, the garden, the mill, and all that belonged to the farm, began to have a double value in my eyes, and to serve as so many cords attached to my heart-strings, and to remind me that the rover

"Drags at each remove a lengthening chain."'

I marvelled at Rupert's tranquility. I did not then understand his character as thoroughly as I subsequently got to know it. All that he most prized was with him in the boat, in fact, and this lessened his grief at parting from less beloved objects. Where Rupert was, there was his paradise. As for Neb, I do believe his head was over his shoulder, for he affected to sit with his face down-stream, so long as the hills that lay in the rear of Clawbonny could be at all distinguished. This must have proceeded from tradition, or instinct, or some latent negro quality; for I do not think the fellow fancied he was running away. He knew that his two young masters were; but he was fully aware he was my property, and no doubt thought, as long as he staid in my company, he was in the line of his legitimate duty. Then it was my plan that he should return with the boat, and perhaps these backward glances were no more than the shadows of coming events, cast, in his case, behind.

Rupert was indisposed to converse, for, to tell the truth, he had eaten a hearty supper, and began to feel drowsy; and I was too much wrapped up in my own busy thoughts to solicit any communications. I found a sort of saddened pleasure in setting a watch for the night, therefore, which had an air of seaman-like duty about it, that in a slight degree revived my old taste for the profession. It was midnight, and I took the first watch myself, bidding my two companions to crawl under the half-deck, and go to sleep. This they both did without any parley, Rupert occupying an inner place, while Neb lay with his legs exposed to the night air.

The breeze freshened, and for some time I thought it might be necessary to reef, though we were running dead before the wind. I succeeded in holding on, however, and I found the Grace & Lucy was doing wonders in my watch. When I gave Rupert his call at four o'clock, the boat was just approaching two frowning mountains, where the river was narrowed to a third or fourth of its former width; and, by the appearance of the shores, and the dim glimpses I had caught of a village of no great size on the right bank, I knew we were in what is called Newburgh Bay. This was the extent of our former journeyings south, all three of us having once before, and only once, been as low as Fishkill

Landing, which lies opposite to the place that gives this part of the river its name.

Rupert now took the helm, and I went to sleep. The wind still continued fresh and fair, and I felt no uneasiness on account of the boat. It is true, there were two parts of the navigation before us of which I had thought a little seriously, but not sufficiently so to keep me awake. These were the Race, a passage in the Highlands, and Tappan Sea; both points on the Hudson of which the navigators of that classical stream were fond of relating the marvels. The first I knew was formidable only later in the autumn, and, as for the last, I hoped to enjoy some of its wonders in the morning. In this very justifiable expectation, I fell asleep.

Neb did not call me until ten o'clock. I afterwards discovered that Rupert kept the helm for only an hour, and then, calculating that from five until nine were four hours, he thought it a pity the negro should not have his share of the glory of that night. When I was awakened, it was merely to let me know that it was time to eat something—Neb would have starved before he would precede his young master in that necessary occupation— and I found Rupert in a deep and pleasant sleep at my side.

We were in the center of Tappan, and the Highlands had been passed in safety. Neb expatiated a little on the difficulties of the navigation, the river having many windings, besides being bounded by high mountains; but, after all, he admitted that there was water enough, wind enough, and a road that was plain enough. From this moment, excitement kept us wide awake. Everything was new, and everything seemed delightful. The day was pleasant, the wind continued fair, and nothing occurred to mar our joy. I had a little map, one neither particularly accurate, nor very well engraved; and I remember the importance with which, after having ascertained the fact myself, I pointed out to my two companions the rocky precipices on the western bank, as New Jersey! Even-Rupert was struck with this important circumstance. As for Neb, he was actually in ecstasies, rolling his large black eyes, and showing his white teeth, until he suddenly closed his truly coral and plump lips, to demand what New Jersey meant? Of course I gratified this laudable desire to obtain knowledge, and Neb seemed still more pleased than ever, now he had ascertained that New Jersey was a State. Travelling was not as much of an every-day occupation, at that time, as it is now; and it was, in truth, something for three American lads, all under nineteen, to be able to say that they had seen a State, other than their own.

Notwithstanding the rapid progress we had made for the first few hours of our undertaking, the voyage was far from being ended. About noon the wind came out light from the southward, and, having a flood-tide, we were compelled to anchor. This made us all uneasy, for, while we were stationary, we did not seem to be running away. The ebb came again, at length, however, and then we made sail, and began to turn down with the tide. It was near sunset before we got a view of the two or three spires that then piloted strangers to the town. New York was not the "commercial emporium" in 1796; so high-sounding a title, indeed, scarce belonging to the simple English of the period, it requiring a very great collection of half-educated men to venture on so ambitious an appellation—the only emporium that existed in America, during the last century, being a slop-shop in Water street, and on the island of Manhattan. Commercial emporium was a flight of fancy, indeed, that must have required a whole board of aldermen, and an extra supply of turtle, to sanction. What is meant by a "literary" emporium, I leave those editors who are "native and to the "manor" born," to explain.

We first saw the State Prison, which was then new, and a most imposing edifice, according to our notions, as we drew near the town. Like the gallows first seen by a traveller in entering a strange country, it was a pledge of civilization. Neb shook his head, as he gazed at it, with a moralizing air, and said it had a "wicked look." For myself, I own I did not regard it altogether without dread. On Rupert it made less impression than on any of the three. He was always somewhat obtuse on the subject of morals.[*]

[Footnote: It may be well to tell the European who shall happen to read this book, that in America a "State's Prison" is not for prisoners of State, but for common rogues: the term coming from the name borne by the local governments.]*

New York, in that day, and on the Hudson side of the town, commenced a short distance above Duane street. Between Greenwich, as the little hamlet around the State Prison was called, and the town proper, was an interval of a mile and a half of open fields, dotted here and there with country-houses. Much of this space was in broken hills, and a few piles of lumber lay along the shores. St. John's church had no existence, and most of the ground in its vicinity was in low swamp. As we glided along the wharves, we caught sight of the first market I had then ever seen—such proofs of an advanced civilization not having yet made their way into the villages of the interior. It was called "The Bear," from the circumstance that the first meat ever exposed for sale in it was of that animal; but the appellation has disappeared before the intellectual refinement of these later times—the name of the soldier and statesman, Washington, having fairly supplanted that of the bear! Whether this great moral improvement was brought about by the Philosophical Society, or the Historical Society, or "The Merchants," or the Aldermen of New York, I have never ascertained. If the latter, one cannot but admire their disinterested modesty in conferring this notable honour on the Father of his country, inasmuch as all can see that there never has been a period when their own board has not possessed distinguished members, every way qualified to act as god-fathers to the most illustrious markets of the republic. But Manhattan, in the way of taste, has never had justice done it. So profound is its admiration for all the higher qualities, that Franklin and Fulton have each a market to himself, in addition to this bestowed on Washington. Doubtless there would have been Newton Market, and Socrates Market, and Solomon Market, but for the patriotism of the town, which has forbidden it from going out of the hemisphere, in quest of names to illustrate. Bacon Market would doubtless have been too equivocal to be tolerated, under any circumstances. Then Bacon was a rogue, though a philosopher, and markets are always appropriated to honest people. At all events, I am rejoiced the reproach of having a market called

"The Bear" has been taken away, as it was tacitly admitting our living near, if not absolutely in, the woods.

We passed the Albany basin, a large receptacle for North River craft, that is now in the bosom of the town and built on, and recognized in it the mast-head of the Wallingford. Neb was shown the place, for he was to bring the boat round to it, and join the sloop, in readiness to return in her. We rounded the Battery, then a circular stripe of grass, with an earthen and wooden breastwork running along the margin of the water, leaving a narrow promenade on the exterior. This brought us to White-Hall, since so celebrated for its oarsmen, where we put in for a haven. I had obtained the address of a better sort of sailor-tavern in that vicinity, and, securing the boat, we shouldered the bags, got a boy to guide us, and were soon housed. As it was near night, Rupert and I ordered supper, and Neb was directed to pull the boat round to the sloop, and to return to us in the morning; taking care, however, not to let our lodgings be known. [...]

I now began to regret that I had not seen a little of the town. In 1797, New York could not have had more than fifty thousand inhabitants, though it was just as much of a paragon then, in the eyes of all good Americans, as it is today. It is a sound patriotic rule to maintain that "our" best is always "the" best, for it never puts us in the wrong. I have seen enough of the world since to understand that we get a great many things wrong-end foremost, in this country of ours; undervaluing those advantages and excellencies of which we have great reason to be proud, and boasting of others that, to say the least, are exceedingly equivocal.

The Last of the Mohicans: A Narrative of 1757. 1826.

Introduction

It is believed that the scene of this tale, and most of the information necessary to understand its allusions, are rendered sufficiently obvious to the reader in the text itself, or in the accompanying notes. Still there is so much obscurity in the Indian

The scout resumed his post in advance, from "The Last of the Mohicans" by James Fenimore Cooper. Photomechical print, c. 1910.

traditions, and so much confusion in the Indian names, as to render some explanation useful.

Few men exhibit greater diversity, or, if we may so express it, greater antithesis of character, than the native warrior of North America. In war, he is daring, boastful, cunning, ruthless, self-denying, and self-devoted; in peace, just, generous, hospitable, revengeful, superstitious, modest, and commonly chaste. These are qualities, it is true, which do not distinguish all alike; but they are so far the predominating traits of these remarkable people as to be characteristic.

It is generally believed that the Aborigines of the American continent have an Asiatic origin. There are many physical as well as moral facts which corroborate this opinion, and some few that would seem to weigh against it.

The color of the Indian, the writer believes, is peculiar to himself, and while his cheek-bones have a very striking indication of a Tartar origin, his eyes have not. Climate may have had great influence on the former, but it is difficult to see how it can have produced the substantial difference which exists in the latter. The imagery of the Indian, both in his poetry and in his oratory, is oriental; chastened, and perhaps improved, by the limited range of his practical knowledge. He draws his metaphors from the clouds, the seasons, the birds, the beasts, and the vegetable world. In this, perhaps, he does no more than any other energetic and imaginative race would do, being compelled to set bounds to fancy by experience; but the North American Indian clothes his ideas in a dress which is different from that of the African, and is oriental in itself. His language has the richness and sententious fullness of the Chinese. He will express a phrase in a word, and he will qualify the meaning of an entire sentence by a syllable; he will even convey different significations by the simplest inflections of the voice.

Philologists have said that there are but two or three languages, properly speaking, among all the numerous tribes which formerly occupied the country that now composes the United States. They ascribe the known difficulty one people have to understand another to corruptions and dialects. The writer remembers to have been present at an interview between two chiefs of the Great Prairies west of the Mississippi, and when an interpreter was in attendance who spoke both their languages. The warriors appeared to be on the most friendly terms, and seemingly conversed much together; yet, according to the account of the interpreter, each was absolutely ignorant of what the other said. They were of hostile tribes, brought together by the influence of the American government; and it is worthy of remark, that a common policy led them both to adopt the same subject. They mutually exhorted each other to be of use in the event of the chances of war throwing either of the parties into the hands of his enemies. Whatever may be the truth, as respects the root and the genius of the Indian tongues, it is quite certain they are now so distinct in their words as to possess most of the disadvantages of strange languages; hence much of the embarrassment that has arisen in learning their histories, and most of the uncertainty which exists in their traditions.

Like nations of higher pretensions, the American Indian gives a very different account of his own tribe or race from that which is given by other people. He is much addicted to over-estimating his own perfections, and to undervaluing those of his rival or his enemy; a trait which may possibly be thought corroborative of the Mosaic account of the creation. The whites have assisted greatly in rendering the traditions of the Aborigines more obscure by their own manner of corrupting names. Thus, the term used in the title of this book has undergone the changes of Mahicanni, Mohicans, and Mohegans; the latter being the word commonly used by the whites. When it is remembered that the Dutch (who first settled New York), the English, and the French, all gave appellations to the tribes that dwelt within the country which is the scene of this story, and that the Indians not only gave different names to their enemies, but frequently to themselves, the cause of the confusion will be understood.

In these pages, Lenni-Lenape, Lenope, Delawares, Wapanachki, and Mohicans, all mean the same people, or tribes of the same stock. The Mengwe, the Maquas, the Mingoes, and the Iroquois, though not all strictly the same, are identi-fied frequently by the speakers, being politically confederated and opposed to those just named. Mingo was a term of peculiar reproach, as were Mengwe and Maqua in a less degree.

The Mohicans were the possessors of the country first occu-pied by the Europeans in this portion of the continent. They were, consequently, the first dispossessed; and the seemingly inevitable fate of all these people, who disappear before the advances, or it might be termed the inroads, of civilization, as the verdure of their native forests falls before the nipping frosts, is represented as having already befallen them. There is sufficient historical truth in the picture to justify the use that has been made of it.

In point of fact, the country which is the scene of the following tale has undergone as little change, since the historical events alluded to had place, as almost any other district of equal extent within the whole limits of the United States. There are fashionable and well-attended watering-places at and near the spring where Hawkeye halted to drink, and roads traverse the forests where he and his friends were compelled to journey without even a path. Glen's has a large village; and while William Henry, and even a fortress of later date, are only to be traced as ruins, there is another village on the shores of the Horican. But, beyond this, the enterprise and energy of a people who have done so much in other places have done little here. The whole of that wilderness, in which the latter incidents of the legend occurred, is nearly a wilderness still, though the red man has entirely deserted this part of the state. Of all the tribes named in these pages, there exist only a few half-civilized beings of the Oneidas, on the reservations of their people in New York. The rest have disappeared, either from the regions in which their fathers dwelt, or altogether from the earth.

There is one point on which we would wish to say a word before closing this preface. Hawkeye calls the Lac du Saint Sacrement, the "Horican." As we believe this to be an appropriation of the name that has its origin with ourselves, the time has arrived, perhaps, when the fact should be frankly admitted. While writing this book, fully a quarter of a century since, it occurred to us that the French name of this lake was too complicated, the American too commonplace, and the Indian too unpronounceable, for either to be used familiarly in a work of fiction. Looking over an ancient map, it was ascertained that a tribe of Indians, called "Les Horicans" by the French, existed in the neighborhood of this beautiful sheet of water. As every word uttered by Natty Bumppo was not to be received as rigid truth, we took the liberty of putting the "Horican" into his mouth, as the substitute for "Lake George." The name has appeared to find favor, and all things considered, it may possibly be quite as well to let it stand, instead of going back to the House of Hanover for the appellation of our finest sheet of water. We relieve our conscience by the confession, at all events leaving it to exercise its authority as it may see fit.

Chapter 1

"Mine ear is open, and my heart prepared:
The worst is wordly loss thou canst unfold:—
Say, is my kingdom lost?"

—Shakespeare

It was a feature peculiar to the colonial wars of North America, that the toils and dangers of the wilderness were to be encountered before the adverse hosts could meet. A wide and apparently an impervious boundary of forests severed the possessions of the hostile provinces of France and England. The hardy colonist, and the trained European who fought at his side, frequently expended months in struggling against the rapids of the streams, or in effecting the rugged passes of the mountains, in quest of an opportunity to exhibit their courage in a more martial conflict. But, emulating the patience and self-denial of the practiced native warriors, they learned to overcome every difficulty; and it would seem that, in time, there was no recess of the woods so dark, nor any secret place so lovely, that it might claim exemption from the inroads of those who had pledged their blood to satiate their vengeance, or to uphold the cold and selfish policy of the distant monarchs of Europe.

Perhaps no district throughout the wide extent of the intermediate frontiers can furnish a livelier picture of the cruelty and fierceness of the savage warfare of those periods than the country which lies between the head waters of the Hudson and the adjacent lakes.

The facilities which nature had there offered to the march of the combatants were too obvious to be neglected. The lengthened sheet of the Champlain stretched from the frontiers of Canada, deep within the borders of the neighboring province of New York, forming a natural passage across half the distance that the French were compelled to master in order to strike their enemies. Near its southern termination, it received the contributions of another lake, whose waters were so limpid as to have been exclusively selected by the Jesuit missionaries to perform the typical purification of baptism, and to obtain for it the title of lake "du Saint Sacrement." The less zealous English thought they conferred a sufficient honor on its unsullied fountains, when they bestowed the name of their reigning prince, the second of the house of Hanover. The two united to rob the untutored possessors of its wooded scenery of their native right to perpetuate its original appellation of "Horican."*

*As each nation of the Indians had its language or its dialect, they usually gave different names to the same places, though nearly all of their appellations were descriptive of the object. Thus a literal translation of the name of this beautiful sheet of water, used by the tribe that dwelt on its banks, would be "The Tail of the Lake." Lake George, as it is vulgarly, and now, indeed, legally, called, forms a sort of tail to Lake Champlain, when viewed on the map. Hence, the name.

Winding its way among countless islands, and imbedded in mountains, the "holy lake" extended a dozen leagues still further to the south. With the high plain that there interposed itself to the further passage of the water, commenced a portage of as many miles, which conducted the adventurer to the banks of the Hudson, at a point where, with the usual obstructions of the rapids, or rifts, as they were then termed in the language of the country, the river became navigable to the tide.

While, in the pursuit of their daring plans of annoyance, the restless enterprise of the French even attempted the distant and difficult gorges of the Alleghany, it may easily be imagined that their proverbial acuteness would not overlook the natural advantages of the district we have just described. It became, emphatically, the bloody arena, in which most of the battles for the mastery of the colonies were contested. Forts were erected at the different points that commanded the facilities of the route, and were taken and retaken, razed and rebuilt, as victory alighted on the hostile banners. While the husbandman shrank back from the dangerous passes, within the safer boundaries of the more ancient settlements, armies larger than those that had often disposed of the scepters of the mother countries, were seen to bury themselves in these forests, whence they rarely returned but in skeleton bands, that were haggard with care or dejected by defeat. Though the arts of peace were unknown to this fatal region, its forests were alive with men; its shades and glens rang with the sounds of martial music, and the echoes of its mountains threw back the laugh, or repeated the wanton cry, of many a gallant and reckless youth, as he hurried by them, in the noontide of his spirits, to slumber in a long night of forgetfulness.

It was in this scene of strife and bloodshed that the incidents we shall attempt to relate occurred, during the third year of the war which England and France last waged for the possession of a country that neither was destined to retain.

The imbecility of her military leaders abroad, and the fatal want of energy in her councils at home, had lowered the character of Great Britain from the proud elevation on which it had been placed by the talents and enterprise of her former warriors and statesmen. No longer dreaded by her enemies, her servants were fast losing the confidence of self-respect. In this mortifying abasement, the colonists, though innocent of her imbecility, and too humble to be the agents of her blunders, were but the natural participators. They had recently seen a chosen army from that country, which, reverencing as a mother, they had blindly believed invincible—an army led by a chief who had been selected from a crowd of trained warriors, for his rare military endowments, disgracefully routed by a handful of French and Indians, and only saved from annihilation by the coolness and spirit of a Virginian boy, whose riper fame has since diffused itself, with the steady influence of moral truth, to the uttermost confines of Christendom.* A wide frontier had been laid naked by this unexpected disaster, and more substantial evils were preceded by a thousand fanciful and imaginary dangers. The alarmed colonists believed that the yells of the savages mingled with every fitful gust of wind that issued from the interminable forests of the west. The terrific character of their merciless enemies increased immeasurably the natural horrors of warfare. Numberless recent massacres were still vivid in their recollections; nor was there any ear in the provinces so deaf as not to have drunk in with avidity the narrative of some fearful tale of midnight murder, in which the natives of the forests were the principal and barbarous actors. As the credulous and excited traveler related the hazardous chances of the wilderness, the blood of the timid curdled with terror, and mothers cast anxious glances even at those children which slumbered within the security of the largest towns. In short, the magnifying influence of fear began to set at naught the calculations of reason, and to render those who should have remembered their manhood, the slaves of the basest passions. Even the most confident and the stoutest hearts began to think the issue of the contest was becoming doubtful; and that abject class was hourly increasing in numbers, who thought they foresaw all the possessions of the English crown in America subdued by their Christian foes, or laid waste by the inroads of their relentless allies.

*Washington, who, after uselessly admonishing the European general of the danger into which he was heedlessly running, saved the remnants of the British army, on this occasion, by his decision and courage. The reputation earned by Washington in this battle was the principal cause of his being selected to command the American armies at a later day. It is a circumstance worthy of observation, that while all America rang with his well-merited reputation, his name does not occur in any European account of the battle; at least the author has searched for it without success. In

this manner does the mother country absorb even the fame,
under that system of rule.

When, therefore, intelligence was received at the fort which covered the southern termination of the portage between the Hudson and the lakes, that Montcalm had been seen moving up the Champlain, with an army "numerous as the leaves on the trees," its truth was admitted with more of the craven reluctance of fear than with the stern joy that a warrior should feel, in finding an enemy within reach of his blow. The news had been brought, toward the decline of a day in midsummer, by an Indian runner, who also bore an urgent request from Munro, the commander of a work on the shore of the "holy lake," for a speedy and powerful reinforcement. It has already been mentioned that the distance between these two posts was less than five leagues. The rude path, which originally formed their line of communication, had been widened for the passage of wagons; so that the distance which had been traveled by the son of the forest in two hours, might easily be effected by a detachment of troops, with their necessary baggage, between the rising and setting of a summer sun. The loyal servants of the British crown had given to one of these forest-fastnesses the name of William Henry, and to the other that of Fort Edward, calling each after a favorite prince of the reigning family. The veteran Scotchman just named held the first, with a regiment of regulars and a few provincials; a force really by far too small to make head against the formidable power that Montcalm was leading to the foot of his earthen mounds. At the latter, however, lay General Webb, who commanded the armies of the king in the northern provinces, with a body of more than five thousand men. By uniting the several detachments of his command, this officer might have arrayed nearly double that number of combatants against the enterprising Frenchman, who had ventured so far from his reinforcements, with an army but little superior in numbers.

But under the influence of their degraded fortunes, both officers and men appeared better disposed to await the approach of their formidable antagonists, within their works, than to resist the progress of their march, by emulating the successful example of the French at Fort du Quesne, and striking a blow on their advance.

After the first surprise of the intelligence had a little abated, a rumor was spread through the entrenched camp, which stretched along the margin of the Hudson, forming a chain of outworks to the body of the fort itself, that a chosen detachment of fifteen hundred men was to depart, with the dawn, for William Henry, the post at the northern extremity of the portage. That which at first was only rumor, soon became certainty, as orders passed from the quarters of the commander-in-chief to the several corps he had selected for this service, to prepare for their speedy departure. All doubts as to the intention of Webb now vanished, and an hour or two of hurried footsteps and anxious faces succeeded. The novice in the military art flew from point to point, retarding his own preparations by the excess of his violent and somewhat distempered zeal; while the more practiced veteran made his arrangements with a deliberation that scorned every appearance of haste; though his sober lineaments and anxious eye sufficiently betrayed that he had no very strong professional relish for the, as yet, untried and dreaded warfare of the wilderness. At length the sun set in a flood of glory, behind the distant western hills, and as darkness drew its veil around the secluded spot the sounds of preparation diminished; the last light finally disappeared from the log cabin of some officer; the trees cast their deeper shadows over the mounds and the rippling stream, and a silence soon pervaded the camp, as deep as that which reigned in the vast forest by which it was environed.

According to the orders of the preceding night, the heavy sleep of the army was broken by the rolling of the warning drums, whose rattling echoes were heard issuing, on the damp morning air, out of every vista of the woods, just as day began to draw the shaggy outlines of some tall pines of the vicinity, on the opening brightness of a soft and cloudless eastern sky. In an instant the whole camp was in motion; the meanest soldier arousing from his lair to witness the departure of his comrades, and to share in the excitement and incidents of the hour. The simple array of the chosen band was soon completed. While the regular and trained hirelings of the king marched with haughtiness to the right of the line, the less pretending colonists took their humbler position on its left, with a docility that long practice had rendered easy. The scouts departed; strong guards preceded and followed the lumbering vehicles that bore the baggage; and before the gray light of the morning was mellowed by the rays of the sun, the main body of the combatants wheeled into column, and left the encampment with a show of high military bearing, that served to drown the slumbering apprehensions of many a novice, who was now about to make his first essay in arms. While in view of their admiring comrades, the same proud front and ordered array was observed, until the notes of their fifes growing fainter in distance, the forest at length appeared to swallow up the living mass which had slowly entered its bosom.

The deepest sounds of the retiring and invisible column had ceased to be borne on the breeze to the listeners, and the latest straggler had already disappeared in pursuit; but there still remained the signs of another departure, before a log cabin of unusual size and accommodations, in front of which those sentinels paced their rounds, who were known to guard the person of the English general. At this spot were gathered some half dozen horses, caparisoned in a manner which showed that two, at least, were destined to bear the persons of females, of a rank that it was not usual to meet so far in the wilds of the country. A third wore trappings and arms of an officer of the staff; while the rest, from the plainness of the housings, and the traveling mails with which they were encumbered, were evidently fitted for the reception of as many menials, who were, seemingly, already waiting the pleasure of those they served. At a respectful distance from this unusual show, were gathered divers groups of curious idlers; some admiring the blood and bone of the high-mettled military charger, and others gazing at the preparations, with the dull wonder of vulgar curiosity. There was one man, however, who, by his countenance and actions, formed a marked exception to those who composed the latter class of spectators, being neither idle, nor seemingly very ignorant. The person of this individual was to the last degree ungainly, without being in any particular manner deformed. He had all the bones and joints of other men, without any of their proportions. Erect, his stature surpassed that of his fellows; though seated, he appeared reduced within the ordinary limits of the race. The same contrariety in his members seemed to exist throughout the whole man. His head was large; his shoulders narrow; his arms long and dangling; while his hands were small, if not delicate. His legs and thighs were thin, nearly to emaciation, but of extraordinary length; and his knees would have been considered tremendous, had they not been outdone by the broader foundations on which this false superstructure of blended human orders was so profanely reared. The ill-assorted and injudicious attire of the individual only served to render his awkwardness more conspicuous. A sky-blue coat, with short and broad skirts and low cape, exposed a long, thin neck, and longer and thinner legs, to the worst animadversions of the evil-disposed. His nether garment was a yellow nankeen, closely fitted to the shape, and tied at his bunches of knees by large knots of white ribbon, a good deal sullied by use. Clouded cotton stockings, and shoes, on one of the latter of which was a plated spur, completed the costume of the lower extremity of this figure, no curve or angle of which was concealed, but, on the other hand, studiously exhibited, through the vanity or simplicity of its owner.

From beneath the flap of an enormous pocket of a soiled vest of embossed silk, heavily ornamented with tarnished silver lace, projected an instrument, which, from being seen in such martial company, might have been easily mistaken for some mischievous and unknown implement of war. Small as it was, this uncommon engine had excited the curiosity of most of the Europeans in the camp, though several of the provincials were seen to handle it, not only without fear, but with the utmost familiarity. A large, civil cocked hat, like those worn by clergymen within the last thirty years, surmounted the whole, furnishing dignity to a good-natured and somewhat vacant countenance, that apparently needed such artificial aid, to support the gravity of some high and extraordinary trust.

While the common herd stood aloof, in deference to the quarters of Webb, the figure we have described stalked into the center of the domestics, freely expressing his censures or commendations on the merits of the horses, as by chance they displeased or satisfied his judgment.

"This beast, I rather conclude, friend, is not of home raising, but is from foreign lands, or perhaps from the little island itself over the blue water?" he said, in a voice as remarkable for the softness and sweetness of its tones, as was his person for its rare proportions; "I may speak of these things, and be no braggart; for I have been down at both havens; that which is situate at the mouth of Thames, and is named after the capital of Old England, and that which is called 'Haven', with the addition of the word 'New'; and have seen the scows and brigantines collecting their droves, like the gathering to the ark, being outward bound to the Island of Jamaica, for the purpose of barter and traffic in four-footed animals; but never before have I beheld a beast which verified the true scripture war-horse like this: 'He paweth in the valley, and rejoiceth in his strength; he goeth on to meet the armed men. He saith among the trumpets, Ha, ha; and he smelleth the battle afar off, the thunder of the captains, and the shouting' It would seem that the stock of the horse of Israel had descended to our own time; would it not, friend?"

Receiving no reply to this extraordinary appeal, which in truth, as it was delivered with the vigor of full and sonorous tones, merited some sort of notice, he who had thus sung forth the language of the holy book turned to the silent figure to whom he had unwittingly addressed himself, and found a new and more powerful subject of admiration in the object that encountered his gaze. His eyes fell on the still, upright, and rigid form of the "Indian runner," who had borne to the camp the unwelcome tidings of the preceding evening. Although in a state of perfect repose, and apparently disregarding, with characteristic stoicism, the excitement and bustle around him, there was a sullen fierceness mingled with the quiet of the savage, that was likely to arrest the attention of much more experienced eyes than those which now scanned him, in unconcealed amazement. The native bore both the tomahawk and knife of his tribe; and yet his appearance was not altogether that of a warrior. On the contrary, there was an air of neglect about his person, like that which might have proceeded from great and recent exertion, which he had not yet found leisure to repair.

The colors of the war-paint had blended in dark confusion about his fierce countenance, and rendered his swarthy lineaments still more savage and repulsive than if art had attempted an effect which had been thus produced by chance. His eye, alone, which glistened like a fiery star amid lowering clouds, was to be seen in its state of native wildness. For a single instant his searching and yet wary glance met the wondering look of the other, and then changing its direction, partly in cunning, and partly in disdain, it remained fixed, as if penetrating the distant air.

It is impossible to say what unlooked-for remark this short and silent communication, between two such singular men, might have elicited from the white man, had not his active curiosity been again drawn to other objects. A general movement among the domestics, and a low sound of gentle voices, announced the approach of those whose presence alone was wanted to enable the cavalcade to move. The simple admirer of the war-horse instantly fell back to a low, gaunt, switch-tailed mare, that was unconsciously gleaning the faded herbage of the camp nigh by; where, leaning with one elbow on the blanket that concealed an apology for a saddle, he became a spectator of the departure, while a foal was quietly making its morning repast, on the opposite side of the same animal.

A young man, in the dress of an officer, conducted to their steeds two females, who, as it was apparent by their dresses, were prepared to encounter the fatigues of a journey in the woods. One, and she was the more juvenile in her appearance, though both were young, permitted glimpses of her dazzling complexion, fair golden hair, and bright blue eyes, to be caught, as she artlessly suffered the morning air to blow aside the green veil which descended low from her beaver.

The flush which still lingered above the pines in the western sky was not more bright nor delicate than the bloom on her cheek; nor was the opening day more cheering than the animated smile which she bestowed on the youth, as he assisted her into the saddle. The other, who appeared to share equally in the attention of the young officer, concealed her charms from the gaze of the soldiery with a care that seemed better fitted to the experience of four or five additional years. It could be seen, however, that her person, though molded with the same exquisite proportions, of which none of the graces were lost by the traveling dress she wore, was rather fuller and more mature than that of her companion.

No sooner were these females seated, than their attendant sprang lightly into the saddle of the war-horse, when the whole three bowed to Webb, who in courtesy, awaited their parting on the threshold of his cabin and turning their horses' heads, they proceeded at a slow amble, followed by their train, toward the northern entrance of the encampment. As they traversed that short distance, not a voice was heard among them; but a slight exclamation proceeded from the younger of the females, as the Indian runner glided by her, unexpectedly, and led the way along the military road in her front. Though this sudden and startling movement of the Indian produced no sound from the other, in the surprise her veil also was allowed to open its folds, and betrayed an indescribable look of pity, admiration, and horror, as her dark eye followed the easy motions of the savage. The tresses of this lady were shining and black, like the plumage of the raven. Her complexion was not brown, but it rather appeared charged with the color of the rich blood, that seemed ready to burst its bounds. And yet there was neither coarseness nor want of shadowing in a countenance that was exquisitely regular, and dignified and surpassingly beautiful. She smiled, as if in pity at her own momentary forgetfulness, discovering by the act a row of teeth that would have shamed the purest ivory; when, replacing the veil, she bowed her face, and rode in silence, like one whose thoughts were abstracted from the scene around her.

Lighthouse, Tarrytown, NY. There are seven lighthouses on the Hudson River, the most famous of which are the Little Red Lighthouse of literary fame, and the Statue of Liberty (which is used as a navigational marker), c. 1900–1920.

Far up the Hudson's silver flood
I hear the Highlands call
With whispering of leafy boughs
And voice of waterfall.

—*Minna Irving*

CHAPTER 15

George P. Morris and Thomas Cole

George Pope Morris (1802–1864) was born in Philadelphia and worked as a printer. In 1823 he moved to New York City and established a literary weekly, *The New York Mirror*. He founded the *National Press* in 1846. After being joined by N.P. Willis as a partner, the title was changed to the *Home Journal* and was published until 1904, forty years after Pope's death in 1864.

Morris wrote a play, *Briar Cliff* (1826); the libretto of an opera, *The Maid of Saxony*; and edited songbooks *Annie of the Vale* and *American Melodies* (1840). *Deserted Bride and other Poems* (1838) was followed by his *Collected Poems* (1853). He also wrote with Willis *Prose and Poetry of Europe and America* (1853).

His residence called Undercliff was on the banks of the Hudson, near Cold Spring.

Poems. 1853.

The Dog-Star Rages

> *Unseal the city fountains,*
> *And let the waters flow*
> *In coolness from the mountains*
> *Unto the plains below.*
> *My brain is parched and erring,*
> *The pavement hot and dry,*
> *And not a breath is stirring*
> *Beneath the burning sky.*

> *The belles have all departed—*
> *There does not linger one!*
> *Of course the mart's deserted*
> *By every mother's son,*
> *Except the street musician*
> *And men of lesser note,*

Whose only earthly mission
Seems but to toil and vote!

A woman—blessings on her!—
Beneath my window see;
She's singing—what an honor!—
Oh! "Woodman, spare that tree!"
Her "man" the air is killing—
His organ's out of tune—
They're gone, with my last shilling,
To Florence's saloon.

New York is most compactly
Of brick and mortar made—
Thermometer exactly
One hundred in the shade!
A furnace would be safer
Than this my letter-room,
Where gleams the sun, a wafer,
About to seal my doom.

The town looks like an ogre,
The country like a bride;
Wealth hies to Saratoga,
And Worth to Sunny-side.
While fashion seeks the islands
Encircled by the sea,

Taste find the Hudson Highlands
More beautiful and free.

The omnibuses rumble
Along their cobbled way—
The "twelve inside" more humble
Than he who takes the pay:
From morn till midnight stealing,
His horses come and go—
The only creatures feeling
The "luxury of wo!"

We editors of papers,
Who coin our brains for bread
By solitary tapers
While others doze in bed,
Have tasks as sad and lonely,
However wrong or right,
But with this difference only,
The horses rest at night.

From twelve till nearly fifty
I've toiled and idled not,
And, though accounted thrifty,
I'm scarcely worth a groat;
However, I inherit
What few have ever gained—

A bright and cheerful spirit
That never has complained.

A stillness and a sadness
Pervade the City Hall,
And speculating madness
Has left the street of Wall.
The Union Square looks really
Both desolate and dark,
And that's the case, or nearly,
From Battery to Park.

Had I a yacht, like Miller,
That skimmer of the seas—
A wheel rigged on a tiller,
And a fresh gunwale breeze,
A crew of friends well chosen,
And all a-taunto, I
Would sail for regions frozen—
I'd rather freeze than fry.

Oh, this confounded weather!
(As some one sang or said,)
My pen, thought but a feather,
Is heavier than lead;
At every pore I'm oosing—
(I'm "caving in" to-day)—

My plumptitude I'm losing,
And dripping fast away.

I'm weeping like the willow
That droops in leaf and bough—
Let Croton's sparkling billow
Flow through the city now;
And, as becomes her station,
The muse will close her prayer:
God save the Corporation!
Long live the valiant Mayor!

Ida or Where Hudson's Wave

Where Hudson's wave o'er silvery sands
Winds through the hills afar,
Old Cronest like a monarch stands,
Crowned with a single star!
And there, amid the billowy swells
Of rock-ribbed, cloud-capped earth,
My fair and gentle Ida dwells,
A nymph of mountain-birth.

The snow-flake that the cliff receives,
The diamonds of the showers,
Spring's tender blossoms, buds, and leaves,

The sisterhood of flowers,
Morn's early beam, eve's balmy breeze,
Her purity define;
Yet Ida's dearer far than these
To this fond breast of mine.

My heart is on the hills. The shades
Of night are on my brow;
Ye pleasant haunts and quiet glades,
My soul is with you now!
I bless the star-crowned highlands where
My Ida's footsteps roam:
O for a falcon's wing to bear
Me onward to my home!

Up the Hudson
Song and Chorus.

Up the Hudson!—Fleetly gliding
To our haunts among the trees!
Joy the gallant vessel guiding
With a fresh and cheerful breeze!
Wives and dear ones yearn to meet us—
(Hearts that love us to the core!)
And with fond expressions greet us
As we near the welcome shore!

Chorus.

Ho! ye inland seas and islands!—
(Echo follows where we go!)
Ho! ye headlands, hills, and highlands!
Ho! ye Undercliffeans, ho!

Up the Hudson!—Rock and river,
Grove and glen pronounce His praise,
Who, of every "Good the Giver,"
Leads us through these pleasant ways!—
Care recedes like water-traces
Of our bark, as on we glide,
Where the hand of nature graces
Homesteads on the Hudson side!

Chorus.

Ho! ye inland seas and islands!—
(Echo follows where we go!)
Ho! ye headlands, hills, and highlands!
Ho! ye Undercliffeans, ho!

Thomas Cole (February 1, 1801–February 11, 1848) was a nine-teenth-century American artist regarded as the founder of the Hudson River School, an American art movement that flourished in the mid-19th century. He also dabbled in architecture and poetry.

Born in England, his family emigrated in 1818. He studied art at the Pennsylvania Academy of the Fine Arts in Philadelphia, then moved with his family to New York City in 1825.

He spent a summer in the Hudson Valley painting landscapes, and upon his return to New York sold works to John Trumbull and became friends with the artists Asher B. Durand and

Thomas Cole, photographed by Mathew Brady's Studio, c. 1844–1848.

William Dunlap. The most famous of his allegorical paintings are "The Course of Empire" and "The Voyage of Life." After 1827 he painted a significant portion of his work in his studio in Catskill, New York. Cole influenced other artists, particularly Asher B. Durand and Frederic Edwin Church, who studied with Cole from 1844 to 1846. Cole spent the years 1829 to 1832 and 1841–1842 in England and Italy.

In 1836 he married Maria Bartow of Catskill, and became a year-round resident. He died at Catskill on February 11, 1848. The fourth-highest peak in the Catskills is named Thomas Cole Mountain in his honor.

The Wild.

Friends of my heart, lovers of Nature's works,
Let me transport you to those wild blue mountains
That rear their summits near the Hudson's wave
Though not the loftiest that begirt the land,
They yet sublimely rise, and on their heights
Your souls may have a sweet foretaste of heaven,
And traverse wide the boundless.

From this rock
The nearest to the sky, let us look out
Upon the earth, as the first swell of day
Is bearing back the duskiness of night.
But lo! a sea of mist o'er all beneath;
An ocean, shoreless, motionless and mute,
No rolling swell is there, no sounding surf;
Silent and solemn all; the stormy main
To stillness frozen, while the crested waves
Leaped in the whirlwind, and the loosen'd foam
Flew o'er the angry deep.

See! now ascends
The Lord of Day, waking with pearly fire
The dormant depths. See how his glowing breath
The rising surges kindles; lo! they heave
Like golden sands upon Sahara's gales.
Those airy forms disporting from the mass,

Like winged ships, sail o'er the wondrous plain
Beautiful vision! Now the veil is rent,
And the coy earth her virgin bosom bares,
Slowly unfolding to the enraptured gaze
Her thousand charms.

John Burroughs, c. 1900–1920.

Ah! how often when I have been abroad on the mountains has my heart risen in grateful praise to God that it was not my destiny to waste and pine among those noisome congregations of the city.

—John James Audubon

John Burroughs (April 3, 1837–March 29, 1921) was an American naturalist and essayist.

Born in the Catskills, he taught school and married Ursula North in 1857. In 1864, Burroughs became a clerk at the Treasury Department in Washington, D.C., and become a federal bank examiner, which he did until the 1880s. Burroughs met Walt Whitman in Washington during the Civil War, and Whitman encouraged Burroughs to develop his nature writing as well as his philosophical and literary essays.

His books and essays increased his popularity. They include *Notes on Walt Whitman as Poet and Person* (1867); *Wake-Robin* (1871); *Winter Sunshine* (1875); *Birds and Poets* (1877); *Locust and Wild Honey* (1879); *Pepaction* (1881); *Fresh Fields* (1884); *Signs and Seasons* (1886); *Riverby* (1894); *Far and Near* (1904); *Ways of Nature* (1905); *Indoor Studies* (1894); *Bird and Bough* (1906); *Camping and Tramping with Roosevelt* (1907); and *Leaf and Tendril* (1908).

In 1874 he settled on a farm at West Park, New York, and also had a summer home in the Catskills called Woodchuck Lodge. Later he bought some land, and in the fall of 1894, began work on a cabin that would be called "Slabsides."

He wrote more than 30 books and published hundreds of essays and poems in magazines. In the late 1880s, in the essay "The Heart of the Southern Catskills," he chronicled an ascent of Slide Mountain, the highest peak of the Catskills range. Slide and neighboring Cornell and Wittenberg mountains, which he also climbed, have been collectively named the Burroughs Range.

Burroughs knew many famous persons of the time, including Theodore Roosevelt, Thomas Edison, John Muir, E.H. Harriman, Henry Ford, and Harvey Firestone.

Burroughs met Clara Barrus in 1901, when she was nearly half his age. She moved into his house after Ursula died in 1917 and was his literary executrix.

He died on a train returning from California in the spring of 1921. He was buried in Roxbury, on the anniversary of his 84th birthday, at the foot of a rock he had played upon as a child. His three homes are all on the National Register of Historic Places.

In the words of his biographer Edward Renehan, Burroughs's special identity was less that of a scientific naturalist than that of "a literary naturalist with a duty to record his own unique perceptions of the natural world."

In the Catskills: Selections from the Writings of John Burroughs. 1910.

The Heart of the Southern Catskills

On looking at the southern and more distant Catskills from the Hudson River on the east, or on looking at them from the west from some point of vantage in Delaware County, you see, amid the group of mountains, one that looks like the back and shoulders of a gigantic horse. The horse has got his head down grazing; the shoulders are high, and the descent from them down his neck very steep; if he were to lift up his head, one sees that it would be carried far above all other peaks, and that the noble beast might gaze straight to his peers in the Adirondacks or the White Mountains. But the lowered head never comes up; some spell or enchantment keeps it down there amid the mighty herd; and the high round shoulders and the smooth strong back of the steed are alone visible. The peak to which I refer is Slide Mountain, the highest of the Catskills by some two hundred feet, and probably the most inaccessible; certainly the hardest to get a view of, it is hedged about so completely by other peaks,—the greatest mountain of them all, and apparently the least willing to be seen; only at a distance of thirty or forty miles is it seen to stand up above all other peaks. It takes its name from a landslide which occurred many years ago down its steep northern side, or down the neck of the grazing steed. The mane of spruce and balsam fir was stripped away for many hundred feet, leaving a long gray streak visible from afar.

Slide Mountain is the center and the chief of the southern Catskills. Streams flow from its base, and from the base of its subordinates, to all points of the compass,—the Rondout and the Neversink to the south; the Beaverkill to the west; the Esopus to the north; and several lesser streams to the east. With its summit as the center, a radius of ten miles would include within the circle described but very little cultivated land; only a few poor, wild farms in some of the numerous valleys. The soil is poor, a mixture of gravel and clay, and is subject to slides. It lies in the valleys in ridges and small hillocks, as if dumped there from a huge cart. The tops of the southern Catskills are all capped with a kind of conglomerate, or "pudden stone,"—a rock of cemented quartz pebbles which underlies the coal measures. This rock disintegrates under the action of the elements, and the sand and gravel which result are carried into the valleys and make up the most of the soil. From the northern Catskills, so far as I know them, this rock has been swept clean. Low down in the valleys the old red sandstone crops out, and, as you go west into

Delaware County, in many places it alone remains and makes up most of the soil, all the superincumbent rock having been carried away.

Slide Mountain had been a summons and a challenge to me for many years. I had fished every stream that it nourished, and had camped in the wilderness on all sides of it, and whenever I had caught a glimpse of its summit I had promised myself to set foot there before another season should pass. But the seasons came and went, and my feet got no nimbler, and Slide Mountain no lower, until finally, one July, seconded by an energetic friend, we thought to bring Slide to terms by approaching him through the mountains on the east. With a farmer's son for guide we struck in by way of Weaver Hollow, and, after a long and desperate climb, contented ourselves with the Wittenberg, instead of Slide. The view from the Wittenberg is in many respects more striking, as you are perched immediately above a broader and more distant sweep of country, and are only about two hundred feet lower. You are here on the eastern brink of the southern Catskills, and the earth falls away at your feet and curves down through an immense stretch of forest till it joins the plain of Shokan, and thence sweeps away to the Hudson and beyond. Slide is southwest of you, six or seven miles distant, but is visible only when you climb into a treetop. I climbed and saluted him, and promised to call next time.

We passed the night on the Wittenberg, sleeping on the moss, between two decayed logs, with balsam boughs thrust into the ground and meeting and forming a canopy over us. In coming off the mountain in the morning we ran upon a huge porcupine, and I learned for the first time that the tail of a porcupine goes with a spring like a trap. It seems to be a set-lock; and you no sooner touch with the weight of a hair one of the quills than the tail leaps up in a most surprising manner, and the laugh is not on your side. The beast cantered along the path in my front, and I threw myself upon him, shielded by my roll of blankets. He submitted quietly to the indignity, and lay very still under my blankets, with his broad tail pressed close to the ground. This I proceeded to investigate, but had not fairly made a beginning when it went off like a trap, and my hand and wrist were full of quills. This caused me to let up on the creature, when it lumbered away till it tumbled down a precipice. The quills were quickly removed from my hand, when we gave chase. When we came up to him, he had wedged himself in between the rocks so that he presented only a back bristling with quills, with the tail lying in ambush below. He had chosen his position well, and seemed to defy us. After amusing ourselves by repeatedly springing his tail and receiving the quills in a rotten stick, we made a slip-noose out of a spruce root, and, after much manoeuvring, got it over his head and led him forth. In what a peevish, injured tone the creature did complain of our unfair tactics! He protested and protested, and whimpered and scolded like some infirm old man tormented by boys. His game after we led him forth was to keep himself as much as possible in the shape of a ball, but with two sticks and the cord we finally threw him over on his back and exposed his quill-less and vulnerable under side, when he fairly surrendered and seemed to say, "Now you may do with me as you like." His great chisel-like teeth, which are quite as formidable as those of the woodchuck, he does not appear to use at all in his defense, but relies entirely upon his quills, and when those fail him, he is done for.

⌒⌒

After amusing ourselves with him awhile longer, we released him and went on our way. The trail to which we had committed ourselves led us down into Woodland Valley, a retreat which so took my eye by its fine trout brook, its superb mountain scenery, and its sweet seclusion, that I marked it for my own, and promised myself a return to it at no distant day. This promise I kept, and pitched my tent there twice during that season. Both occasions were a sort of laying siege to Slide, but we only skirmished with him at a distance; the actual assault was not undertaken. But the following year, reinforced by two other brave climbers, we determined upon the assault, and upon making it from this the most difficult side. The regular way is by Big Ingin Valley, where the climb is comparatively easy, and where it is often made by women. But from Woodland Valley only men may essay the ascent. Larkins is the upper inhabitant, and from our camping-ground near his clearing we set out early one June morning.

One would think nothing could be easier to find than a big mountain, especially when one is encamped upon a stream which he knows springs out of its very loins. But for some reason or other we had got an idea that Slide Mountain was a very slippery customer and must be approached cautiously. We had tried from several points in the valley to get a view of it, but were not quite sure we had seen its very head. When on the Wittenberg, a neighboring peak, the year before, I had caught a brief glimpse of it only by climbing a dead tree and craning up for a moment from its topmost branch. It would seem as if the mountain had taken every precaution to shut itself off from a near view. It was a shy mountain, and we were about to stalk it through six or seven miles of primitive woods, and we seemed to have some unreasonable fear that it might elude us. We had been told of parties who had essayed the ascent from this side, and had returned baffled and bewildered. In a tangle of primitive woods, the very bigness of the mountain baffles one. It is all mountain; whichever way you turn—and one turns sometimes in such cases before he knows it—the foot finds a steep and rugged ascent.

The eye is of little service; one must be sure of his bearings and push boldly on and up. One is not unlike a flea upon a great shaggy beast, looking for the animal's head; or even like a much smaller and much less nimble creature,—he may waste his time and steps, and think he has reached the head when he is only upon the rump. Hence I questioned our host, who had several times made the ascent, closely. Larkins laid his old felt hat upon the table, and, placing one hand upon one side of it and the other upon the other, said: "There Slide lies, between the two forks of the stream, just as my hat lies between my two hands. David will go with you to the forks, and then you will push right on up." But Larkins was not right, though he had traversed all those mountains many times over. The peak we were about to set out for did not lie between the forks, but exactly at the head of one of them; the beginnings of the stream are in the very path of the slide, as we afterward found. We broke camp early in the morning, and with our blankets strapped to our backs and rations in our pockets for two days, set out along an ancient and in places an obliterated bark road that followed and crossed and recrossed the stream. The morning was bright and warm, but the wind was fitful and petulant, and I predicted rain. What a forest solitude our obstructed and dilapidated wood-road led us through! Five miles of primitive woods before we came to the forks, three miles before we came to the "burnt shanty," a name merely,—no shanty there now for twenty-five years past. The ravages of the barkpeelers were still visible, now in a space thickly strewn with the soft and decayed trunks of hemlock-trees, and overgrown with wild cherry, then in huge mossy logs scattered through the beech and maple woods. Some of these logs were so soft and mossy that one could sit or recline upon them as upon a sofa.

But the prettiest thing was the stream soliloquizing in such musical tones there amid the moss-covered rocks and boulders. How clean it looked, what purity! Civilization corrupts the streams as it corrupts the Indian; only in such remote woods can you now see a brook in all its original freshness and beauty. Only the sea and the mountain forest brook are pure; all between is contaminated more or less by the work of man. An ideal trout brook was this, now hurrying, now loitering, now deepening around a great boulder, now gliding evenly over a pavement of green-gray stone and pebbles; no sediment or stain of any kind, but white and sparkling as snow-water, and nearly as cool. Indeed, the water of all this Catskill region is the best in the world. For the first few days, one feels as if he could almost live on the water alone; he cannot drink enough of it. In this particular it is indeed the good Bible land, "a land of brooks of water, of fountains and depths that spring out of valleys and hills."

Near the forks we caught, or thought we caught, through an opening, a glimpse of Slide. Was it Slide? was it the head, or the rump, or the shoulder of the shaggy monster we were in quest of? At the forks there was a bewildering maze of underbrush and great trees, and the way did not seem at all certain; nor was David, who was then at the end of his reckoning, able to reassure us. But in assaulting a mountain, as in assaulting a fort, boldness is the watchword. We pressed forward, following a line of blazed trees for nearly a mile, then, turning to the left, began the ascent of the mountain. It was steep, hard climbing. We saw numerous marks of both bears and deer; but no birds, save at long intervals the winter wren flitting here and there, and darting under logs and rubbish like a mouse. Occasionally its gushing, lyrical song would break the silence. After we had climbed an hour or two, the clouds began to gather, and presently the rain began to come down. This was discouraging; but we put our backs up against trees and rocks, and waited for the shower to pass.

"They were wet with the showers of the mountain, and embraced the rocks for want of shelter," as they did in Job's time.

But the shower was light and brief, and we were soon under way again. Three hours from the forks brought us out on the broad level back of the mountain upon which Slide, considered as an isolated peak, is reared. After a time we entered a dense growth of spruce which covered a slight depression in the table of the mountain. The moss was deep, the ground spongy, the light dim, the air hushed. The transition from the open, leafy woods to this dim, silent, weird grove was very marked. It was like the passage from the street into the temple. Here we paused awhile and ate our lunch, and refreshed ourselves with water gathered from a little well sunk in the moss.

The quiet and repose of this spruce grove proved to be the calm that goes before the storm. As we passed out of it, we came plump upon the almost perpendicular battlements of Slide. The mountain rose like a huge, rock-bound fortress from this plain-like expanse. It was ledge upon ledge, precipice upon precipice, up which and over which we made our way slowly and with great labor, now pulling ourselves up by our hands, then cautiously finding niches for our feet and zigzagging right and left from shelf to shelf. This northern side of the mountain was thickly covered with moss and lichens, like the north side of a tree. This made it soft to the foot, and broke many a slip and fall. Everywhere a stunted growth of yellow birch, mountain-ash, and spruce and fir opposed our progress. The ascent at such an angle with a roll of blankets on your back is not unlike climbing a tree: every limb resists your progress and pushes you back; so that when we at last reached the summit, after twelve or fifteen hundred feet of this sort of work, the fight was about all out of the best of us. It was then nearly two o'clock, so that we had been about seven hours in coming seven miles.

Here on the top of the mountain we overtook spring, which had been gone from the valley nearly a month. Red clover was opening in the valley below, and wild strawberries just ripening; on the summit the yellow birch was just hanging out its catkins, and the claytonia, or spring-beauty, was in bloom. The leaf-buds of the trees were just bursting, making a faint mist of green, which, as the eye swept downward, gradually deepened until it became a dense, massive cloud in the valleys. At the foot of the mountain the clintonia, or northern green lily, and the low shadbush were showing their berries, but long before the top was reached they were found in bloom. I had never before stood amid blooming claytonia, a flower of April, and looked down upon a field that held ripening strawberries. Every thousand feet elevation seemed to make about ten days' difference in the vegetation, so that the season was a month or more later on the top of the mountain than at its base. A very pretty flower which we began to meet with well up on the mountain-side was the painted trillium, the petals white, veined with pink.

The low, stunted growth of spruce and fir which clothes the top of Slide has been cut away over a small space on the highest point, laying open the view on nearly all sides. Here we sat down and enjoyed our triumph. We saw the world as the hawk or the balloonist sees it when he is three thousand feet in the air. How soft and flowing all the outlines of the hills and moun-

tains beneath us looked! The forests dropped down and undu-
lated away over them, covering them like a carpet. To the east
we looked over the near-by Wittenberg range to the Hudson and
beyond; to the south, Peak-o'-Moose, with its sharp crest, and
Table Mountain, with its long level top, were the two conspicuous
objects; in the west, Mt. Graham and Double Top, about three
thousand eight hundred feet each, arrested the eye; while in our
front to the north we looked over the top of Panther Mountain
to the multitudinous peaks of the northern Catskills. All was
mountain and forest on every hand. Civilization seemed to have
done little more than to have scratched this rough, shaggy surface of the earth here and there. In any such view, the wild, the
aboriginal, the geographical greatly predominate. The works of
man dwindle, and the original features of the huge globe come
out. Every single object or point is dwarfed; the valley of the
Hudson is only a wrinkle in the earth's surface. You discover
with a feeling of surprise that the great thing is the earth itself,
which stretches away on every hand so far beyond your ken.

The Arabs believe that the mountains steady the earth and
hold it together; but they have only to get on the top of a high
one to see how insignificant mountains are, and how adequate
the earth looks to get along without them. To the imaginative
Oriental people, mountains seemed to mean much more than
they do to us. They were sacred; they were the abodes of their
divinities. They offered their sacrifices upon them. In the Bible,
mountains are used as a symbol of that which is great and holy.
Jerusalem is spoken of as a holy mountain. The Syrians were

beaten by the Children of Israel because, said they, "their gods are gods of the hills; therefore were they stronger than we." It was on Mount Horeb that God appeared to Moses in the burning bush, and on Sinai that He delivered to him the law. Josephus says that the Hebrew shepherds never pasture their flocks on Sinai, believing it to be the abode of Jehovah. The solitude of mountain-tops is peculiarly impressive, and it is certainly easier to believe the Deity appeared in a burning bush there than in the valley below. When the clouds of heaven, too, come down and envelop the top of the mountain,—how such a circumstance must have impressed the old God-fearing Hebrews! Moses knew well how to surround the law with the pomp and circumstance that would inspire the deepest awe and reverence.

But when the clouds came down and enveloped us on Slide Mountain, the grandeur, the solemnity, were gone in a twinkling; the portentous-looking clouds proved to be nothing but base fog that wet us and extinguished the world for us. How tame, and prosy, and humdrum the scene instantly became! But when the fog lifted, and we looked from under it as from under a just-raised lid, and the eye plunged again like an escaped bird into those vast gulfs of space that opened at our feet, the feeling of grandeur and solemnity quickly came back.

The first want we felt on the top of Slide, after we had got some rest, was a want of water. Several of us cast about, right and left, but no sign of water was found. But water must be had, so we all started off deliberately to hunt it up. We had not gone many hundred yards before we chanced upon an ice-cave beneath some rocks,—vast masses of ice, with crystal pools of water near. This was good luck, indeed, and put a new and a brighter face on the situation.

Slide Mountain enjoys a distinction which no other mountain in the State, so far as is known, does,—it has a thrush peculiar to itself. This thrush was discovered and described by Eugene P. Bicknell, of New York, in 1880, and has been named Bicknell's thrush. A better name would have been Slide Mountain thrush, as the bird so far has been found only on this mountain.[1] I did not see or hear it upon the Wittenberg, which is only a few miles distant, and only two hundred feet lower. In its appearance to the eye among the trees, one would not distinguish it from the gray-cheeked thrush of Baird, or the olive-backed thrush, but its song is totally different. The moment I heard it I said, "There is a new bird, a new thrush," for the quality of all thrush songs is the same. A moment more, and I knew it was Bicknell's thrush. The song is in a minor key, finer, more attenuated, and more under the breath than that of any other thrush. It seemed as if the bird was blowing in a delicate, slender, golden tube, so fine and yet so flute-like and resonant the song appeared. At times it was like a musical whisper of great sweetness and power. The birds were numerous about the summit, but we saw them nowhere else. No other thrush was seen, though a few times during our stay I caught a mere echo of the hermit's song far down the mountainside. A bird I was not prepared to see or to hear was the black-poll warbler, a bird usually found much farther north, but here it was, amid the balsam firs, uttering its simple, lisping song.

[Footnote 1: Bicknell's thrush turns out to be the more southern form of the gray-cheeked thrush, and is found on the higher mountains of New York and New England.]

The rocks on the tops of these mountains are quite sure to attract one's attention, even if he have no eye for such things. They are masses of light reddish conglomerate, composed of round wave-worn quartz pebbles. Every pebble has been shaped and polished upon some ancient seacoast, probably the Devonian. The rock disintegrates where it is most exposed to the weather, and forms a loose sandy and pebbly soil. These rocks form the floor of the coal formation, but in the Catskill region only the floor remains; the superstructure has never existed, or has been swept away; hence one would look for a coal mine here over his head in the air, rather than under his feet.

This rock did not have to climb up here as we did; the mountain stooped and took it upon its back in the bottom of the old seas, and then got lifted up again. This happened so long ago that the memory of the oldest inhabitants of these parts yields no clew to the time.

A pleasant task we had in reflooring and reroofing the log-hut with balsam boughs against the night. Plenty of small balsams grew all about, and we soon had a huge pile of their branches in the old hut. What a transformation, this fresh green carpet and our fragrant bed, like the deep-furred robe of some huge animal, wrought in that dingy interior! Two or three things disturbed our sleep. A cup of strong beef-tea taken for supper disturbed mine; then the porcupines kept up such a grunting and chattering near our heads, just on the other side of the log, that sleep was difficult. In my wakeful mood I was a good deal annoyed by a little rabbit that kept whipping in at our dilapidated door and nibbling at our bread and hardtack. He persisted even after the gray of the morning appeared. Then about four o'clock it began gently to rain. I think I heard the first drop that fell. My companions were all in sound sleep. The rain increased, and gradually the sleepers awoke. It was like the tread of an advancing enemy which every ear had been expecting. The roof over us was of the poorest, and we had no confidence in it. It was made of the thin bark of spruce and balsam, and was full of hollows and depressions. Presently these hollows got full of water, when there was a simultaneous downpour of bigger and lesser rills upon the sleepers beneath. Said sleepers, as one man, sprang up, each taking his blanket with him; but by the time some of the party had got themselves stowed away under the adjacent rock, the rain ceased. It was little more than the dissolving of the nightcap of fog which so often hangs about these heights. With the first appearance of the dawn I had heard the new thrush in the scattered trees near the hut,—a strain as fine as if blown upon a fairy flute, a suppressed musical whisper from out the tops of the dark spruces. Probably never did there go up from the top of a great mountain a smaller song to greet the day, albeit it was of the purest harmony. It seemed to have in a more marked degree the quality of interior reverberation than any other thrush song I had ever heard. Would the altitude or the situation account for its minor key? Loudness would avail little in such a place. Sounds are not far heard on a mountain-top; they are lost in the abyss of vacant air. But amid these low, dense, dark spruces, which make a sort of canopied privacy of every square rod of ground, what could be more in keeping than this delicate musical whisper? It was but the soft hum of the balsams, interpreted and embodied in a bird's voice.

It was the plan of two of our companions to go from Slide over into the head of the Rondout, and thence out to the railroad at the little village of Shokan, an unknown way to them, involving nearly an all-day pull the first day through a pathless wilderness. We ascended to the topmost floor of the tower, and from my knowledge of the topography of the country I pointed out to them their course, and where the valley of the Rondout must lie. The vast stretch of woods, when it came into view from under the foot of Slide, seemed from our point of view very uniform. It swept away to the southeast, rising gently toward the ridge that separates Lone Mountain from Peak-o'-Moose, and presented a comparatively easy problem. As a clew to the course, the line where the dark belt or saddle-cloth of spruce, which covered the top of the ridge they were to skirt, ended, and the deciduous woods began, a sharp, well-defined line was pointed out as the course to be followed. It led straight to the top of the broad level-backed ridge which connected two higher peaks, and immediately behind which lay the headwaters of the Rondout. Having studied the map thoroughly, and possessed themselves of the points, they rolled up their blankets about nine o'clock, and were off, my friend and I purposing to spend yet another day and night on Slide. As our friends plunged down into that fearful abyss, we shouted to them the old classic caution, "Be bold, be bold, "be not too bold." It required courage to make such a leap into the unknown, as I knew those young men were making, and it required prudence. A faint heart or a bewildered head, and serious consequences might have resulted. The theory of a thing is so much easier than the practice! The theory is in the air, the practice is in the woods; the eye, the thought, travel easily where the foot halts and stumbles. However, our friends made the theory and the fact coincide; they kept the dividing line between the spruce and the birches, and passed over the ridge into the valley safely; but they were torn and bruised and wet by the showers, and made the last few miles of their journey on will and pluck alone, their last pound of positive strength having been exhausted in making the descent through the chaos of rocks and logs into the head of the valley. In such emergencies one overdraws his account; he travels on the credit of the strength he expects to gain when he gets his dinner and some sleep. Unless one has made such a trip himself (and I have several times in my life), he can form but a faint idea what it is like,—what a trial it is to the body, and what a trial it is to the mind. You are fighting a battle with an enemy in ambush. How those miles and leagues which your feet must compass lie hidden there in that wilderness; how they seem to multiply themselves; how they are fortified with logs, and rocks, and fallen trees; how they take refuge in deep gullies, and skulk behind unexpected eminences! Your body not only feels the fatigue of the battle, your mind feels the strain of the undertaking; you may miss your mark; the mountains may outmanoeuvre you. All that day, whenever I looked upon that treacherous wilderness, I thought with misgivings of those two friends groping their way there, and would have given much to know how it fared with them. Their concern was probably less than my own, because they were more ignorant of what was before them. Then there was just a slight shadow of a fear in my mind that I might have been in error about some points of the geography I had pointed out to them. But all was well, and the victory was won according to the campaign which I had planned. When we saluted our friends upon their own doorstep a week afterward, the wounds were nearly healed and the rents all mended.

When one is on a mountain-top, he spends most of the time in looking at the show he has been at such pains to see. About every hour we would ascend the rude lookout to take a fresh observation. With a glass I could see my native hills forty miles away to the northwest. I was now upon the back of the horse, yea, upon the highest point of his shoulders, which had so many times attracted my attention as a boy. We could look along his balsam-covered back to his rump, from which the eye glanced away down into the forests of the Neversink, and on the other hand plump down into the gulf where his head was grazing or drinking. During the day there was a grand procession of thunderclouds filing along over the northern Catskills, and letting down veils of rain and enveloping them. From such an elevation one has the same view of the clouds that he does from the prairie or the ocean. They do not seem to rest across and to be upborne by the hills, but they emerge out of the dim west, thin and vague, and grow and stand up as they get nearer and roll by him, on a level but invisible highway, huge chariots of wind and storm.

In the afternoon a thick cloud threatened us, but it proved to be the condensation of vapor that announces a cold wave. There was soon a marked fall in the temperature, and as night drew near it became pretty certain that we were going to have a cold time of it. The wind rose, the vapor above us thickened and came nearer, until it began to drive across the summit in slender wraiths, which curled over the brink and shut out the view. We became very diligent in getting in our night wood, and in gathering more boughs to calk up the openings in the hut. The wood we scraped together was a sorry lot, roots and stumps and branches of decayed spruce, such as we could collect without an axe, and some rags and tags of birch bark. The fire was built in one corner of the shanty, the smoke finding easy egress through large openings on the east side and in the roof over it. We doubled up the bed, making it thicker and more nest-like, and as darkness set in, stowed ourselves into it beneath our blankets. The searching wind found out every crevice about our heads and shoulders, and it was icy cold. Yet we fell asleep, and had slept about an hour when my companion sprang up in an unwonted state of excitement for so placid a man. His excitement was occasioned by the sudden discovery that what appeared to be a bar of ice was fast taking the place of his backbone. His teeth chattered, and he was convulsed with ague. I advised him to replenish the fire, and to wrap himself in his blanket and cut the liveliest capers he was capable of in so circumscribed a place. This he promptly did, and the thought of his wild and desperate dance there in the dim light, his tall form, his blanket flapping, his teeth chattering, the porcupines outside marking time with their squeals and grunts, still provokes a smile, though it was a serious enough matter at the time. After a while, the warmth came back to him, but he dared not trust himself again to the boughs; he fought the cold all night as one might fight a besieging foe. By carefully husbanding the fuel, the beleaguering enemy was kept at bay till morning came; but when morning did come, even the huge root he had used as a chair was consumed. Rolled in my blanket beneath a foot or more of balsam boughs, I had got some fairly good sleep, and was most of the time oblivious of the melancholy vigil of my friend. As we had but a few morsels of food left, and had been on rather short rations the day before, hunger was added to his other discomforts. At that time a letter was on the way to him from his wife, which contained this prophetic sentence: "I hope thee is not suffering with cold and hunger on some lone mountain-top."

Mr. Bicknell's thrush struck up again at the first signs of dawn, notwithstanding the cold. I could hear his penetrating and melodious whisper as I lay buried beneath the boughs. Presently I arose and invited my friend to turn in for a brief nap, while I gathered some wood and set the coffee brewing. With a brisk, roaring fire on, I left for the spring to fetch some water, and to make my toilet. The leaves of the mountain goldenrod, which everywhere covered the ground in the opening, were covered with frozen particles of vapor, and the scene, shut in by fog, was chill and dreary enough.

We were now not long in squaring an account with Slide, and making ready to leave. Round pellets of snow began to fall, and we came off the mountain on the 10th of June in a November storm and temperature. Our purpose was to return by the same valley we had come. A well-defined trail led off the summit to the north; to this we committed ourselves. In a few minutes we emerged at the head of the slide that had given the mountain its name. This was the path made by visitors to the scene; when it ended, the track of the avalanche began; no bigger than your hand, apparently, had it been at first, but it rapidly grew, until it became several rods in width. It dropped down from our feet straight as an arrow until it was lost in the fog, and looked perilously steep. The dark forms of the spruce were clinging to the edge of it, as if reaching out to their fellows to save them. We hesitated on the brink, but finally cautiously began the descent. The rock was quite naked and slippery, and only on the margin of the slide were there any boulders to stay the foot, or bushy growths to aid the hand. As we paused, after some minutes, to select our course, one of the finest surprises of the trip awaited us: the fog in our front was swiftly whirled up by the breeze, like the drop-curtain at the theatre, only much more rapidly, and in a twinkling the vast gulf opened before us. It was so sudden as to be almost bewildering. The world opened like a book, and there were the pictures; the spaces were without a film, the forests and mountains looked surprisingly near; in the heart of the northern Catskills a wild valley was seen flooded with sunlight. Then the curtain ran down again, and nothing was left but the gray strip of rock to which we clung, plunging down into the obscurity. Down and down we made our way. Then the fog lifted again. It was Jack and his beanstalk renewed; new wonders, new views, awaited us every few moments, till at last the whole valley below us stood in the clear sunshine. We passed down a precipice, and there was a rill of water, the beginning of the creek that wound through the valley below; farther on, in a deep depression, lay the remains of an old snow-bank; Winter had made his last stand here, and April flowers were springing up almost amid his very bones. We did not find a palace, and a hungry giant, and a princess, at the end of our beanstalk, but we found a humble roof and the hospitable heart of Mrs. Larkins, which answered our purpose better. And we were in the mood, too, to have undertaken an eating-bout with any giant Jack ever discovered.

Of all the retreats I have found amid the Catskills, there is no other that possesses quite so many charms for me as this valley, wherein stands Larkins's humble dwelling; it is so wild, so quiet, and has such superb mountain views. In coming up the valley, you have apparently reached the head of civilization a mile or more lower down; here the rude little houses end, and you turn to the left into the woods. Presently you emerge into a clearing again, and before you rises the rugged and indented crest of Panther Mountain, and near at hand, on a low plateau, rises the humble roof of Larkins,—you get a picture of the Panther and of the homestead at one glance. Above the house hangs a high, bold cliff covered with forest, with a broad fringe of blackened and blasted tree-trunks, where the cackling of the great pileated woodpecker may be heard; on the left a dense forest sweeps up to the sharp spruce-covered cone of the Wittenberg, nearly four thousand feet high, while at the head of the valley rises Slide over all. From a meadow just back of Larkins's barn, a view may be had of all these mountains, while the terraced side of Cross Mountain bounds the view immediately to the east. Running from the top of Panther toward Slide one sees a gigantic wall of rock, crowned with a dark line of fir. The forest abruptly ends, and in its stead rises the face of this colossal rocky escarpment, like some barrier built by the mountain gods. Eagles might nest here. It breaks the monotony of the world of woods very impressively.

I delight in sitting on a rock in one of these upper fields, and seeing the sun go down behind Panther. The rapid-flowing brook below me fills all the valley with a soft murmur. There is no breeze, but the great atmospheric tide flows slowly in toward the cooling forest; one can see it by the motes in the air illuminated by the setting sun: presently, as the air cools a little, the tide turns and flows slowly out. The long, winding valley up to the foot of Slide, five miles of primitive woods, how wild and cool it looks, its one voice the murmur of the creek! On the Wittenberg the sunshine lingers long; now it stands up like an island in a sea of shadows, then slowly sinks beneath the wave. The evening call of a robin or a veery at his vespers makes a marked impression on the silence and the solitude.

The following day my friend and I pitched our tent in the woods beside the stream where I had pitched it twice before, and passed several delightful days, with trout in abundance and wild strawberries at intervals. Mrs. Larkins's cream-pot, butter-jar, and bread-box were within easy reach. Near the camp was an unusually large spring, of icy coldness, which served as our refrigerator. Trout or milk immersed in this spring in a tin pail would keep sweet four or five days. One night some creature, probably a lynx or a raccoon, came and lifted the stone from the pail that held the trout and took out a fine string of them, and ate them up on the spot, leaving only the string and one head. In August bears come down to an ancient and now brushy bark-peeling near by for blackberries. But the creature that most infests these backwoods is the porcupine. He is as stupid and indifferent as the skunk; his broad, blunt nose points a witless head. They are great gnawers, and will gnaw your house down if you do not look out. Of a summer evening they will walk coolly into your open door if not prevented. The most annoying animal to the camper-out in this region, and the one he needs to be most on the lookout for, is the cow. Backwoods cows and young cattle seem always to be famished for salt, and they will fairly lick the fisherman's clothes off his back, and his tent and equipage out of existence, if you give them a chance. On one occasion some wood-ranging heifers and steers that had been hovering around our camp for some days made a raid upon it when we were absent. The tent was shut and everything snugged up, but they ran their long tongues under the tent, and, tasting something savory, hooked out John Stuart Mill's "Essays on Religion," which one of us had brought along, thinking to read in the woods. They mouthed the volume around a good deal, but its logic was too tough for them, and they contented themselves with devouring the paper in which it was wrapped. If the cattle had not been surprised at just that point, it is probable the tent would have gone down before their eager curiosity and thirst for salt.

The raid which Larkins's dog made upon our camp was amusing rather than annoying. He was a very friendly and intelligent shepherd dog, probably a collie. Hardly had we sat down to our first lunch in camp before he called on us. But as he was disposed to be too friendly, and to claim too large a share of the lunch, we rather gave him the cold shoulder. He did not come again; but a few evenings afterward, as we sauntered over to the house on some trifling errand, the dog suddenly conceived a bright little project. He seemed to say to himself, on seeing us, "There come both of them now, just as I have been hoping they would; now, while they are away, I will run quickly over and know what they have got that a dog can eat." My companion saw the dog get up on our arrival, and go quickly in the direction of our camp, and he said something in the cur's manner suggested to him the object of his hurried departure. He called my attention to the fact, and we hastened back. On cautiously nearing camp, the dog was seen amid the pails in the shallow water of the creek investigating them. He had uncovered the butter, and was about to taste it, when we shouted, and he made quick steps for home, with a very "kill-sheep" look. When we again met him at the house next day, he could not look us in the face, but sneaked off, utterly crest-fallen. This was a clear case of reasoning on the part of the dog, and afterward a clear case of a sense of guilt from wrong-doing. The dog will probably be a man before any other animal.

Our River

"Rivers are as various in their forms as forest trees. The Mississippi is like an oak with enormous branches. What a branch is the Red River, the Arkansas, the Ohio, the Missouri! The Hudson is like the pine or poplar—mainly trunk. From New York to Albany there is only an inconsiderable limb or two, and but few gnarls and excrescences. Cut off the Rondout, the Esopus, the Catskill and two or three similar tributaries on the east side, and only some twigs remain. There are some crooked places, it is true, but, on the whole, the Hudson presents a fine, symmetrical shaft that would be hard to match in any river in the world. Among our own water-courses it stands preeminent. The Columbia—called by Major Winthrop the Achilles of rivers—is a more haughty and impetuous stream; the Mississippi is, of course, vastly larger and longer; the St. Lawrence would carry the Hudson as a trophy in his belt and hardly know the difference; yet our river is doubtless the most beautiful of them all. It

Coxsakie

pleases like a mountain lake. It has all the sweetness and placidity that go with such bodies of water, on the one hand, and all their bold and rugged scenery on the other. In summer, a passage up or down its course in one of the day steamers is as near an idyl of travel as can be had, perhaps, anywhere in the world. Then its permanent and uniform volume, its fullness and equipoise at all seasons, and its gently-flowing currents give it further the character of a lake, or of the sea itself. Of the Hudson it may be said that it is a very large river for its size,—that is for the quantity of water it discharges into the sea. Its watershed is comparatively small—less, I think, than that of the Connecticut. It is a huge trough with a very slight incline, through which the current moves very slowly, and which would fill from the sea were its supplies from the mountains cut off. Its fall from Albany to the bay is only about five feet. Any object upon it, drifting with the current, progresses southward no more than eight miles in twenty-four hours. The ebb-tide will carry it about twelve miles and the flood set it back from seven to nine. A drop of water at Albany, therefore, will be nearly three weeks in reaching New York, though it will get pretty well pickled some days earlier. Some rivers by their volume and impetuosity penetrate the sea, but here the sea is the aggressor, and sometimes meets the mountain water nearly half way. This fact was illustrated a couple of years ago, when the basin of the Hudson was visited by one of the most severe

New York City as seen from New Jersey, across the Hudson River

droughts ever known in this part of the State. In the early winter after the river was frozen over above Poughkeepsie, it was discovered that immense numbers of fish were retreating up stream before the slow encroachment of salt water. There was a general exodus of the finny tribes from the whole lower part of the river; it was like the spring and fall migration of the birds, or the fleeing of the population of a district before some approaching danger: vast swarms of cat-fish, white and yellow perch and striped bass were en route for the fresh water farther north. When the people along shore made the discovery, they turned out as they do in the rural districts when the pigeons appear, and, with small gill-nets let down through holes in the ice, captured them in fabulous numbers. On the heels of the retreating perch and cat-fish came the denizens of the salt water, and codfish were taken ninety miles above New York. When the February thaw came and brought up the volume of fresh water again, the sea brine was beaten back, and the fish, what were left of them, resumed their old feeding-grounds.

Aerial view of New York City from two miles
in the air, c. 1922.

Selected References

Adams, Arthur G. *The Hudson River in Literature*. New York: Fordham University Press, 1988.

Bruce, Wallace. *The Hudson: Three Centuries of History, Romance and Invention*. New York: Bryant Union Co., 1907.

Burroughs, John. *In the Catskills: Selections From the Writings of John Burroughs*. Boston, New York: Houghton Mifflin Co., The Riverside Press, 1910.

Cooper, James Fenimore. *The Last of the Mohicans: A Narrative of 1757*. London: John Miller, 1826.

Drake, Joseph Rodman. *The Culprit Fay, and Other Poems*. New York: G. Dearborn, 1835.

Irving, Washington. *A History of New York: From the Beginning of the World to the End of the Dutch Dynasty, by Deidrich Knickerbocker*. New York: Inskeep & Bradford, 1809.

Janvier, Thomas A. *Henry Hudson: A Brief Statement of His Aims and His Achievements*. New York, London: Harper & Bros., 1909.

Macfarlane, James. *An American Geological Railway Guide.* 2nd ed., rev. and enl. New York: Appleton, 1890.

Morris, George Pope. *Poems.* New York: Scribner, 1854.

Noble, Louis L. *Course of Empire, Voyage of Life, and Other Pictures of Thomas Cole, N.A.* New York: Cornish, Lamport & Co., 1853.

Skinner, Charles M. *Myths and Legends of Our Own Land*, vol. 1. Philadelphia: Lippincott Co., 1896.

Index

About Cider Mill Press

Good ideas ripen with time. From seed to harvest, Cider Mill Press strives to bring fine reading, information, and entertainment together between the covers of its creatively crafted books. Our Cider Mill bears fruit twice a year, publishing a new crop of titles each spring and fall.

Visit us on the web at

www.cidermillpress.com

or write to us at

12 Port Farm Road

Kennebunkport, Maine 04046